The Addict

by

Richard Galvan

Authors Library Press

The Addict
Published by The Authors Library Press in the United Kingdom 2024
Tel: +44(0)1304 449 413
https://www.authorslibrarypress.com/
info@authorslibrarypress.com
ISBN 978-1-0687946-0-5
Copyright ©Richard Galvan
All rights reserved.
Typesetting by Authors Library Press
Cover Design by: Hollybookstore

In 2023 120,000 Americans died from a drug overdose
-Center for Disease Control-

That's the equivalent of 37 9/11 terrorist attacks

Contents

- Preface 8
- Introduction 10
- Part One: 14
- DRUGS WERE NOT MY PROBLEM, THEY WERE MY SOLUTION 14
- LIKE A VIRGIN 17
- DAMIEN 19
- DIGRESSIONS OF A TEENAGE MIND 22
- PAUL KERSEY 27
- BASKETBALL DIARIES 30
- I WONDER IF HELL HAS PAWN SHOPS 34
- GOD CALLED IN SICK TODAY 37
- UNDER THE BRIDGE 40
- BUT NOWHERE IS HOME 42
- PRIMITIVE ACTS OF KINDNESS 47
- BREAKFAST OF CHAMPIONS 49
- THE JENNY CRANK DIET 52
- RAMBO MODE 53
- THE KEISTER BUNNY 54
- CABRON 58
- THE MAN WITHOUT A PLAN 60
- SOMEBODY PLEASE… 64
- WINNERS DO WHAT THEY GOTTA DO 69

SUB ZERO	71
LOVE DON'T LIVE HERE ANYMORE	74
MOCKING BIRD	76
VENTURA HIGHWAY	80
ANIMAL FARM	83
ANTHONY BOURDAIN	88
GET BUSY LIVING OR GET BUSY DYING	92
Part Two	98
THE ADDICT	98
GOD LEAVES THE ROOM WHEN YOU START DOING IT FOR MONEY	100
SHALLOW HAL	105
DR. CONRAD MURRAY	107
TO SERVE MAN- IT'S A COOK BOOK! OH NO WAIT, IT'S A JOB DESCRIPTION...	110
CULTURE VULTURE	114
IF YOU BABY'EM YOU BURY'EM	115
TOUGH LOVE IS BETTER THAN LOST LOVE	119
Part Three	126
THE ADDICT MUST DIE	126
... AND THEN YOU WOKE UP	126
ONLY FEAR OF DEATH	129
TIME TO SCORE	134
SURRENDER	135
(Identifying the problem)	138

COMMIT	140
COMPLETE ABSTINENCE OR MODERATION?	145
ON THE MIND	151
KEEP CHANGING THE DIAL TILL YOU FIND YOUR STATION	156
2001: A SPACE ODYSSEY	160
LIKE MIKE	166
YOU ARE WHAT YOU THINK	168
ON THE BODY	171
COME FOR REHABILITATION LEAVE ON MEDICATION	177
ON THE SPIRIT	182
-The Lion, the Snitch and the Wardrobe	182
SERVICE IS FOOD FOR THE SOUL	188
HIGHER POWER	191
G.O.D = GET- OUT- DO SOMETHING ABOUT IT	194
WHO DO YOU BELIEVE IN?	199
OVERVIEW	204
FEAR	209
JULIA GULIA??	210
FEAR OF PEOPLE UNLIKE OURSELVES	214
ORIGIN STORY	216
THE GROUCH AND THE BRAINSTORM	218
INVENTORIES	222
RESENTMENT INVENTORY	222

FEAR INVENTORY	238
THE MATRIX	242
IF YOUR LIFE WAS A MOVIE, WOULD PEOPLE FALL ASLEEP IN THE THEATRE?	246
16 CLUMSY AND SHY	249
REPAIR	253
THE IMPOSSIBLE LIST	260
EVOLVE	264
DAILY OVERVIEW	266
THE FIVE VIRTUES	267
Part Four:	269
BECOME WHO YOU ARE	269
WHAT IF I'M WRONG?	269
NOW WHAT?	271
GRATITUDE	276

Preface

How does one go from a giggling toddler learning to walk, to a heroin-addict gang member living on the streets? What went wrong? Was it one significant event, or a series of small deviations? Maybe the better question is: How does one get out of the deepest of gutters and into the sunshine? I started writing this book in an attempt to answer those questions. Not only for you, but for myself. I spent my late teens and early 20's addicted to heroin and crack -a true nightmare of an existence- homeless living on skid row, in and out of jails, psych wards, hospitals and treatment centers. Then in 2004 I got sober and have spent the past 20 years working with other addicts to help pull them out of the depths of hell. After a decent amount of success in life, and helping people get sober via Alcoholics Anonymous, I decided to open my own treatment centers. My personal experience, as well as being on the clinical and altruistic side of helping addicts has allowed me to gain a clear picture on the problems at hand. I'll talk about the things that worked for me, as well as what didn't; and doesn't seem to work well for others either. This book contains what I feel is a more effective and practical recovery process called SCORE. I've distilled the 12-steps down to its very essence, burning off any archaic dogmas and infusing principles for your health, along with aspects for the mind and spirit. This book is not just for addicts, but for anyone struggling or in need of a drastic change in life. The elements in this program are what changed *my* life and pulled me out of the lowest places a human can go. There was no pre-existing familial structure to fall back on, no mentors, no money, no education, no talent, no good looks, or charming character. Just the things I picked up along the way from life, books and a few friends. I've travelled all around the world with my pen and stack of notebooks trying to pour out everything from my head into these pages- hoping to leave my daughters and the world a better place, with the lessons of my life and its misfortunes.

Introduction

I've spent the past two decades watching thousands of addicts try to get sober and fail miserably, hilariously and fatally. Why do so very few get it? Being an obsession of mine, I found some serious flaws in how we go about treating addiction. Why are treatment centers and 12-step programs our best options when they have such low first-time success rates? The treatment industry's generic model is to medicate and sit in group sessions all day. Groups don't keep anyone sober. In the evenings clients are shuttled to a 12-step program in desperate hopes they work the steps. All of us in treatment industry know there's almost no chance of them staying sober if they don't. Or if it's a religious program, they better find god and fast. Either situation, the treatment center is banking on a third-party spiritual solution to carry the load after discharge. The truth is once the client leaves the facility, they have no idea how to actually keep someone sober. "Just say NO" and avoiding "triggers" doesn't work. Information has no power over an addict. Every addict knows exactly how dangerous drugs are. I don't know how many times I've met people that know the AA book or the Bible front to back but can't still stay sober. Expecting an addict to abide by a treatment plan isn't very effective either. Might as well tell them they can't use drugs because it against the law. It all sounds good on paper but isn't strong enough to keep a needle out of someone's arm.

The 12-step programs themselves leave lots of room for improvement. For instance, the 12-steps written in the 1930's aren't always easily digestible to the newcomer and the steps require you to have a sponsor. A sponsor is member of the program that has a working knowledge of the 12-steps. This can be someone with 20 days or 20 years of experience. I've seen some horrible sponsors as well as some amazing ones. I can tell who is a good or bad sponsor within five minutes of talking to someone. The problem in the sponsorship method is that it's up to the addict to pick their sponsor. This often results in the addict picking the person that looks the "coolest". I see women pick a young pretty woman with a flock of girls around her and newly sober, over a humble older woman with 30 years of sobriety that has been getting women sober for decades. Same goes for men. Many of my sponsees admitted to only picking me because I drive nice cars or wear nice watches. So that's what we're dealing with.

 Even the most experienced of sponsors still have different interpretations of how the steps are to be worked. Some go through all the steps in a day. Some (like me) took years to complete them. Step 1 which is arguably the most important of them all has no clear-cut procedure in the Alcoholics Anonymous book. If I was a struggling alcoholic without access to a decent sponsor or meeting, how would I complete the steps? Even with access, not everyone can muster up the courage to go to a 12-step meeting. They're weird. Then you have to stand up and announce to everyone your problem. Next, (like a teenager asking a girl to a prom) have the balls to ask a stranger to sponsor you. After that, make plans with that stranger to work on the steps once a week. Hopefully this stranger knows what he or she is doing. What if someone works and has kids and can't make it to the meetings? There's a lot of hoops to jump through just to even get started. Saying one *needs* a sponsor to get sober, is like saying one *needs* a personal trainer to get in shape. Who knows how many people have died or are still suffering before they even got a chance- because of these barriers. Don't get me wrong, 12-step programs are undoubtedly the most solid chance a person has to stay sober; I owe everything I have to AA. It does produce what it promises -a spiritual awakening- which is usually what the *real addict* requires to stay sober. 12-step programs just make it a little more difficult than it needs to be. They also leave out some of the most important aspects of your life such as your health; which has everything to do with your chances of *staying* sober. Being grateful and an admirer of the 12-steps I only want to add to, and contribute to, the world of recovery with the SCORE program. It's been almost 100 years since the Alcoholics Anonymous book was written; it might be time for a fresh look at things. Think of the 12-step process as a hamburger- SCORE is just *The Cheeseburger*. This book is here not just to help the addicts but *anyone* in need of a spiritual awakening. Whether you suffer from depression, fear, anxiety, or just need a fresh outlook on life, you'll find answers in these pages. How can I be so sure? Because this book doesn't just explore my life, it explores- *yours*.

"I hope the lord will forgive me, I was a G and getting high was a way of being free..." *Death around the corner – Tupac Shakur*

Part One:

DRUGS WERE NOT MY PROBLEM, THEY WERE MY SOLUTION

Spring, the year 2000, Downtown Los Angeles- I'm standing there, age seventeen smoking crack with a man in his sixties called "Hollywood." We were standing on the sidewalk watching a group of kids my age cross the street. They were all snazzy and dressed up for what looked to be prom. White teeth smiling ear to ear, with that distinct chatter, hooting and laughter made only by high-schoolers having the time of their lives. While they took pictures next to their limo, I took a hit off the crack pipe and held it in as long as I could. Hollywood was standing there staring at me with an angry and confused look on his scruffy black face. I let out a huge puff of smoke along with a little cough. As the rush of the cocaine hits my brain Hollywood intensifies his stare. *What?* I asked him, annoyed that he was fucking up my high. I passed him the pipe as he shook his head in disbelief, he asked; "Man what the fuck is you doing here?" Confused and getting more annoyed, I replied: *What the fuck ARE YOU doing here? What kind of stupid question is that, take your hit already.* He just kept shaking his head as he loaded the pipe with more crack and barked at me; "Yo ass should be out there living yo life like them (gesturing towards the festive teens) What the fuck is you doin here with me? You young you got yo whole life ahead of you!"

Ouch. That hit me hard. What on earth was I doing there? I think that was the first time I realized what a fucked up situation I was in. It had all happened so fast. How did I get to this? How do I get out? I remember thinking- *this is just my life*. Going to prison, overdosing or getting murdered was all I had to look forward to.

Walk with me a bit, I'll tell you the whole story. We have to rewind the tape back to my first drink. That first drink not only changed my life, it saved it. It was the summer of 6th grade going into 7th. I was a shy insecure punk with glasses, braces and a lumpy broken nose. I sucked at sports, my grades were bad, and I hated school. I hated my home life even worse. I didn't want to be at home or at school, both places were filled with tears and turmoil. If there were tears at home, I'd be fighting at school. If there was fighting at home, there would be tears at school. Both made me hate living. There was no escaping. I didn't know why, everyone else seemed to blend in just fine at school and their home. When I say, "hate living", what I felt was a yearning to die. It's funny to think about now, back then I didn't even realize that was a thing, to not want to live anymore. I wasn't familiar with the term suicide and that people killed themselves yet, I just knew life wasn't for me. The only time I felt ok was when I was out roaming around with friends, the streets were my happy place. Vandalizing and shop lifting were my sports.

We had just got a little apartment in a good neighborhood in the northern part of Los Angeles. I hated it, even though it was a huge improvement from the drug infested gang neighborhood we had just come from. I just wasn't adapting very well -a fish out of water. You would think going from a bad neighborhood to a good one would make a kid's life easier, it was the opposite. The dramatic change was shocking and stressful for a kid like me. In the neighborhood I just came from our lives revolved around the park. My friends and I hung out there all day till it got dark just getting into trouble. We all looked up to the gang members, graffiti artists and drug dealers; they seemed so cool compared to my dorky ass. Nothing was more exciting than watching them fight, tag up walls and chase each other. Every so often one would get killed. A friend's brother, a neighbor or someone we were scared to even walk by or look at. Everyone I knew was from some type of dysfunctional home. Maybe a single mom on welfare, or the classic alcoholic dad. Hoarders, immigrants even whole families that belonged to the same gang. It was a wholesome place.

In contrast, the new neighborhood was like being warped into an episode of *Leave it to Beaver*. These "rich kids" (as I saw them) were all from good wholesome families. Their parents were involved in everything they did, afterschool sports, activities and even their friends. They talked, dressed and acted different. Funny how in LA every mile is a different world. I wasn't fitting in and didn't have the baked-in social skills or desire to adapt. In addition, with my mom's boyfriend living with us, I wasn't fitting in at home either. When he came into the picture, I was an undisciplined delinquent driving my mom insane. He wasn't having it and we clashed constantly. The next thing I knew my mom was dropping me off at my dad's house. I was bitter. While playing Gameboy on the couch, my dad walked up and broke the news to me. The reason I was there was because my mom and her boyfriend were getting married. Like a judge sentencing me to a lifetime in prison the wind was knocked out of me. It devastated me. I hated every man my mom ever brought home, but they all eventually left and peace was restored. This man wasn't going anywhere. Later on in my adult life he would play a big roll but at that time it was my worst nightmare

LIKE A VIRGIN

One night my mom and my new step-dad went out for the evening and I had the place to myself. Being left alone was no big deal, normally I'd just play some video games all night. That particular evening a brand-new thought emerged from my mind; LET'S DRINK! Even though people had been drinking and doing drugs around me my whole life the thought had never occurred to me before. None of my peers in the new town were drinking yet so there was no peer pressure, it was an organic thought. I opened the freezer and grabbed the ice-cold frosty bottle of vodka. I had seen it so many times when reaching for frozen burritos or TV dinners but never paid it any mind. I poured myself about the amount of a double shot and replaced what I took with water. I don't remember what I was thinking before I took the shot but I do remember what I thought after: HELL YEAH LET'S DO ANOTHER!

I repeated the same thing again, pour a shot refill with water, repeat. Buzzed and giddy I bounced around the apartment dancing and lip singing music videos with the TV turned up full blast. Then the thought hit, "This feels great let's drink a little more" so this time I hit the E&J brandy. A little more jumping on the bed and rapping over Ice Cube songs then it was time for another drink. At this point I was pretty drunk and feeling on top of the world with that beautiful first buzz, if only they were all like that... What in hindsight can only be described as the phenomenon of craving I went to the fridge compelled to drink more. This time it was my mom's wine jug. I took a few drinks and on the last one it slipped out of my hand and smashed onto the kitchen floor breaking into dozens of small razor-sharp pieces of glass. Wine and glass coated the floor of our tiny kitchen. Soon blood would join the mixture as I cut myself trying to clean up in a drunken stupor. It looked like a murder scene. After a while I said *fuck this* and left the mess. I jumped in the shower desperately trying to sober up before my mom got home.

Once they got back, I couldn't hide the mess, so I fessed up to what I did. I don't remember whether they were mad or not, probably. I could be mistaken but I almost feel like they were somewhat amused at the situation. It must've been a tragically funny sight to come home and find your place thrashed with your drunken kid laying there. What I do remember is laying in my bed, head still spinning, hearing them say to each other: "He's going to be hurting tomorrow..." All I could think was: I CANT WAIT TO TELL MY FRIENDS, I WANT TO DO THIS EVERY DAY.

The next day I acted as if I felt sick, hoping I could dodge punishment if they thought I learned my lesson. In reality I felt amazing (Fun fact: Not only did I not have a hangover that day but I would never have a hangover in my entire drinking career). That night was the best night of my life up to that date. I can't think of a happier day prior to that. Alcohol was a miracle to me at the time, a saving grace. It offered temporary escape from the life I hated so much.

Now that I knew there was a solution to my anxiety and depression, I never wanted to go back to my old feelings again. Why the fuck would I do that when I could be buzzed and happy? I vowed to be *High till I die* as we'd say. I went from suicidal to excited about life overnight. Looking back, I realize I had that alcoholic tendency right from the start. There was no gradual descent, I drank every day right from the beginning. I couldn't stop even when I wanted to. It's safe to say I drank and/or did drugs everyday possible for the next 10 years straight.

The very next school day I was stealing a bottle of Bacardi rum and *Aftershock* (a cinnamon flavored liquor) from the local supermarket. Not only did alcohol take the pain away but it made me a part of something, for once I had a way to bond with my peers. The climate in school also changed. One day sports was life to these kids and I sucked at sports, therefore I sucked... Now it was all about partying, and I was not only a pioneer of drugs 'n alcohol to most of my peers but also a provider. I had value to bring to the table (drugs and alcohol) which boosted my social status. All of a sudden, I felt like I belonged and life could be fun. It actually gave me something to look forward to when I woke up.

DAMIEN

I would steal a bottle or two of liquor from a different store every day so I had pretty much an endless supply. The kid with the alcohol was king in my school. The star of the party welcomed everywhere and if you could hold your liquor, even better. Some kids were afraid to hang with me.

I would drink like a madman every day before, during and after school. Whoever was around me was getting pressured to drink too, and I was very persuasive. Kids got alcohol poisoning hanging with me. In no time all my friends were drinking daily too. I seemed to be the only one that would go home and drink alone though.

We ended up moving again, same town but to its one and only crappy pocket. By this time selling stolen bottles started to put money in my pocket. My bed had 3 drawers under it, when you pulled out the drawers there was a hidden space. I had this area lined the entire length of my bed with various liquor bottles. Everything from *Wild turkey whiskey* to *Boones farm* wines. Anything you wanted I'd get it. This was a good little hustle for an 8th grader and all the older Mexican dads in the neighborhood bought bottles off me. I also caught the attention of the local drug dealers and nearby cholos ("Cholo" is a slang term for a Hispanic gang member). I would trade bottles of liquor for weed. Neither the dealers nor cholos trusted me with the harder drugs (which I always asked for).

Fortunately for me (unfortunately for society) one day the school recommended I get a psych evaluation due to my behavior and bad grades. I left that psych appointment with a prescription for Ritalin. The Ritalin was supposed to help me with ADHD, but what do you think I did with it?

Did I take the medication as prescribed and start to improve in school? I'm sure by now you can guess the answer. If you guessed: I snorted and sold them all. You guessed correctly. I only sold them to kids in my school because I didn't want to get robbed by the cholos. One day I mustered up the balls and offered one of the main gang members a line of Ritalin. He was called *Shadow*. Shadow sucked his teeth and said "Nah homie, I got the real shit." *Well what's up, bust it out then* I said. He did, and so I did my first lines of cocaine. I liked it but it wore off a little too fast.

A few days later I stopped by Shadow's house. Him and a bunch of other cholos were smoking and snorting peanut butter crank (an old version of methamphetimine). I jumped right in, DING! Now this I liked. Meth filled my heart with joy, like a warm hug and loving smile from God himself. I was sitting there, getting high with dudes I used to be afraid to even walk by. Some of which were about 10 years older than me. Drinking beer listening to oldies, boxing each other, and just hanging out till the sun came up felt like heaven to me. I felt like Henry Hill in *Good Fellas* working at the cab stand. Needless to say, I got jumped in the gang shortly after- twice. Now listen, I'm not trying to give anyone the impression that I was some hard-core gang member. I was just a knuckle head that *happened* to be into the same activities that the cholos liked to do. There was no effort, I fitted right in, even though I was 60% goofy ass kid, 40% gangster. I guess I was like a LEGO Cholo if you will.

Shadow had become like a big brother to me; I wanted to be just like him, he had hot girls, drugs, cash, and most of all people respected him. I remember one of the first times I hung out with him he wanted me to steal some liquor from the nearby Ralphs supermarket. I told him I couldn't, I was burned there; last time they chased me out and threatened to call the cops as soon as I walked in. Shadow said: "Nah homie they ain't gonna do shit. Let's go." *Ok fuck it, let's go...* I said as I looked at my friend Adam. Adam was about 10 or 11 years old, I was about 13 maybe. We walked up to the Ralphs, and Shadow walked in and stood in the doorway. He waved us in and we walked fast to the liquor isle and started grabbing as many bottles as we could. I peeked over and saw the nerdy clerk and fat white lady that chased me out before just standing there watching. Then I heard Shadow call the guy over, I couldn't make out what they were saying but the guy was scared. We ran out, Shadow walked out. Me and Adam thought that was the most bad-ass thing ever. *That-* is what I wanted to be like.

    I stole from that store every week for the next few years and never had any problems again. I remember being about 16 trying to show off for some girls; I walked into that Ralphs and grabbed two Alize bottles. As I was walking out, I looked at that same hefty lady and held up the bottles as if to say- *Hey, just grabbing some drinks for the night, carry on, have a good evening.* This was mid 90's, you weren't able to loot in LA freely like you can now; a clerk would beat your ass and hold you till the cops came back then. I was no John Gotti, but to a kid like me who always felt so weak, any little feelings of power or respect was like hitting a home run to the kids that play baseball. A couple years later Shadow was deported back to Guatemala. Soon after his arrival he was murdered, shot point blank with a shot gun while talking on a payphone.

DIGRESSIONS OF A TEENAGE MIND

    Ninth grade. More dealers than teachers would see the likes of my face that year. In order to stay high eight days a week I graduated from selling alcohol to weed, meth, mushrooms, LSD or whatever prescription drugs I could raid from my mom's medicine cabinets. I was also my best customer. My friends and I loved Vicodin's, Valiums, cough syrups or whatever narcotic we could find, all was welcome. This was before Google, so if we weren't sure what a medication was, or did, we would just take a bunch and find out. As long as it had the "May cause drowsiness" label I was game to try. Down the hatch! Sometimes I'd pass out, sometimes I'd get high. Other times my menopausal symptoms were relieved, or my cholesterol was lowered. Not even the air fresheners around the house were safe. I would throw a sock over any aerosol can I could find to inhale the nitrous oxide out of it. I did it all, I was what they call a trashcan addict.

Now, as many drugs as I was doing, the only one I felt I couldn't go without- was marijuana. I wouldn't call it an addiction but definitely a bad habit for a 14-year-old. Then again, I did smoke a bowl of seeds and stems one night when I ran out of weed. I couldn't sleep without it.

My drinking was getting worse too. So much so that I'd wake up with the shakes. I couldn't even talk to anyone till Ray the local crack head got back from the store with my two 32 oz'ers of *King Cobra* malt liquor. I'd guzzle the first one with the urgency of a dehydrated man in the desert. By the second one I'd be able to light a cigarette and talk. Some days I would finish a whole fifth of Bacardi by myself. Even the old winos would be like *Damn slow down kid.*

Once my friends went home, you could find me in the back of the apartments with the winos and tweakers. Drunk and singing oldies songs till I mustered up the courage to go home. I wasn't getting beat or anything, it was just the last place I wanted to be. I knew my mom and step-dad couldn't stand me. Could I really blame them? I can't imagine my kids doing the stuff I was. I'd be pissed and wouldn't know what to do either. Anytime we interacted it was a fight, so I just tried to stay out of their hair as much as possible.

On what started as a slow weekend morning turned into a heated argument with my step-dad. Over my dog or his droppings which I forgot to clean I think. I heard him tell my mom "Either he goes, or I go," So my mom sent me to live with my dad.

At that time I had never really spent more than a night or two at his house. Each time I went my step-mom and sister would pick me apart. They loved to talk about how ugly I was, what a bitch my mom is, pinch, scratch, throw shit at me- whatever they could do to fuck with me. They hated me coming over and I hated going even more. As for my dad, he was like a stranger being used as a disciplinary tool. It was a forced situation and super awkward. Getting sent to live there was a common threat by my mom, so when she actually kicked me out I was shattered. The betrayal I felt that she chose a man over me and effectively severed what little connection we had left, was shocking. It filled me with an anger and sadness that would last for more than a decade. It warped my life and changed my entire personality. I guess only a mother can have that power over a man.

The next few months were rough. I missed my baby brother and sister, even my mom. I didn't want my siblings growing up not knowing me or losing our bond, which eventually happened. After the move and all the chaos in my life, every time I would visit I was just a stranger now, pulling them from what they were doing. They didn't remember how close we used to be. I'd get that same feeling each time I'd see my mother again as well.

On a better note- as much as my step-mom and sister

disliked me prior; once my mom kicked me out, strangely they welcomed me in. Maybe they felt bad for me- or just understood my situation a little better. Eventually I settled into my new life and got to know my Mexican side of the family better. Being mixed (Mexican/White) meant I was both, but at the same time neither. On the Italian side of the family, I was the Mexican kid. On the Mexican side I'm the white boy. No matter where I go, I'm an outsider.

It was a tough adjustment at first, there was a lot more of what they called "rules" and structure. Every day was pretty much a rinse and repeat (still is over there). We all cooked and ate dinner together every day. I couldn't just wake up and leave like I used. I actually had to go to school every day, and do the work. Plus, I slept on the couch so there was no privacy at all. At my mom's I could go out freely and, if I was home, I was watching TV or playing video games. I would drink a 6 pack of sodas and eat mostly cereal and frozen pizzas. My step-dad and mom tried to push chores on me but there was so much resentment everything was a battle. My dad had a much different approach, a lot calmer. With him I wasn't allowed out as much or as easily and I had a curfew. Home life was yard work, cleaning and schoolwork. No video games whatsoever.

Surprisingly I listened (for a time) and actually felt better with discipline in my life. This slowed down my drinking and drugging initially. I had to be a lot more discreet and creative. Another thing that took some getting used to was the bluntness of my step-mom and sister. They liked to make fun of me and point out any and all flaws. My bent up glasses, tired style and especially my messed up nose. I had broken it doing flips in a bounce house a few years back but never saw a doctor to get it fixed. "We gotta get that nose fixed" was a term flung around daily. So they took me to the doctor where I had to have somewhat of a nose job to fix the crookedness and take out the bone fragments that were floating around beneath my skin. This helped a great deal with my confidence (though it would be broken twice more in fights over the next 2 years).

At this point I pretty much stopped smoking weed. I felt it slowed me down too much and started making me paranoid. I stuck to drinking, and meth on the weekends. I was fighting more often and needed to be sharp, the weed made me feel vulnerable. My new high school was growing on me. Mostly as a place to meet girls, but my school work did improve. At this point (around 10th-11th grade) I had grown to 6' 200 lbs. and was no longer being bullied but had became a bully. I replaced sadness with anger, which is a much more tolerable feeling. At least anger can be used as fuel. Even so, I still had that underlying sorrow. A feeling of not really belonging anywhere or having any purpose. When nobody and nowhere feels like home.

Playing house at my dad's didn't last very long. My nature is too restless. I defaulted back to drugs, girls and gang life. What initially felt good about the gang culture was having a bunch of homies that would do anything for you. You protected each other, threw up on one another, shared food and clothes and went to jail together. Then it just became all about violence and revenge. Really that's all gang banging boils down to, a sport of revenge. When there are no enemies at the present, you go create some. There's obviously a deeper issue in that but honestly, I was pretty mild in comparison to some of my friends who seem to be made for gore. Random acts of violence was never my thing.

Even though I despised anyone with a *good life*, I only had an urge to hurt people that actually did something wrong to me. I also tried very hard to outsmart the police when committing crimes. I never understood how my friends kept going to prison for crimes I was committing more often than they were. Believe it or not I had friends whose ultimate goal was life in prison and to run things from in there. They didn't want to be rich and famous on the outside, they wanted to be rich and famous on the inside. But at least they had goals. I was a feather in the wind being blown from fire to fire. Have you ever had a long hard day at work and couldn't wait for it to be over? Drinking coffee after coffee to pull through. Saying to yourself *Fuck it's only 1:00! Will this day ever end?* Well that's how I felt about my life. Somebody shoot me already. I felt like death was looming, but wished it would hurry the fuck up.

PAUL KERSEY

Late 90's. A warm summer night deep in the San Fernando Valley. The smell of weed smoke and Cool Water cologne was in the air. The mixture of blasting music from dozens of cars blends into one inaudible noise. Girls everywhere, standing around or in backseats cackling, dudes hollering *Was up mija!* as they drive by honking. Summer nights when you're a teen are a magical time in life - the best- I mean do you ever really have better summers again?

My friends and I were out that night cruising Laurel Canyon Boulevard. Laurel Canyon was the cruising strip of the Valley. Kind of like our Whittier or Crenshaw Blvd. Low riders, girls, and gangsters, you better be prepared for anything. You never knew what you were going to get into. Might get in a fight or get shot. Might get laid. Maybe go to jail. Maybe all 4.

Two carloads full, we stopped at a gas station. Me and my friend "Joey" were walking towards the counter laughing and talking about getting a girl's number or something when a car pulled up pulled up. "WHERE YOU FOOLS FROM?" the passenger yelled out as he kicked the door open and pointed a shot gun at us. As we yelled out our neighborhoods he cocked the gun. "OH SHIT!" we yelled and scattered as he opened fire. BOOM! BOOM! Both of us scrambled back to the car. Joey limped behind and dove in the back seat laying across three of our laps. "THEY SHOT ME IN THE ASS!" Then we looked down at his back pockets and saw the peppered holes starting to saturate with blood. We all looked at each other again "OH SHIT!" Then after a slight pause, out of nowhere we all burst into laughter (except Joey). No matter how hard we tried we couldn't hold it in. It was just the funniest thing ever, for some reason. Who would've thought such a scary moment would turn into one of the hardest laughs I ever had. We brought Joey back to the house and tried to remove the bullets ourselves with eyebrow tweezers. That didn't go so well. It was a bloody mess and he was screaming in pain so we took him to the hospital. Later on that night, must've been around 3 or 4 am, I was sitting in the waiting room with his family. They didn't speak much English so we couldn't really talk. I had the ridiculous thought that he was lucky. He got shot so he had the better night, I was just the chump in the waiting room. Probably not the way of thinking most kids had. That was just my mentality at the time.

A little after that, some friends and I were pulling out of a liquor store parking lot and got ambushed by 3 cars. As the cholos in the cars pointed guns at us another jumped out pointing some sort of rifle at me. He came right up to my window and "hit me up." In LA getting "hit up" is when a gang member asks you "where you from?" meaning what gang are you in. So I told him. "What about you fools?" He shouted to my "friends" in the backseat who were so stunned they didn't respond. So I replied for them too. The driver of our car was just an Asian dude buying meth off me. He had no affiliation, so he was crapping his pants. Even though we were from a rival gang the gunman had respect that I didn't bitch out like the dudes in the back seat did. He said they were on a mission looking for some guys in particular from another gang in the area and took off. Normally if your homies don't speak up in a situation like that there's repercussions, but I didn't even say anything or care. I was the one with a death wish not them. Again I didn't think *Phew we got lucky*. I thought *I wish somebody would kill me already,* and that's exactly the attitude I walked around with. This attitude never got me killed obviously but I sure did get my ass kicked a lot. I also had the pleasure of being stabbed, teeth knocked back, broken noses, fractured cheek bone, a few concussions, and plenty of other little flesh wounds.

BASKETBALL DIARIES

Let's get back to high school and when things really went down hill. As I had mentioned I was doing all types of drugs, I was even smoking crack in cigarettes between classes. However nothing quite grabbed me by the balls, till one lunch break in a McDonalds bathroom.

That morning in weight training class my friend asked me: "Are you ready to try the mother of all drugs? "Negra." As he said that he opened a little folding of foil with a small piece of tar heroin on it. I don't remember my reply but it was probably something to the tune of *Fuck yeah*. I recall him warning me that a lot of people get sick and throw up the first time. That you either hate it, or love it. But now I wonder, what if it's the other way around? Maybe it hates or loves you. What if it chooses you? If so it definitely chose me that day.

This wasn't really comparable to my other first experiences with drugs, like my first alcohol buzz or first time I got high off weed. Those were fun, this wasn't in the territory of "fun" or "good times." This was in the elevated realm of bliss and ecstasy. An overwhelming feeling of true love towards everyone around me. At that moment I couldn't hate anyone if I tried. You've got to remember this is coming from a guy that walked around daily in a general state of anger, pessimism or indifference. To me this wasn't like "getting high" this was more like a revelation of the spirit. How could this drug have such a bad rap? Maybe they're wrong, after all they used to think marijuana was deadly. This is glorious, now I know what Heaven must be like. Little did I know later on it would come with the price of knowing Hell too. What happened to me in that dingy McDonalds bathroom is what my teenage daughter would call a CANON EVENT in my life.

Why can't I sleep? I kept asking myself in the middle of the night as I tossed 'n turned, sweaty and aching. I need to get some rest; I have to get up at 7 am to do my Community Service. My legs were aching, and I couldn't get comfortable. Must be because I haven't been working out lately. At least that's what I thought at the time. On no sleep and a few bites of the MRE (meals ready to eat) they gave us at Community Service, I muddled through the day. Felt like it was in slow motion. Afterwards I walked over to my friend Raffa's house. He was also my heroin connection.

"Damn homie I couldn't sleep at all last night, my legs were killing me and I had the chills" I told Raffa as I shook his hand and gave him a hug. Raffa looked at me and chuckled.

"You're Malias homie" Malias was a Spanish term for being sick from heroin withdraw. That news came as a shock to me and was definitely not what I wanted to hear. That would mean I was getting addicted. I always thought addiction was something that only happened to weak people, not to someone with as much drug experience as me. After all, I had been doing meth, coke, and every other drug they say is highly addictive for years and never had any type of hard withdraws. Even when I would have to wake up and drink, all I had to do was switch to meth and pills for a few days and I was fine. Maybe that's all I had to do now. I was trying to take in what he just told me but was sceptical. Also, why the hell was he laughing? Raffa then said "You don't believe me? Here take a hit and tell me if you feel better." I took the hit and sure enough I was magically cured of all cramps, chills, tiredness and any other type of pain in my body. Damn... I knew I was in trouble and had a big problem on my hands. I'll worry about it tomorrow.

Tomorrow wouldn't come for years. What did happen was the forfeiture of all things worthwhile in life. School, friends, family, health, freedom, they'd all disappear like dust in the wind. A month or two later I'd be what the local Methadone Clinic would say was their youngest patient ever. I would end up maxing out my 5 per year detox attempts every year at that clinic and various others around LA. I just couldn't shake it.

One day I did a little too much dope in the bathroom of my dad's house, I ended up passing out cold on the toilet. I woke up to the sound of my step-mom screaming and pounding on the door "WAKE THE FUCK UP! OPEN THE FUCKING DOOR!"

I fumbled to pull up my pants, put my needle and lighter in my pocket and walked out of the bathroom as if nothing happened.

"Oh sorry, I was super tired from last night and fell asleep for a minute" Deny, deny, deny was my motto. This time however I must've dropped or left my dope on the floor in my flustered attempt to flee the bathroom. I found this out from an ear shattering scream;

"WHAT THE FUCK IS THIS!!" She came out of the bathroom with the little piece of plastic bag my nugget of heroin was in. I didn't have a room or anyplace to get away from the madness so I just had to sit there and endure it or leave. So I left.

I was allowed back the next day under the condition that I would go stay with my aunt and grandma in Mexico to sober up. I agreed, but first I had to make a quick trip downtown to load up on benzos to help me through the kick. I found my connection and got an assortment of pills to last me about 2 weeks. The plan was to take one in the morning for the pain and one in the night to help me sleep. Solid plan. Now off to Mexico! My sister came along for support. The bus trip felt like it took over 24 hours, or maybe it was 1 hour. I don't remember much. What I do remember is I kept taking the pills I was supposed to be rationing out. The higher I got the more I took. I ended up taking them all before I even got there.

We arrived at my aunt's house in the middle of the night. There wasn't much of a welcoming because everyone was sleeping so she just showed me to my bed. I was already starting to feel the pre-sick panic of knowing I had no dope. As soon as I put my stuff down, I told her I wanted to go for a walk to get some fresh air. Of course, this seemed extremely bizarre considering it was about 2 am and I had just arrived. Not to mention it was a less than safe area of Mexico and everyone just wanted to go back to sleep.

I didn't care, I couldn't care. Heroin takes away all common courtesies when the sickness kicks in. I could've been about to meet the President or out on a date with a super model, doesn't matter. Wife is in labor? Ok we just gotta swing by the projects really quick, It's on the way. Jesus is back and in the clouds? Ok I'll be out of the bathroom in a few minutes. When heroin says it's time to go, it's time to go. I set out to find a 24 hour pharmacy to buy some opiates or a dope man. I walked and walked. I didn't know where the fuck I was anymore. This is before smart phones. Instead of finding a pharmacy I found a dude that robbed me. Then I found my way to the inside of a Mexicali jail cell. While wandering around looking for the guy that robbed me I was stopped by the cops. When they searched me they found my notorious little key chain knife. They held up the blade against two fingers to check the length. The cop shook his head. I said no, four fingers is legal. He said "No in Mexico is two." Fuuuuck... So off to jail I went. I was only there for a day then they let me go. Eventually I wound up in San Diego. A kind-hearted marine paid for my train ticket right as security was about to throw me out of the station. I landed back in downtown L.A and used my last $10 to buy a $4 balloon of heroin, a $1 needle and a $4 hit of crack.

As soon as I injected the dope and exhaled, the next thought in my head was WHAT THE FUCK DID I JUST DO? Heroin withdrawal, or even just the fear of it puts your mind and body in a state of panic. You get stricken with intense panic and tunnel vision until you take that first shot. Then you are released temporarily and the clarity of whatever you just did hits. I left my sister in Mexico! How would I explain this? Turns out I wouldn't have to. I didn't talk to my dad's side of the family again for a few years. I didn't bring up Mexico till the amends with my sister almost 10 years after the fact.

I WONDER IF HELL HAS PAWN SHOPS

The next few months I would spend hustling in L.A's Skid Row and Hollywood. I got to experience all the fine Skid Row accommodations like the Hotel Cecil, Rosslyn, Frontier, St.George, Huntington and a few others. Along with every available tent and staircase I could find.

I can even recall the day I transitioned from staying in hotels to becoming a homeless person. It was a warm night with perfect L.A. weather. I was sitting on the hood of a car with a friend, both of us trying to sell the last of our dope to call it a night. It was probably around midnight, we were laying back on the windshield talking, feeling the nice summer breeze coming through the buildings. Carrying with it the smell of piss and spilled beer from the alley. I had just eaten a $6 soul food plate from a guy we called The Dinner Man. He sold food from a cart on the corner of 5th and main. There was ambient funk music in the background from a boom box amongst the cussing and chatter of the skid row crowd. Dimly lit figures walking by us coming in and out of the streetlights selling everything from single cigarettes to crack. I thought to myself: Why waste $40 on a motel? It's already midnight, I'm not gonna sleep anyways, plus it's so nice out. We can just take turns napping on this car and save the money. So I slept on the car that night and washed up in a parking garage bathroom the next morning. From then on I couldn't rationalize spending money on a hotel that could be better spent on drugs. I'd rather be high on the street than sick in a hotel. Thus began my homeless years.

Every so often I could convince my Nana & Papa that I was going to change and stay with them for a brief stint. Now to me my Nana and Papa were the only people on earth that truly loved me. They were actually my great grandparents on my mother's side. My maternal grandpa died of alcohol related cirrhosis of the liver. My grandmother was a recovering heroin addict living in Arizona, I don't remember much of her. My Paternal grandfather was killed when my dad was young, the man I considered grandpa and my grandma were living in Mexico.

Nana and Papa were the only people on earth left that I had a bond with. I tried my best to shield them from the chaos that was my life but in the end, I think they got the worst of it all. I caused them immense grief in their golden years and am forever saddened for it. You have to understand that I was their golden boy. I was named Richard after their late son that died of a heart condition as a teenager. They had high hopes and dreams for me as a kid.

In their final years they saw me shrivel down from a 220 lb. muscular teen to 130 lb. dope-fiend pan handler with the body of Mr. Burns from *The Simpsons*. They had to witness my spectacular crash and were caught in the explosion. My Nana cried every time she found me passed out with a needle in my arm. Needles I had stolen from her for her diabetes. As shitty as that was, stealing bags of clean needles from my Nana probably saved me from getting AIDS and bad track marks on my arms. They were crushed when they found out I had been stealing money from the shoe box of cash they kept for savings. Both of our biggest disappointments in me was when I grabbed a ring that looked expensive from my Nana's jewellery box and pawned it. I was desperate and sick. I got $30 for it. I had no idea it was their original wedding ring worth a few thousand. I got home that day to find my Nana crying. My Papa stood up and asked me where her wedding ring was. FUCK! I ended up telling them the friend I was with must've stole it. I got on a fake call with my "friend" and started cussing him out demanding he told me where he sold the ring and how to get back. I told them he said he pawned the ring for $90 and if they gave me the money I would go get it back. Which I did, after I used the extra $60 to go buy more dope. I'm not proud of these things I did, I carried horrible shame for years. Drugs had a death grip on me so strong that not even love could stand in the way. I too suffered seeing the look in their eyes as these scenarios and many others unfolded. It's an horrendous look of disappointment and disgust that stabs you in the heart like a red hot dagger. Most people on earth will never know this particular type of pain, it's reserved for the lowest of the low. The reason I'm sharing these stories with you is for those other dope fiend scumbags like me that think they are the only ones. You aren't the only one. If you have a family member like me, they're not the only ones. Known for shooting dope in the church bathroom, I felt like I was the sole biggest piece of shit on earth. Come to find out there was a lot of people like me. People that did some pretty shameful things in their using days but were still able to turn their lives around and become someone they can look in the mirror and be proud of once again. Unfortunately, my Papa would never live to see me sober. He passed away while I was in jail and my Nana would die an even sadder death while I was in rehab. When they died, so went a piece of me and the last people on earth whom I truly loved.

GOD CALLED IN SICK TODAY

The day my Papa died I was sitting in a rowdy sweltering hot LA county jail dorm. If I remember correctly, I was just hanging out playing cards, drinking coffee and clowning around with the homies. I remember the Spanish TV show *Caliente* (kind of like a Mexican version *of Soul Train*) was playing on the big screen TV. It was rumoured that the TV's were donated by Robert Downey Jr. during his stay a few years prior. "GALVAN GET DRESSED!" blasts over the speaker interrupting our game. "Oh shit you got a visit" "Nah you're probably getting an add charge, it's too early for visits" We were all wondering why I was being called out. I got dressed and stood waiting by the door hoping maybe it was a visit or even better maybe my charges were going to be dropped. The door popped open and I stepped out. A deputy was there waiting to walk me down. "Hey deputy, any idea where I'm going?" I asked. "Chaplin." He replied with the same voice and cold demeanour as *The Terminator*. I thought to myself: *Chaplin? What the fuck is that?* But I didn't feel like being told to shut the fuck up so I didn't ask. We walked down the long mural covered halls of the Men's Central Jail till we came upon a small office. I walked in and a man that looked like a priest said hello and asked me to have a seat. "Mr. Galvan I'm sorry to inform you that your grandfather has passed away" I looked at him for a second, then asked "What do you mean?" So he said it a little louder "Your Grandfather has died." "Which one?" I asked, still not fully grasping what was going on. He then picked up the office phone and handed it to me saying "Why don't you give your mother a call, she is the one we spoke to." My mom picked up right away. She was crying, that's when I knew it was my Papa. I still had no reaction though. It wasn't like in the movies where someone gets horrible news and starts freaking out, or drops the phone and faints. I was unaffected. Keep in mind this is the most important person not only in my life but also to my whole family. My mom was on the phone hysterically crying as she told me my Papa died then handed the phone to my Nana who was equally distraught. I could hardly understand either one. I didn't know what to say other than *I'm sorry*. I told my Nana I loved her and everything was going to be alright. I got off the phone and the Chaplin briefly gave me his condolences, then seemed to hurry me out as if he had another appointment. On the way out he asked me if I wanted a Bible. "Sure." I got back to my dorm and everybody was asking me what happened. At first, I said "nothing" and tried to brush it off but realized they might think I was talking to a detective or something, so I told them that it was the Chaplin and that my grandpa died. For some reason I also said, "It's all good I didn't know him very well." I don't know why I said that. I think I just didn't want to talk about it. In a daze I tried to go about the rest of my day like normal. Later on I sat on my bunk and just started reading the Bible. In fact it's all I did during down times for the next few weeks (that's also when I realized how fucked up and weird some of the shit in there is). Maybe I was looking for comfort, or meaning. When the lights went out that night, I pulled the covers over my head and tried to make myself cry. I didn't understand why I wasn't feeling anything. I was thinking about him nonstop and how messed up it was that all this was happening while I was in jail. I missed him and I missed my Nana. I knew this was a sad day but there was just no emotions tied to my thoughts. I cried when my dog died, I cried when my mom sent me away, I cried many a night sitting alone in stairwells, so why couldn't I cry now? I wasn't worried about looking hard or anything. Contrary to what most people might think about jail or gang culture, nobody is going to think you're a punk if you cry when a loved one dies. Actually, the homies probably would've shown me lots of love, I just didn't want any attention. Ever since I was kid my biggest fear was my Nana or Papa dying, I dreaded this day my whole life. This was the most cherished important man in my world but all I could think about was how bad I felt for my Nana. I wish I could have been there to comfort her. It was our loss together, we were a trio.

UNDER THE BRIDGE

    A few weeks later I was released from the L.A. county jail around 3 am with about $12 to my name and an extreme case of what is known in Alcoholics Anonymous as "The phenomenon of craving." It's the unshakeable craving that drives people to the baffling behaviors drug addicts are known for- like the people that steal from their Nana & Papa. Then there's the women and men that sell their bodies and even their babies for drugs. The menacing demon that drives people to commit robberies and murders just to get enough money for one more fix.
    That night my craving was in the driver's seat, I was just along for the ride. Immediately upon release I power-walked the few miles from the county jail to the alley where my connections tent was. Once there I rapped on the tent and woke up my dealer. He went by the name of "Dread." Dread was probably mid 60's in age. An old, skinny dreadlocked Jamaican dude. I'm not even sure he was really Jamaican but he definitely played up the part. Boy was he was pissed that I woke him up and even more upset that I didn't have $20 (his minimum). He gruffly let me know that he didn't even have any dope to sell me. After some arguing back and forth (because I didn't believe him) he said; "Look man all I got is my morning fix and I shot up part of it before I went to sleep. It's got blood in it man." For those that don't know, in order to inject drugs into your blood stream with a hypodermic needle you need to hit a vein. The way you

know you hit a vein is when your blood starts rushing in the needle. So basically the needle he had with dope in it, also was mixed with his blood. He rattled that sentence off as a last resort to shut me up so he could go back to sleep. He didn't realize I was in demon mode. The grips of that phenomenon of craving had me. The grief from my Papa just passing didn't help either. I wasn't ready to deal with any of it, especially my poor Nana who I knew was in pieces. I handed him the cash and said "Give it to me." Once again I saw that distinct look of shock and disgust in someone's eyes. On the streets money is money. He handed the needle over. Actually, his old white girlfriend gave it to me. I prepped to shoot it immediately. They stared at me in the same manner one would gaze upon a deadly car accident. I balled my fist, slapped my vain, then injected myself with the concoction of old homeless man blood and low grade heroin. I felt a slight rush, then as the phenomenon of craving left my common sense kicked back in. I got hit with that scary feeling again; WHAT THE FUCK DID I JUST DO?

Later on I would be diagnosed with a roaring case of hepatitis C. Fortunately I was able to get it under control and fully cured a few years later. Not sure if I got it from the Dread incident, or one of the other many times I shared needles. Back when I first started hanging out with Shadow, there would be a bathroom full of us all sharing 1 needle. The needle would be so dull we'd have to sharpen it with a match book and almost hammer it into our skin. When I would complain, Shadow would tell me how when he was locked up they would shoot up with a needle made from a sharpened chicken bone and the finger of a latex glove. He said it was a bloody mess but it worked. I was also having unprotected sex with half of the female homeless pop. Not to mention coming in contact with every type of filth imaginable on the street. It's a miracle I didn't have anything worse. HIV and Herpes were pretty common on the streets of Skid Row and Hollywood. Although I was so skinny I think my family assumed I probably had AIDS, or Leprosy by the way I was shunned. In fact AIDS was actually seen as a come up to many die hard addicts. It was a ticket to some of the best prescription drugs you could get. This equated to better drugs and free housing in addition to a bunch of other county benefits. I'm not condoning it, I definitely didn't want AIDS. I'm just giving you a glimpse into the thought process of skid row addicts. You know you're in the wrong place when getting AIDS is cool.

BUT NOWHERE IS HOME...

What happens when you become homeless? Nothing. It's not until you look the part that you lose your humanity.

Ever wonder what it's like to be a beggar? You know the ones you see asking for change outside the market or trying to hustle you out of a dollar on the train. Probably never crossed your mind what it's like but I'll tell you anyways. It sucks. My literary skills may not quite be sufficient enough to paint an accurate picture for you but I'll do my best. To say it's humiliating would be like saying getting ripped apart alive by a shark "hurts". Humiliating is what it feels like the first few times. After days, weeks, months, you sink past the gates of humiliation on through shame and mortification. You go further and further into the abyss till you've scorched through the different atmospheric layers of mental torture. Whoooosh.... Now you're in the black quiet nothingness of your mind. No more pain. No more happiness either. You also notice society silently revokes your membership as a human being. Congratulations you are now tossed into the same category as the cockroach and rats. You thought you were lonely on a rainy day at home alone. Or when a person you loved died or broke up with you. You still had some friends and family though, they just weren't physically there. This is different. You're alone in another dimension of existence. You can see people, but they can't see you. Nor do they want to. No one wants anything to do with you. The entire human population including everyone you know is shunning you. It's the last level of hell. To be outcast and shunned by your species is the deepest nightmare of many. And if you ever do make it back nothing is the same. Everyone smiles and welcomes you home, but, there's no rejoice. You've seen beneath the masks. Once you find out Santa Claus is a lie there is no going back. Once you've seen the dark side you can't unsee it. Everyone you ever meet again, you will be all too aware of just how conditional your relationship is. No matter how much someone says they love you. No matter how deep their undying devotion may seem, once everything is taken, they too will turn their backs. Life, is now like going to a kids birthday party with a partner you know cheated. No one knows you know, you're going along with everything. You're singing happy birthday and trying to enjoy the party but in the back of your mind you're thinking; this bitch is a snake. Everyone seems fake now that you've seen the cardboard and Styrofoam behind the facade. But wait! There is one true soul that will stick by your side through the darkness and keep the pilot light of your spirit from flickering out. A dog. Your dog (or cat) doesn't care if everyone hates you. He doesn't care if you're ugly or broke or smelly. He loves you still, and is all the more happy to see you. I remember showing up at my mother's house one evening, tired, hungry, broken. I hadn't seen or spoken to anyone for a few months and didn't know how I would be received. I wasn't looking for money or anything in particular, just some respite from the elements. Maybe the chance to talk to a friendly face. Instead the reaction I got was; What are you doing here? You can't be here. What do you want? No you can't come in. I can hear yelling in the background. My little siblings aren't even cracking a smile, they're falling in with the reaction of their parents. All I get is frowns. In the midst of all this though my dog Blue is running in circles, sniffing, barking and trying to get past my mom. Finally he makes it to me and is uncontrollably excited to see his old friend. Trying not to be tackled I kneel down to give him kisses and hug his muscular neck, although he can hardly stay still. It only lasts a minute or so till he's wrangled back in the house and I have to leave. But man, what a great feeling. What a great friend. He too would pass before I could make it back. He lives on as a tattoo on my arm and a legend in my heart.

A few weeks ago I met a gorgeous Italian woman in an Amex lounge at the Naples airport. I gave her my number and told her to call me when she gets home. She must've been homeless too.

Oh well... back to our topic. We all hate being talked down to. There's always that one person that thinks they're better than us. Many only have to swallow these types of interactions from a boss or snobby acquaintance. Irritating yes, but we can just vent to a friend about it later and have a laugh. Now picture EVERY single person you encounter looking at you in disgust. Or even worse, not looking at you. That awkward avoidance of any eye contact. *I don't have time and don't want to deal with it.* I'm sure you've done it. I have. If someone does interact with you it's to toss you some change and give themselves a feather in their cap. Mothers bring in their children to shield them from you. Don't even try to pet or be friendly to someone's dog, they tug on their leash and shoot you dirty looks in fear you might sully up the pooch. Or you might hear someone mumble *GET A JOB*. Thanks lady! No shit... Of course I wanted a job. But what do I do for tonight? I tried hard to get work when I was on the streets but when you have no home you have no bathroom. When you have no bathroom you have no shower, no soap, no toothpaste, no shaver etc. Not to mention no changes of clothes or socks. No washer or dryer. If it rained last night and you got wet, you're sleeping in wet clothes. Might take a day or so to dry. I walked around applying for jobs all the time. I didn't even have an ID for a year because my wallet had been stolen and no address to mail the ID to. I even offered to work for free at some places. I was shooed out as if I was radioactive. I also got turned down by a few places for having visible tattoos. Back then it was a sign you were a bad guy. This is before Mr. Cartoon started tattooing celebrities like Justin Bieber and other mainstream stars making tattoos more acceptable. Now don't get me wrong, I'm not really a homeless advocate. Most belong in a mental hospital, rehab or prison. I've never met any homeless person that was "just down on his luck." I for sure don't know the solution to the homeless problem. There are definitely some dangerous malicious people on the streets. I was one at times. Even though I was robbing people, I honestly did not want to. I would try and get work, sell drugs or panhandle first. I wasn't sleeping in my car or couch surfing, like most people are actually doing when they say they were homeless. Sometimes I'd still be starving, cold thirsty and broke praying to God to help me not have to hurt anyone. I hated robbing people. One tourist in Hollywood I stuck up at knifepoint was about to fight back or yell but then looked in my eyes and saw I was almost crying and said, "Hey man its cool here" and gave me some money. He also gave me the worst look of pity ever. Once I was walking down Van Nuys Blvd. in Pacoima looking for people to rob. It was like 1 am. I saw a dude walking towards me so I clutched the gun in my hoodie pocket to get ready. As we crossed paths the fucker pulled a gun out and robbed me! I told him "I ain't got nothing I'm doing the same shit bro" and showed him my gun. He said, "Alright then" and kept walking. I finally came up with a less aggressive way to rob someone without actually robbing them. I would walk up to someone and pull out my gun or knife and say (in an aggressive way) "Hey you wanna buy this gun? How much you got?" Most people got the hint and said "Here (handing over cash) keep the gun" if not I would insist. Again, last resort.

 Keep in mind though many homeless people were once little goofy cute kids too. They've probably walked with their mother and asked; *Mommy why are those people sleeping on the street*? I remember asking questions of the sort when I was little. *Why didn't they just work?* I would think to myself. I didn't understand or like street people. A neighborhood friend of ours was raped at the park by one of the homeless crowd that camped there. I had already moved but from what I heard it was one of the guys that used to buy everyone beer. We only saw her once more after the incident, then her and her family moved away too. I was disgusted by bums and wondered how they could let themselves go so low. I even used to knock out or harass homeless junkies as if they were NPC's (Non Player Characters) in a video game. But now in a cruel (but possibly deserving) twist of fate the tables have turned, YOU are now the person kids are asking their parents about. Every now and again an old girlfriend, high school buddy or friend of your mom will stumble upon you. You pray they don't recognize you, but then you meet eyes and catch that glimmer of recognition. Just as a smile is about to be cracked you see the confusion take hold of their face. They try their best to mask the shock of seeing your current situation. Sometimes they stop for a chat. Their eyes start to get red and tear up in the midst of small talk. You can see your old friend's mind trying to wrap their head around what they are seeing. What happened to the person they once knew? How did it get to this? Is he still in there? If you're lucky they don't stop, they just keep walking.

PRIMITIVE ACTS OF KINDNESS

That's not to say there isn't an occasional heart-warming interaction. I was standing out front of a K-Mart when a Hispanic dude probably in his mid 30"s walked by. "Hey can I buy a smoke for a quarter?" I asked with a defeated spirit. The dude pulled 2 cigarettes out. He put one in his ear and lit up the other. He then tossed me the rest of the pack. He leaned up against the wall and started talking to me while we both smoked our cigarettes. It was mostly small talk, I don't remember all the details. I do remember him mentioning that he had been through some pretty rough times in his younger days too and not to worry. He said I seemed like a smart kid and assured me things would work out in time. This got me choked up. He was trying to encourage me and give me hope. It was a comforting conversation. Now that I think of it I guess he ended up being right. As he departed he shook my hand then pulled out a $5 and gave it to me. Not in a belittling charity way, but in the same manner your uncle might slip you some cash. Right then he broke me, I started crying. Or should I say I was trying my best not to, but couldn't hold it anymore. The man had a deep effect on me. At the time it felt like he was an angel sent to keep me going.

    I hadn't really just *talked* to someone in a while. At least without being scolded or judged. This was simply a nice guy that stopped and spent a few minutes to chat with a down and out kid. He genuinely seemed to care and it mattered to me. Eyes watering, nose sniffling I thanked him as he smiled and left. I didn't quite know what to say or why my physical reaction was to cry. Sure the smokes and few bucks in my pocket was a cool start to my evening. To me, it meant so much more than that. In normal life we meet nice people and have good conversations all the time. It's nothing. But to someone typically avoided by the human race who is often treated with less regard than a dog, it can mean the world. We take for granted the small surge of respect we receive from someone shaking our hand. The brief but important connection we feel from a hug. Or just being able to shoot the shit with a friend. Man is a social creature and not only enjoys interacting with his or her fellows but actually depends on them for his very sanity. Strip him of his companions and community so go with it his humanity. He is left with nothing. He becomes an insect. This is why solitary confinement is currently our highest level of punishment, surpassed only by execution. I'll never forget that experience. So simple, so base, but yet so powerful. I guess when starvation sets in even a plain slice of bread can seem like the best tasting thing on earth. I can only aspire to be as kind of a soul as that dude was to me. I would almost say my entire beggar experience can be justified by the lesson in humanity I received. Just two guys smoking a cigarette in front of K-mart.

BREAKFAST OF CHAMPIONS

How do winners start their day? I don't know, but here's how I started mine. 5 am the methadone clinic opens and I take my methadone dose washed down with four to six 2 mg Klonopins. Jump on the subway from Hollywood to downtown. Once there I'll smoke a little crack and hustle for a few hours. Then, to come down off the crack, I have to shoot some heroin, preferably timed after taking a few more Klonopins. The heroin doesn't hit as hard because of whatever opiate blockers are in the methadone. It still does the trick after you've been smoking crack all day, especially mixed with some pills. Once I feel levelled-out I might do some shop-lifting from a hardware store so I could return the goods for cash or credit. Walk in to a Home Depot, walk out with 4 or 5 diamond blades (for skill saws) under my shirt. Walk back in the other door and return them for cash. Home Depot used to have a good no receipt return policy. Worst case, I sell the tools at a construction site. If shop lifting wasn't feeling right I might take the bus to rich areas and break into cars. Possibly steal some bikes, or whatever other hustle I have going on at the time. Robbing rookie crack dealers is always a good one, or collecting debts for other dealers. Maybe even stealing steaks and sea food from the market. Diapers, baby formula, Mach 3 razors, I'd turn the bus into a flea market on wheels.

Once night hit, I'd be back in Hollywood selling off my crystal meth. In those days it was almost impossible to sell meth downtown. I couldn't even give it away there. Skid Row was comprised mostly of older black and Mexican addicts wanting crack, heroin, pills or weed. Crystal meth was like a suburban designer drug to them I guess. Sounds stereotypical but back then it seemed mostly a Mexican and white drug, black dudes wouldn't touch it. They wouldn't even try it for free! But at the clubs and bars in Hollywood it would fly out of my hands. The gay guys flocked to me like a Lady Gaga concert. I used to hang in the alley between Greco's pizza place and a porn arcade off of Cahuenga and Hollywood Blvd. This was a convenient location because my methadone clinic was basically across the street.

I'd take customers into a booth in the porn arcade and separate out the amount they wanted. I know what you're thinking, but the porn arcade was kind of like a safe zone. The cops seemed to have no interest whatsoever in the shenanigans that went on in that porn arcade. And boy that was a weird place. Plus, the security guard let me do my thing. He was a meth head and "john" from my pimping days that me and my friend Temper had to beat down once (I'll touch on that later). He never sweated me. Try to do the same stuff in the alley, on the street or in a club and you're going to jail. I didn't pre bag individual portions any more. That was an open and shut sales case which at that time meant prison. After catching a sales case that I fought and got dropped down to possession, I was much more cautious. That possession case qualified me for a program the state had going on at the time called prop 36. They were just starting to NOT send you to prison for personal use drugs. Crack and heroin were still felonies but now they were giving you a chance to get help first. Individually bagging would have disqualified me if I was caught. I wasn't Scarface selling kilos or anything, I was just trying to stay numb and survive.

Around 2 am when police presence went up on the streets I'd head back into one of the porn arcade booths to call it a night. I could only be in the booth if I was spending money. I'd try to find the longest videos possible, usually like a 4 hour porn. $6 was the cost, cheaper than a hotel. I could unwind and shoot some dope to the finest cinematic experience the bottom scrapings of the porn industry had to offer. Trying to catch a good night's sleep could be challenging. First off you have the moaning of the movie, even if you turn the volume off, you can bet your neighbor has his on blast. Police sirens, and the drunk Hollywood Blvd. crowd filled in any gaps of silence. The most startling was the "psssst" and knocks on your door from pervs fishing for random encounters. Always make sure you grab a paper towel to stuff in the little peep holes made in some of the booth walls. Even then, every so often you'll see the wad of paper fall to the ground or get pulled through and replaced by an eyeball staring at you. I still get flooded with flashbacks every time I smell someone cleaning their floors with Fabuloso which was the smell the porn arcade had from the constant mopping. Right around the time the Asian granny pirate was receiving her money shot and the movie was coming to a conclusion, the methadone clinic was opening up at 5 am. Then I'd start my day and do it all over again.

THE JENNY CRANK DIET

In case you're wondering how I sustained my 130 pound skeletal physique, well I had a few things on the menu. There was the bag of chips from 7-11 that I would fill up with nacho cheese, Jalapeños and chili for 99 cents. During the day I'd go to downtown LA's Grand Central Market and buy a bollio (Mexican bread roll) for 25 cents, then take it to one of the Mexican food stands and pay them 50 cents to put a little beans and rice in it. I'd throw in a few Jalapeños, radishes and onions and I'd have a pretty good sandwich. Still a comfort food to this day.

For a late night snack the Midnight Mission used to give away free doughnuts at midnight, so I'd scarf down a few. Or I could get a meal from the center over on San Julian but the line was always so long and I didn't want my fellow street hustlers catching me in the food line it was a bad look. If I felt like splurging, I'd buy a $2 ceviche tostada, or a bacon wrapped hot dog at a little Mexican stand. $1 elotes (corn on a stick with mayo, butter, parmesan and chili powder) were a go-to. To feast I'd walk through a Shakey's or Round Table Pizza and swipe whatever leftover slices of pizza and chicken legs were left by diners.

RAMBO MODE

Of course life on the street wasn't always chicken legs and pizza. Once you cross a certain line in appearance and familiarity you are no longer welcome in any commercial establishment. The instant my dirty pair of Nikes crossed the threshold I was met with hostility and ushered back out. This only heightened my frustration and caused a scene. Now my mere presence warrants a call to the police. This was before California had become a homeless safe haven. The more doors that slammed in my face the narrower my options got. Crime or hunger is what it boiled down to. Even the locations where meals and services were provided had become danger zones in enemy territory. All bridges had been burnt. Aggressive action becomes necessary just to eat and stay well. Before, I was just a nuisance, now I had become a menace. No more Mr. Nice guy. Wanted by the police, drug dealers, gangsters and even other homeless people. Hardly a day went by without action. At that point you're constantly in a state of what I like to call RAMBO mode. Just like Buck the dog in *The Call Of The Wild*, humans too can go from civilized to wild beast once those dormant primordial instincts come out. When you're in a constant state of danger with no means of food or shelter these dead instincts kick in. It's "Law of the club and fang." You gotta do what you gotta do, your moral compass is now a liability. You're either predator or prey. Everyone you encounter on the streets needs to be sized up in an instant. You have to learn to read people and fast. One minute you're just walking down the street smoking a cigarette, then in a flash you could be fighting, running or being approached by someone trying to set you up. Skid Row in the late 90's early

2000's was a wild place. L.A. in general. I couldn't walk from one destination to another without an incident occurring. Either dope fiends trying to rob me, or a rival trying to catch me off guard. Not to mention cops, both regular and under cover. I was getting into some form of fight or incident almost every day, sometimes straight out of a dead sleep. The upside to all that is, once you've been in "Rambo mode" you forever have an added confidence knowing you have the ability to kick into gear at anytime. The downside, regular life seems to be in slow motion. The decompression takes years and never fully leaves. You start to crave chaos, it becomes nostalgic like a meal your grandma used to make.

THE KEISTER BUNNY

Downtown LA from Broadway to San Pedro, in-between 2nd to 9th was my Disneyland. Everyone was there; Mickey, Dopey, Sleepy, Drowsy, Grumpy. They were characters alright but not cartoons. Two main gangs (at the time) controlled the downtown LA Skid Row drug trade. One of them my dad and uncle were from so I was able to play that up a little and get a pass (although it was a little more complicated and took a few scuffles).

The other gang didn't sweat me much at first. Then of course shit happens. One of their main dealers called Gato landed in a county jail dorm with me. I used to buy packs (a bundle of 12 $5 heroin balloons) off him on the street so when he arrived, I was happy to see him. He didn't look too comfortable being in jail though. The dorm I was in had pretty strict jail politics and high tension. Oh you stepped off the bunk without shoes on? You're getting beat up. A black dude gave you an apple? You're getting beat up. You peed in the toilet for shitting? 113 burpees. Any little infractions of the jail code got you a 13 second beating or 113 burpees. I once saw a dude get jumped for not wiping when he got up from the toilet. Harsh maybe, but there are some dirty nasty people in there.

Jails and institutions didn't bother me. I actually welcomed the bed, 3 meals and making some friends. I had a lot of good times in jails and have friends I met in there to this day. The part I dreaded and made me fear police was having to kick dope raw, especially in that setting. Once that part was over, I was comfortable. Not like I had anything better going on out there. Gato on the other hand was visibly intimidated and was relieved to set eyes on a familiar face.

This was an odd situation for me because on the street he was higher up the food chain and well respected. He would never say more than 2 words to me. To see him afraid and looking to me for safety was weird. We all love when the tables turn on someone right? I had been in that dorm a while, through a riot and the week of torture we got from the sheriffs after. A beating, and a week in an ice-cold dorm with only boxers. Let me say that again ICE COLD. They blasted the AC so hard on our bare bruised bodies it felt like a week in Guantanamo bay. No shoes, no blankets no mattresses, just metal and concrete covered in tear gas residue. The ten of us (alleged) riot antagonists slept huddled up together to keep our bodies warm. The hot breath of your homie smashed up against you felt like a warm Caribbean breeze on the 2 inches of your body it brought warmth to. Two sack lunches a day that only had the sandwich and apple. I've never been so cold and so

hungry in my life. But it bonded us. After that week new inmates trickled in the dorm that we now were kings of. One of them was Gato. I brought him over to my bunk and as he sat there eating his sack lunch along with some chips I brought out, he told me he had swallowed 5 balloons (of heroin) when he got busted. On the streets we kept our heroin balloons in our mouths as opposed to in our hand or pockets. This way we could just swallow them if the cops pull up. I don't know why he told me this, maybe he was just glad to see me and talking out of his ass. I wouldn't have told anyone. Either way he said it, and once the cat was out of the bag there was no putting it back in. I told him the rules; we've got to give a 3rd to the homies upstairs (Mexican Mafia) a 3rd to the homies in the dorm (shot caller), and me & him will split the rest. I assured Gato he'd be alright. I brought him to my boy running the dorm and floor of the jail. This guy was the biggest most intimidating dude I had ever seen in person. His arms were were bigger than my legs and he had a hair temper. I saw him beat a few people pretty bad. Not beat up like you'd see in a bar fight, I mean till a guys head looked like a bloody pink pumpkin. He was a heroin addict too and we got along good. We were both excited for what the keister bunny had brought us.
Keister bunny: A parody of the easter bunny and a funny name for someone bringing drugs into the jail via the anal cavity.

 If you had to swallow a balloon only for a short period of time you would just take a sip of shampoo and throw it back up. Gato had it in him for hours so we had to put him on potty watch. This meant every time he went to the bathroom someone went with him so he could shit in a clear trash bag. They would get the trash bag with shit in it and add water, mixing it up till it was a transparent tea like liquid. Then poke a hole in the corner of the bag so all the liquid could drain leaving only the undigested solids (like drug balloons) in the bag. Bag after bag we were disappointed, no balloons were turning up. The second day of potty watch we were getting pretty irritated and started wondering if he was full of shit (no pun intended).

That night I was awoken from a light sleep by what sounded like an earthquake or an elephant stampede. Then as grunts and smacks were added to the mix I knew what was going on. Someone was getting beaten, nothing out of the ordinary. Should be over in a few seconds. I got mentally ready in case whatever was happening spilled over my way or turned into another riot. Around the time it should've been over I started hearing squeals, head cracks, and other gut-wrenching noises. Dang, this guy was getting beat really bad and it's going on forever. As tough as I thought I was, the sounds were making my stomach turn. My instinct was telling me to break it up or help whoever it was. The rule is to mind your business though. Still in my bunk I finally sat up on my elbows to see what was going on. I caught a glimpse of the last few stomps to the guys head and saw them drag him to the door. They knocked on the window of the sherif's booth. The door popped open, they drug him out, left him there, then came back in. No one seemed thrilled. There was no reenacting blows landed or bragging, just heavy breathing amongst the silence.

The dude was an unrecognizable bloody pulp so I couldn't tell who it was. Then someone whispered to me "That was your boy." It was Gato. I guess that last potty watch was the straw that broke the camels back and they decided he was lying. All that shit sifting was for nothing and boy did they make him pay. I never saw Gato again in person. None of his dealers would ever sell to me again when I got out and avoided me like the plague. I kept my distance. A few months later one of his boys caught me with my girlfriend at a taco stand. We used to be cordial but I saw his eyes turn to anger when he saw me. I hoped he'd keep walking. Instead he looked at me, sat down right next to my girlfriend and started whispering in her ear and playing with her hair. She recoiled and started cussing, of course then me and him start fighting. Once the scuffle was over he started running off. I thought; *yeah you better run!* Then the taco lady started pointing at me and saying something in Spanish. My girlfriend's eyes flung open as she looked at me "Oh my god look!" As she said that I looked at the X-Acto knife on the ground, then at my shirt. I was wet. I lifted up my shirt and saw 2 small bloody slits below my chest. *Mutha fucker stabbed me...*

CABRON

Slightly after that another situation that had been stewing was about to culminate. Things would get even hotter on the streets for me. Prior to the Gato incident, I used to buy dope from another dude in that gang called Malo. One day, on my way to score, I ran into Malo on the train downtown and bought some balloons off him. Since I was already getting sick I went ahead and smoked some dope under a staircase at the train station. Malo stayed and chatted with me a minute while I smoked. Since I had what I came for I didn't even need to go up. I jumped back on the train and Malo continued out of the station. I didn't see him again after that for a while.

About two years later- I'm minding my own business walking down Broadway. A car screeches up, out comes an excessively muscular cholo in a white muscle shirt. This guy is furious and barking in my face saying I got him locked up. "Who the fuck are you? What are you talking about?" He didn't bother explaining he just swung at me and we started fighting. Then his boys got out of the car and tried to jump me. I didn't even know who or why I was fighting. This was happening on a crowded downtown street and someone tried to break it up or something. I'm not sure but I was able to get separated from the melee and get the hell out of there.

   I found out later that the buffed out cholo was Malo! Last I saw him he was as skinny and strung out as I was. I guess he had just got out of prison. He must've been lifting weights and eating good in there because he was unrecognizably huge. From what I was told by a mutual acquaintance, that day I scored from him and started smoking in the train station, someone had reported it to the metro cops. So the police were waiting for us at the entrance of the station. But since I jumped back on the train they only got Malo. The cops found his dope and he caught a new case sending him to prison. He blamed me.

He must've been stewing on his anger towards me like Robert De Niro's character in that movie *Cape Fear* because he was angry and out for revenge. Every time I set foot in that area it was on. This is where I scored my dope so I didn't really have a choice. I just had to be careful and get in and out of there fast. One occasion him and his friends caught me off guard outside of Grand Central Market which resulted in another wild street brawl spilling on and off of a bus that left one of his boys with a disfigured face and me missing a shirt and shoe. Another time it was an all out chase on foot through a crowded Broadway boulevard. I want to say I even caught him first once. As much as I tried to avoid trouble, I still couldn't help but see these altercations as fun and exciting.

THE MAN WITHOUT A PLAN

The situation started getting too hot for me and was getting old fast. I tried one night to sell off my dope in a less risky area that we called The Circles. I must've been a little too loaded that night because some junkies I was about to sell to, tried to snatch the dope out of my hand and run. I caught them and there was a small scuffle. I was scratched up and my shirt was stretched out but I got my dope back. Now from what I was told, me and the dudes were fighting, then they both ran across the street. We were both yelling something at each other, then I checked my pockets, lit up a cigarette, sat down then passed out on one of the circled planters. I was so high that once I lit the cigarette and sat down I must've forgot what was going on (Benzos have that effect) and nodded off. The low life robbers saw this and came back over to try again. This time they got everything including my cell phone and money. A dude I had sold to before them was in his car shooting up and saw it all go down. He woke me up and brought me to his car. Once in the car he asked where I wanted to be dropped off but I passed out again and wouldn't wake up. When I did come to, the next day, I didn't know what the hell happened. I woke up in the passenger seat of a car by myself. I had absolutely no idea where I was, or how I got there. I just knew all my stuff was gone and I would be sick soon. I got out of the car and realized I was in the parking lot of a car wash in Echo Park. I was broke with no dope to do or sell and no phone. At first I thought he was probably involved somehow in the robbery, but then I slowly remembered the scuffle and how it went down. Who knows maybe he was involved. You couldn't trust anybody, it was like *Game of Thrones* on the streets. Either way I needed to get right. I had him drive me to a rich neighborhood in the valley so I could try to come up somehow. After another bizarre twist of events I ended up getting in a fight with an off-duty cop. I walked by a house and grabbed what I thought was a violin in its case. It was just sitting there next to a stand on a lawn. Easy come up I thought. Then right as I was walking away a little girl came out and was confused asking a parent what happened. It was hers. She was like 8 or 9. Even I'm not that low... I turned around and walked back; I went up to the grandpa and said (in a friendly voice as not to worry the kid): *Hey sorry I picked this up on accident I thought someone left it.* The grandpa looked confused but then caught on to what was happening and thanked me. I apologized again and told him I had a rough day and didn't mean to do something stupid. We talked for a minute then he shook my hand and even gave me a water I think. I walked away relieved I was able to smooth things over and not ruin that kids or her grandpas day. I actually felt kind of proud of myself, and had a good heart to heart with grandpa. About halfway down the block out of nowhere I was tackled like a football player on to a lawn. POW!! WHAT THE FUCK? Next thing you know I'm fighting with this guy trying to restrain me. I flipped on top of the dude and started pummeling him. This grown man in his 40's with a stereotypical cop mustache started screaming at the top of his lungs for help like he was a woman being violated. His high pitch screeches were so unexpected and loud that they even scared me. It made me panic. I was just trying to knock him out now so I could get the hell out of there. All of a sudden, every husband in the neighborhood is out there trying to figure out what to do. The guy is yelling for someone to help and no one is helping him. They were just circling us as this guy is trying and failing every wrestling move, he could think of. The husbands continued to argue amongst each trying to figure out what to do. Again, I don't want to hurt this guy I just want to get out of there. Then one of the dads leaps on me and the others jump in too. Each fat couch potato husband grabs one of my limbs and they crucify me onto the lawn. There was like 6 guys on me, as in actually sitting on me- I could hardly breathe. Once again I was off to jail. While in a holding cell at the local station, a group of sheriffs walked over to peek in on me. They were laughing, I guess the screaming man that tackled me was an off-duty Glendale police officer. The sheriffs and the Police department had a friendly rivalry so they were laughing that it took so much man power to subdue my skinny ass. "He stated that you had super human strength and must've been high on PCP" they laughed. I was far from high and in fact was in withdrawal. The sheriffs crowded the cell as I told them the whole story. "Then he started screaming like a bitch I should've just back handed him!" They were dying laughing, it felt like I was telling a story to my friends at a bar- he must've not been very popular. Luckily he ended up dropping the assault charges but I stayed in jail for the theft of the violin (that I gave back), him and the grandpa showed up in court to testify.

At that point I was pretty much burned everywhere. Especially down town which is bad news for an LA junky. It was like a fisherman being banned from the lake. On top of that my drug tolerance was getting so high that the dope wasn't working anymore. The euphoria was gone, felt like I depleted my brains supply of dopamine. I couldn't get high, at least not in my price range. Remember I wasn't Kieth Richards or some rockstar that could afford a $5000 a day habit. My addiction to opiates, meth and benzos wasn't sustainable in my situation. I couldn't keep up. Any variation in doses was a disaster. I was hurled into painful withdrawal if I took less than normal. I was overdosing in a bathroom if I tried to do more than normal. No one likes being kicked awake in the El Pollo Loco bathroom by a teenage employee trying to mop.

I knew it was only a matter of time before something was going to happen. What would happen I didn't know, but this couldn't go on. I assumed I'd either overdose and die, get killed or go to prison. The thought of getting sober wasn't even in my mind. I had tried countless times before and couldn't last a day. Heroin allows you to feel like heaven in a shit storm. As many lives as drugs have taken they've also probably saved quite a few from taking their own. However, when the drug stops working you pay the price back tenfold. The pain is worse than ever. Your once moderately bad situation is now severe in all aspects. When someone goes to prison in movies big black Bubba saves the new prisoner from other inmates harassing him. Unaware of the debt he's taken on, the naive prisoner thinks he's made a friend. Until they get back to Bubbas cell. The unsuspecting prisoner discovers to his horror that he now has a new master. He is raped repeatedly and is now one of Bubbas bitches. The inmate would've been far better off just getting his ass kicked while learning to acclimate to his new environment. To me the addict and the archetypal prison bitch have a lot in common. Anyone caught in the grips of heroin knows this analogy isn't too far off.

SOMEBODY PLEASE...

I heard a guy in a meeting say his rock-bottom was when he found his best friend hanging dead, and the first thing he did was search his pockets for money or drugs. My rock bottom was less eventful but just as devastating (to me); the drugs stopped working. Simple as that. You can be in a hot musty Skid Row Port o Potty yet be transported to the Elysian fields with a good shot of dope. But when the drugs stop working the reality of your situation grabs you by the balls and peels your eyes open. *NO BLINKING BITCH! LOOK AT YOUR LIFE!* That's what was happening. The drugs were my last friend, I had lost everything else. Did I mind being homeless? Not really anymore, I had grown accustomed. Did I mind having nothing and no one? No. There's no shame in looking stupid if no one's around to see it. Did I fear dying? No. The sooner the better. What I did fear was kicking. What I did mind was having to face reality unfiltered. All the painful things and piles of shit that didn't get dealt with were all waiting patiently for me. As I said before drugs were not my problem they were my solution. Was it time to end it all? Seemed like the best option.

So what ended up happening you ask? After about five years of streets, jails, psych wards, institutions and a life even fellow junkies looked down at, the never ending nightmare would finally come to an end.

On a typically sad day hanging out at a park, the thought came to me to call my mom. Now, I hadn't spoken to my mom in months and we weren't exactly on friendly terms. It's possible I was hoping for some change of heart, or just a friendly voice. Who knows, but I decided to call her for some reason. Maybe it's a primitive instinct to turn to our mother for help in crisis. She did end up helping me, just not in the way I hoped.

Me: "Hey ma, it's Richard"

Mom: "What do you want?"

Me: "I'm just calling to say hi, see how you guys are doing."

Mom: "We're fine Richard. Why are you calling here?"

Me: "What do you mean? I'm just calling to talk. Whatever.. bye.."

Mom: "Do me a favor don't call here anymore till you get your shit together and have some respect for yourself."

Me: "Whatever... Bye..."

I hung up the phone pissed off. *Why the fuck is she so cold to me?* Then it dawned on me, she has a point. I've got to do something.

The next thought was to call my public defender Silvia Patton (bless her soul).

"Hi Mrs. Patton it's Richard "

"Mr. Galvan, how can I help you?"

I admitted to Mrs. Patton that I had a drug problem and I needed help. I told her I wanted to get off drugs but rehabs don't work for me because I can just leave. The only place that can get me sober is jail. I asked her if I can get some jail time first, then go to a rehab. Mrs. Patton knew I had a drug problem but seemed delighted to hear me finally admit it. She then told me: "Well you're in luck because you have a few warrants issued for your arrest and I'll do my best to get you back in a program (I had left the previous ones). Can you come in to court tomorrow?"

"Tomorrow! Ouch. (In the back of your mind you always hope they say no) Yeah I can be there." The next day I showed up to court, got booked and was headed back to L.A. county jail. It was in that hell hole that I would experience the worst and final kick in my life. Knock on wood.

I remember hearing the voice from *The Candy Man* movie in my head "The pain I assure you will be exquisite..." and it was. I would spend the next 5 or 6 weeks of my county jail visit in agony.

The entire stay I didn't sleep more than 10 minutes at a time which in itself was torture. My mind and body were exhausted and in pain but I couldn't sleep. I would get these painfully aggressive yawns. The methadone kick had my bones and joints in excruciating pain like a 190-year-old man. The physical pain was miserable, but the emotional and mental torment was much worse. Your mind and body are in a constant state of panic and anxiety. There was absolutely no relief. No good feelings for weeks, not even for a minute.

To top it off here came the head-twisting seizures from the benzodiazepine withdraw (which can actually kill you and I was hoping it would). One seizure happened in the middle of the day and caused everyone in the dorm to freak out. I was laying on my bunk already in pain when all of a sudden I lost control of my neck muscles. My head started trying to turn like it wanted to do an Exorcist 360. It felt as if there was an invisible ogre trying to snap my head off. My body then started convulsing. I thought I was going to die. "HE'S HAVING A SEIZURE!" The homies grabbed hold of the sides of my mattress like a casket carrying me to the sherifs booth. "MAN DOWN! MAN DOWN!" They yelled as they knocked on the window (someone better be dying or dead to knock on the sheriffs window or you might find yourself kissing a flashlight). A monotone voice comes through the speaker: "Put him in the hall" then the gate pops open. I laid seizing out in that freezing hall way staring at the Baker to Vegas murals for what seemed like hours. Even when it was over I was still in shock. I laid there afraid to move or do anything in fear it might come back. That, my friends, was a little slice of hell on earth. Not just the pain of kicking with the added twist of a seizure, but that hard shot of fear the seizure gave me. Real fear, because you don't know what's happening. Am I gonna die? Will I mess up my spine and be crippled? Maybe end up in a coma or a vegetable? Maybe the wrong deputy will walk by and beat the shit out of me if I can't snap out of it. I didn't know what was happening and there was no friend or even a doctor to say those words everyone wants to hear "You're gonna be alright."

At some point a deputy did stop to ask why I was still lying there and what was going on. I told him I needed to see a doctor, I was kicking benzodiazepines and just had a seizure. The deputy just said to his partner as he called it in "He probably took someone else's psych meds". Even worse that's what the deputies told the doctor when they brought me down. In fact the opposite was true, I hadn't taken any meds. Back then they used to give you Thorazine when you were kicking and that made you feel even worse. It made you feel like you were a brain-dead zombie. Eventually the doctor saw me but all he did was check my blood pressure and give me Benadryl then sent me back to the dorm. Gee thanks doc...

    Once the seizures and restless leg thrashing phase passed, I was left with the most intense case of hot/cold flashes and chills you could imagine. Time slowed to make sure I felt every moment of agony. Each minute seemed like an hour. Every day felt like a week-long endurance marathon of pain. Almost like in that movie *Interstellar* when they're on a different planet and 1 hour there is equivalent to 7 years on earth. That's what it was like but 1 hour felt like 7 years. The only thing that seemed to help was taking hot showers. I was showering as much as possible whenever it was my race's turn. Speaking of races, I also had to keep up with the jail politics and racial boundaries. Since you're segregated by race as well as gang affiliation, it forces you to act as if a racist while you're in there. This behavior not coming natural to me I ended up getting in trouble twice for dealings with my black friends. First time was a warning, the second time I had to do 113 Burpees. For those of you that aren't familiar, a Burpee is kind of like a push-up, squat and jump rolled into one repetition. Other rules also called for exercise every day, which I normally would've loved but I could hardly even do one push up at the time. I was a frail bag of bones fresh off the needle. No one believed me at 130 pounds of boney flesh that I was once a muscular 220lb. I was so skinny that when I would shower a thimble of water would pool up at the top of my sternum. More than once someone has told me I was the skinniest person they had ever seen. I looked like someone you'd see in a photo of the holocaust. I was as weak as I could be. The county jail is definitely not an ideal situation for someone withdrawing from drugs.

    5 or 6 weeks doesn't seem that long to the layman but in

kicking terms that's an eternity of suffering. I was in pain nearly every second I was in there. I couldn't imagine not being in agony. I really mean that. The days of feeling good or even just "normal" (whatever that was) were just beyond my ability to recall. I wondered if this epoch of misery would ever be over. Had I gone too far to come back? Maybe I did so many drugs that I used up all my endorphins. Is it possible to never be able to feel good again and live one's life out in a constant state of discomfort?

This went on for weeks, looking back I can't believe I made it through. How the fuck did I do it? I don't think I would ever be able to do that again. The only thing that kept me going was telling myself: *This is the last time I am ever going through this. This has to end at some point. The hard part is almost over.*

WINNERS DO WHAT THEY GOTTA DO
(LOSERS DO WHAT THE FUCK THEY FEEL LIKE DOING)

Towards the end, my physical pain mellowed out a bit, but I still wasn't sleeping. Going weeks without more than five-minute cat naps put me in a weird exhausted mind numbing dream like state. I tried everything to get some sleep but nothing helped. Everyone had some suggestion they knew would work. "Try drinking lots of milk," "Wear out your body with exercise till you're exhausted, then you'll fall asleep!", "Try to meditate", I tried it all nothing could put me to sleep more than a few minutes.

Finally after the long wait a rehab came to pick me up.

This wasn't the type of rehab you see on TV with a manicured lawn and pool, this is where you went when you had nowhere else to go. The place was a state funded facility for people that were court mandated and fresh out of jail or prison. Located on the corner of Crack and Gang, it was just blocks away from the drug haven MacArthur Park just outside Downton LA. I was back in my old stomping grounds. The residents and environment didn't differ that much from the jail I had just left (at least not on the surface). Great, how am I supposed to stay sober here? It wasn't until that first night, in the rickety but comforting rehab bed that I got my first good night's sleep again. I even slept straight through the first day of groups then woke up for dinner and ate like a king. They definitely fed you good, way better than the streets and jail at least. I ended up spending 364 days in there. I would also secretary the Sunday night AA meeting there for the next 18 years. That place truly saved my ass. It was the most productive year in my life since the one when I learned to walk and use the potty. Here's a few things I got out of my time there: I got my General Education Diploma (with the intent to join the military but my criminal record disqualified me). I cleared up all my open court cases and restitutions. I learned how to drive and got my license. I met two life-long friends. I picked up some of the principles that would drive my life and my favorite saying; *Winners do what they gotta do, losers do what the fuck they feel like doing.* I proudly discharged my Probation and Proposition 36 cases early (I even got a hug from the DA). I started my first career, got my first apartment and my first car. It was on the front steps of that rehab when I was handed a piece of paper with two storks on it that said CONGRATULATIONS A BABY IS ON THE WAY! One of the best memories of my life. My oldest daughter Isabel was born a few months after I discharged. What a difference a year can make. The jail van dropped me off at The Royal Palms a disaster of a human with nothing to live for. I left that place a smiling man with a fighting chance to make it in life.

SUB ZERO

Why did I make it when so many others don't? Two reasons; desperation, and I actually got a sponsor and worked the 12-steps wholeheartedly. Working the steps was 100 percent a deciding factor. This came after some bucking and disbelief of course. The steps were the last thing I ever wanted to do. I used to think: What a lame program, how is a book going to keep a needle out of my arm and fix my fucked up life? That stuff might work for some average Joe that drank a little too much. *Oh you lost your job? Poor thing.* I was sleeping under a parked semi with a 60 year old prostitute, smoking crack with a broken pipe and cigarette butts I picked off the ground. Get the fuck out of here...

Let me tell you what rocked my world and changed my mind. While in rehab out on a weekend pass, I drank (for the second time). While drinking I got a frightening taste of something they talked about in the AA meetings. They called it the "phenomenon of craving." It was the term Dr. Silkworth (a co-author of the Alcoholics Anonymous book) used to describe what happens when an alcoholic consumes alcohol as opposed to a non-alcoholic person. The alcoholic can feel completely normal, then drink some alcohol and be taken over by an uncontrollable craving that kicks in. This *phenomenon of craving* is overwhelming and the person can't stop even when he wants to. The alcoholic will often continue even when faced with ultimate sacrifices. This craving is said to be the manifestation of an allergy that non alcoholics do not have according to Dr. Silkworth.

    I used to think it was all just bullshit, till that day. As I was calmly drinking my 32oz Corona all of a sudden my heart started beating faster, my adrenaline started pumping and the thought came in my head to score some dope. I had absolutely no desire and was adamant not to get high prior to drinking. I recognized this feeling creeping in and what was about to happen next. I was scared. All those times I had started a night off with the old "I'll just have a beer or two" or "Let me just take one hit" but ended up going on a raging bender instead, it was this *phenomenon of craving* kicking in. It had happened before so many times, now I had a name for it. Immediately I realized what they meant by not being able to safely drink or use again. Even though I didn't consider myself an "alcoholic" since heroin was my drug of choice, drinking still kicked it off. I freaked out, capped the bottle right away and went back to the rehab. That's not a summarization, that's exactly what I did. Next day I went to a meeting and got a sponsor.

    After being sober a couple months I had a little epiphany. I was dead broke, and my life was still a pile of wreckage with no sign it was going to get better anytime soon, but I was still sober. Most of all I was happy. My circumstances were shit yes, but I was slowly cleaning things up. Not only was I repairing my life but I was helping others repair theirs. I felt better than ever. I had always assumed you had to be living a good life to be happy. I didn't realize you could be happy at the bottom with so many problems. Was I mentally deranged?

What reason did I have for being happy? I had lots of effort and some progress but no real results yet. I didn't understand it but I sure felt good. I remember the exact moment it hit me. I was walking down the rehabs old musty red carpet hallway (think The Overlook Hotel from *The Shining*) after a workout and I thought to myself: "I'm happy. If I could always feel this way without drugs, I can stay sober forever." I really didn't think it was possible to feel this good without some mind-altering substances.

They say you stop maturing when you start regularly using drugs. I started at the end of 6th grade and to say I was as immature as a 6th grader wouldn't have been a complete lie. Although I did leave that place sober and had made huge leaps forward, my problems were far from over. I wasn't starting from zero, I was deep in the negative. It took a lot of hard work just to get up to ZERO that's how far down I was. I wasn't a normal person with nothing starting fresh. I was a high school dropout gang member with felonies on my record and no family support. I had a fucked up mentality and emotional wiring, I was prone to violence and would lose it over the most simple dilemmas or disagreements. I was highly ignorant and uneducated with no social skills or self-esteem. No financial support, not even for gas money let alone the deep debts and collections I had from credit cards, fines and restitutions mandated by the court. I was so broke I ended up having to do jail time (sober) for some of the tickets I owed. I also owed banks money too so I was on Check Systems and couldn't open any types of accounts. I had no family or friends that would let me stay with them, no mentors, no one to talk to or give me advice. To top it all off I had a baby on the way! A buddy in rehab had just got out from a long stretch in prison, learned a trade in there, had no debts, no kids and was able to live with his mother till he got on his feet. The dude was still whining that he had to start over even with such a head start. I did have a few things going for me though, my willingness and ignorance.

LOVE DON'T LIVE HERE ANYMORE

I soon learned that not everybody will celebrate your sobriety and things don't always go as expected. Sometimes your old relationships don't get repaired and that's ok too. While in rehab everybody was repairing relationships and reconnecting with their family. I assumed I was supposed to be doing the same. At that time, before the world lost my Nana she was living with my mom. I would try to visit her and my mom for an hour or so on my weekly passes. Nana left the earth a few months before my 1 year clean. Afterwards I tried to continue stopping by my mom's house here and there hoping to maybe be a part of the family. Maybe even gain some sense of normalcy. Not that there ever was one, but both sides of my family seemed to be doing well so I thought maybe this could be a new chapter. When I finally got my 1 year sober I stopped by my mom's house eager to share the news. To my surprise her attitude was; "What are you doing here?" Confused, I asked her what she meant. She said: "You can't just show up. Why do you keep coming here?" Still wondering what the problem was, I told her "I'm just visiting" it's not like I was asking for money or favors. I was honestly just trying to visit my mother and rebuild (or build) some sort of relationship. I don't remember her exact words but it was something disheartening. She basically told me to stop coming. I proudly mentioned to her and my stepfather that I just got 1 year sober and was doing good. My step-dad then barked out: "So what? You should've never been doing drugs in the first place." Which I guess was true, but damn...

My real dad had somewhat of a similar reaction. I reconnected with him and that side of my family with whom I hadn't talked to in almost 2 years. When I told him I was sober now and my girlfriend was pregnant, all they did was try to convince me to get an abortion and gave off the same stranger danger unwelcoming vibes that I got from my mother. My family's lack of enthusiasm didn't shock me, eventually they'd warm up a little. What finally hit me though was the gravity of my Nana and Papa being gone. It was like Mike Tyson punched me in the chest when I realized that I would never see either one of them again. I would never get another warm heavy perfumed hug from my Nana. No more grabbing a soda from the fridge, plopping on the plastic covered sofa and telling them my prospects (real or made up). My Papa would never look me in the eyes again and tell me what a smart kid I was and that I could do "good things" with my life if I "just applied myself". Just a few loving words and moments of eye contact into his wise greying eyes could rally my down 'n out junky heart. If only for a while. Never again, they were gone. All that was left for me now was my fair-weathered family. Good for holiday visits and about an hour worth of small talk. Any attempts of conversation beyond the surface level turned into a heated argument. My presence past the meal was met with yawns and hints towards the door. I had nobody left, at least no real relationships. Nobody to report my accomplishments to, nobody to make proud, there was nobody on my team... The entire planet felt like enemy territory in a foreign country.

MOCKING BIRD

Then, January 11, 2006 in the middle of a late night rerun of *Seinfeld* my daughter Isabel was born.

Once the night settled down all the nurses left the room. The lights were off and her mother was knocked out. Isabel was bundled up like a burrito lying there in a little plastic tray softly lit by a warm heating lamp. I was just sitting there staring at her, watching this little baby sleep so peacefully. It was then that the feeling of love started to make its return back into my system. As happy as I was to have this baby laying in front of me, the happiness was soon replaced with a deep pity. This poor baby had just lost the birth lottery. I felt so sorry for her. The poor kid has no idea what a loser her dad is. Her mother wouldn't end up doing very well either. Any baby born to us must've really pissed someone off. Somewhere there's a baby being born to a big loving family of doctors or scholars. This kid was dropped off to a guy that almost got beat up for misspelling his own gang in big graffiti block letters. I hardly had enough gas in my bucket to drive us home. But that night I made a promise to the baby. I vowed that I would be the best father I could be and do everything in my power to give her a good life. I would sooner set the whole world on fire before I would ever let her down.

As hard as I tried to make things work, within a few

months of Isabel being born her mother and I split up. She wanted gangster Richard, I just wanted to be regular ass guy Richard. She moved to the Jordan Downs projects in Watts and laughed at me for having a regular job. Yours truly wasn't going back to jail or drugs, I was trying to change my life. The shame I felt for bringing an innocent baby into this mess was deep. The odd jobs I was doing for my step-dad and his friends paid little or nothing at the time. We would do 12-18 hour days, I was exhausted but it gave me a shot to learn a trade (studio lighting for television). In the meantime, I was dead broke putting $1.60 worth of gas in coins. I couldn't even donate blood for cash because I had Hepetitis C. My car would overheat every few miles and I'd have to stop and fill the radiator with water. One day I took Isabel to the mall just to get out of the house. We strolled into a children's clothing store, nothing fancy just a little mall store. Isabel was just excited to be out in the mall hoping to get something. I saw parents picking out piles of outfits like nothing. I grabbed a matching pair of shorts and shirt to show it to Isabel. It was so cute, she smiled and liked it! I checked the price. I just saw a few days' worth of gas and put it back. She looked confused. I felt like such a fucking loser. I told Isabel Santa would bring it for her. Later on I called my mom and asked if she could please buy it as a Christmas present to Isabel, and she did. There was no pride in me, I certainly didn't feel like a man, I felt like a worm. Maybe her mother was right, I'm just a sucker. Sucker or not Isabel was all I had, and I made her a promise that I'd do whatever it takes.

 Hoping for some respite from my day, I dozed off with Isabel for a daytime nap. I woke up, feeling like shit before my eyes even opened up of course. Isabel was laying next to me still asleep. I looked over at her beautiful face sleeping in such peace. She always woke up in the happiest of moods. So innocent, so full of joy. I contemplated that the only thing I could ever do for this kid was fuck that all up. Unbelievable how this wonderful being was left here with me to care for it. I probably couldn't keep a pet roach alive. I just kept staring at her and staring at her. Then, I must've fell into some type of deep meditation or trance. Something happened that I had never experienced. Out of nowhere my entire body felt like it was being flooded with the feeling of pure love. That's the best way I could describe it. It was like someone connected a hose to my brain and opened up the faucet, filling my entire dry shrivelled body with hydrating love. No fear, no shame, that was washed away, just love. The experience was brief but extremely powerful. I consider this somewhat of a spiritual event in my life. It changed me. It really did. It was a moment of bliss without any drugs or spectacular event happening. I was just laying there staring at a baby. Maybe some baked-in paternal instinct knew I needed a massive shot of endorphins to keep going? Maybe since I had been doing drugs for so long my natural reserves needed lots of time to rebuild. Now that I had been sober about 2 years maybe my body had such a huge reserve of these chemicals that when it tried to give me a little it accidentally let loose. I have no clue what it was to be honest. Whether it was a freak event of the body or a deity, either way; good looking out, I needed it. That might've been the happiest I have ever been in my entire life, even to this day. It was a beautiful moment. I don't know how long it lasted, maybe 2 minutes give or take. Unfortunately, the moment faded and the details of my life started to creep back in. I was back, but to a new baseline with a lingering happiness that stayed with me for years. My pessimistic nature was swapped out for new shiny optimism. I had a whole new disposition to life and again it lasted for years. I'd say I kept this general happiness as a default for about 15 years. I'm not saying I was always happy for 15 years straight. I'm saying that even when bad things hit it would only mess me up for a couple hours and then I would work my little AA program and default back to a general mood of feeling pretty damn good. Maybe that's what normal people always feel like, I don't know. It was like a brand new car to me. Much better than the "I'm a piece of shit, fuck my life and fuck you" default I had been living with since I could remember. I knew now true joy *was* possible without drugs, but could I possibly induce that feeling again and make it last longer?

    Isabel came to live with me when she was about 3- for the next few years I *happily* struggled as a single dad. Had to briefly dabble back into selling guns, which caused the gang life to creep back in a bit, but I quickly course corrected. My career working in the studios finally started to pick up. I made decent money consistently. Isabel spent a few weekends a month with her mother, which allowed me a dating life. I ended up getting into a relationship that lasted about 2 years. Let's just say I still had plenty of character defects lingering. Around this time I finished my 4th and 5th steps (getting rid of resentments) this played a huge role in my life. What a weight off my shoulder that was. More on resentments later.

VENTURA HIGHWAY

At nine years came my next big leaps in life. I met my first wife and mother of my youngest children and bought a house. This is about 2013 at the tail end of the 2008 financial crisis years. With $1500 in my bank account, I put an offer on a house. Then I borrowed from my girlfriend and friend Ruben the rest of the down-payment and bought my first house. What a great feeling, especially after 3 failed escrows. Growing up moving place to place never really having anywhere that felt like "Home" it was always my dream to buy a house.

Around the same time, I had done all the amends I could in my 9th step. Which meant I was basically done with my steps because 10,11 and 12 were ongoing and already in practice. Yes, it took me that long to complete my steps meeting with my sponsor once a week. No, it is not typical in AA, but it was typical in the group my sponsor was from, called the 4th dimension in Los Angeles. What took the bulk of that time was my 4th and 5th step. I had hundreds of names. It took me about two years to finish the writing (working on it 10-60 minutes a day) and another two years to read it out to my sponsor. We dissected each resentment sufficiently. I couldn't imagine it being as effective or powerful if we did it any less thoroughly. The 9th step took a couple years too, just because there were so many people I had to find and at the right time. Once I was done with my amends though, wow, being freed from years of guilt was liberating. I had what they call in AA, a spiritual awakening. When I use the term "spiritual awakening" you probably have some picture in your mind of a hippie falling on his knees as God blasts him with a ray of light. That's not what I mean. For our purpose it's just a term used to describe a radical change in one's thinking and perspective. People describe having these types of occurrences after a near death experience, like a horrible car crash or winning a battle with cancer. Something that shook their life to the core.

Some people get sober after having one of these experiences. Mine came years after I got sober and was able to unpack the events of my past and repair whatever damage I could. I wouldn't say my experience was supernatural or religious in nature, but I could see how someone could believe they were touched by their god. It was profound. Not in a feel-good way like that first experience, this one made me realize how much damage I had done. All the people I hurt. How hurt I was. The way I had been warped by my world. It was all so clear. I got a whole new perspective on my life, past, present, and in general. I saw that the thug mentality I had been walking around with for most of my life was no longer necessary. It was old software that needed to be updated. I was operating with personality traits that had been downloaded as a kid to cope with family, friends and environment. These traits may have been needed for survival growing up and coming of age but now were obsolete. Some acted more like viruses and needed to be deleted. I was a man in my 30's walking around with my teen identity. No wonder I hadn't felt right. Realizing all this gave me hope that better days were ahead. Things started to make sense now. I had a new appreciation for my life. I no longer took my time for granted.

One of the first things I thought was no more wasting life in a career I didn't like anymore. No more working on someone else's dreams. I realized I was working Isabels childhood away. 10-16 hours a day 5-7 days a week up to 30 plus days straight sometimes. I wanted to spend more time with my woman and kid, build something, with them. I developed a hunger for knowledge and started reading, listening to audiobooks and watching *YouTube* videos on starting businesses and real estate investing. My girlfriend and I saw an opportunity so I took out a personal loan from the bank and maxed out all my credit cards. We opened up a dance studio together in LA near Universal Studios called 101 Dance Center.

Soon after that I traded in my BMW for a used fiat, then put our house up for rent. I moved us all into a cramped 1 bedroom apartment near the dance studio in order to pay down debt and save up to buy another house. This put a strain on my relationship, we broke up for a while during that period. Eventually we reconciled and got married. Even though I wasn't able to save up much, where there's a will there's a way. We ended up getting my wife's mom to come live with us and pitch in on the down payment to buy another house. A year later after paying down my debts, I used up all my credit cards and lines of credit again to buy some properties abroad. Next year I bought another house in Woodland Hills and moved us again. Eventually I was able to quit my career and live off my rental income and businesses. The newest one being a Sober Living and an online drug treatment program. This was around 2018 pre Covid so treatment via FaceTime and Zoom was not yet accepted, in fact most people called me unethical. That was of course till Covid hit and everyone jumped on the treatment via ZOOM train. I don't know if I was the first (it depends on who you ask) but I was definitely one of the first three pioneering batch of online drug treatment in the US. There were no actual results when you Googled online drug treatment, aside from one or two that seemed to be more therapy than drug treatment.

ANIMAL FARM

By fifteen years sober the seeds I had planted years earlier were starting to bear fruit. I was living a life I could only dream of when I was on the streets. I had a bunch of properties, a house on the beach in Malibu, nice cars and a different Rolex everyday. I wasn't Jeff Bezos rich or anything like that but I definitely wasn't tearing up from not being able to buy my kid a slice of pizza anymore. Most importantly unlike Jeff Bezos or all the other rich people I was familiar with, I owned pretty much all my time. That was my real goal. Who cares if you have a bunch of money if you don't own your time. I was able to go anywhere, anytime for however long I want. Everything I touched seemed to bloom. Real estate, businesses, stocks, crypto, all my picks were doing well.

A few years prior, nobody, I mean nobody, wanted anything to do with any ventures I had. I would spend all day going door to door, business to business trying to push whatever I was doing. Then I'd pick up Isabel from school and keep going. I took Isabel everywhere with me like the guy in *There Will Be Blood*. Whether I was promoting the dance studio, trying to find properties, get loans or treatment centers to work with me. Even though we struck out 95% of the time, I still loved just being out with her. My little road dog. Eventually the tides turned, people started blowing me up wanting *me* to be a part of *their* deals. Funny how that works. Reminds me of what Malcom X says in *The Autobiography of Malcom X*: "Sometimes if you want something you have to look like you already have it."

I didn't use to care about the money all that much. Especially since it just seemed to make friends and family resent me. I just wanted enough so I didn't have to sell off my life off anymore. I wanted to use my time for travel, family, and to be of service. But then something weird started to happen, greed kicked in. Almost like a gold fever. My dream was just to live on the beach, surf every day and not have to worry about money. I was there, why wasn't that enough?

One afternoon a friend stopped by for a walk and talk on the beach. We were joking around about how I stood out like a sore thumb in the neighborhood. We laughed at what the rich old white people must've thought of me. I don't look like an athlete or a rapper, I definitely don't look like a business man, I look more like the gardener or liquor store clerk. I always tried to downplay everything by saying I was the poorest person in Malibu. It started as a joke, but it stuck in my mind. It drudged up a little self-consciousness. As civilized as I appeared to be on the outside, the insecurities of that feral street kid getting shooed out of stores still lingered. Dormant for years, the feeling of being "less than" was now reignited. I felt as if I looked poor. I wanted to make sure everyone knew I wasn't broke the minute they laid eyes on me. But why? Why did I care what strangers I'd never even meet think about me? Why couldn't I just be satisfied with my life as is? I don't know if man is wired for satisfaction (at least not this man). Wired to seek satisfaction yes, but once we top a peak, we see another just beyond. *Maybe if I can just reach that next peak I'll be ok...just one more...*That is what I like to call the disease of MORE. "Bro you got MOREliosis!"

I remember, middle of the night being freezing cold in a parking garage. Curled up in a ball inside my t shirt praying for either sleep or morning to come. I thought: all I want is a warm spot to sleep at night and I'd be happy. Not even a room, just a warm safe nook in a staircase or something. When I got to the treatment center and had a warm place to sleep, I thought: all I need is an apartment now and I'll be good. After I got a one bedroom apartment I thought: I just need a 2 bedroom so Isabel and I don't have to be crammed. Then it was a house, then a bigger house, then a nicer area. Now I just needed a vacation house, then another. Same situation when I was on the bus: I just need a car, any car and I'll be happy. I'm sure you can guess how that went. It made me think of a time back when I worked in television. We were shooting a reality show at this spectacular 30-million-dollar mansion in Bel Air. The location guy told me that when he got hold of the owner to ask about renting the house for the shoot, the owner had forgotten he still owned it! Imagine forgetting you own a 30-million-dollar mansion. I thought: I bet the guy with the 30 million dollar mansion is dissatisfied and envious of the people with 100 million dollar mansions. The people with $100 million dollar mansions are probably envious of the cat that has five of em. The cat with five $100 million mansions is envious of the dude with a private island. The dude with a private island is envious of the king that rules a small country. The king that rules a small country is envious of the men that rule the major countries and they all want to rule the world. There is no end when someone suffers from MOREroids. So what do we do?

 I used to always say- the tortoise wins the race. I liked to do things slower and steady; work smarter not harder. I had no desire for gambling or get-rich-quick schemes. Once I got MOREpox I started making rash decisions to make money faster. This is mid covid times so things were all up in the air. I sold my rental properties to invest in stocks, crypto and NFT's. Which I had been doing good in for a while. I should've just stuck to what I did know which was L.A real estate. I made a lot of money at first, then things started heading downhill fast. The market started dropping, crypto started dropping and at the same time my treatment center was taking hits. We were going through an audit from one of the biggest insurance companies and that seemed to affect all our payouts so there were no profits coming in. For more than a year no money came in and all my investments were just sinking. The only thing that didn't go down was my monthly bills which were in the mid 5 figures. This caused me to act in fear and make other dumb moves and lose more money. I even created my own Non Fungiblee TokenI hired my favorite graffiti artist and spent a bunch of money. Unfortunately, when launch time came I only sold two. Now I was Mush from *The Bronx Tale* everything I touched turned to shit. The snowball just got bigger as it rolled down the mountain. Eventually I was upside down and had to start selling off assets at the worst time possible, at a loss. 15 years of work; one bad year. I blinked and everything was gone.

Now I had taken plenty of loses before, none had ever really affected my psyche. I once bought some beach houses and land in San Juan Del Sur but after a political uprising had to sell them at a total loss. I wasn't really bothered. I used to proudly say: "nothing can upset me for more than a couple of hours." I was that solid on my feet and mind for a long time. My confidence was concrete and I stayed in a general state of happiness for over a decade. The first few years sober, people in AA would say: "You're just in the pink cloud phase, wait till life hits you. Then we'll see how happy you are!" I figured those people were just doing it wrong because life did hit me plenty of times and I still felt great. I was in that "pink cloud" for about 15 years straight. It was no pink cloud or supernatural phenomenon. I was just living by a personal program that worked.

I've never been good at obeying rules, especially following directions mindlessly. AA has some great concepts, I took what I liked and left the rest. Books, programs, philosophies, lifestyles, cultures; I plucked the fruits I liked and made my own smoothie. I had to piece together something that fitted and made sense to me. I wasn't satisfied with just being sober. Yes that was a must, but also a bare minimum. People in 12-step programs seemed to treat sobriety as the final stage, to me it was just a beginning. I didn't share my Frankenstein'd program with my sponsees or others in the rooms out of respect for AA. Plus, AA people tended to be pretty evangelical when it came to deviations. Tell someone in AA you are doing things differently and they'll say you're headed towards a relapse and running on "self will." *Self will* they use in kind of a derogatory way to describe someone that is not following "Gods will" (whatever that is) or the AA program as it is laid out. Neither are laid out clear enough to actually know whether you're following them or your own will. Unless something doesn't go right then obviously it must've been "self-will" of course. Life's perfect when following "Gods will," good luck trying to figure that out. I never could or even tried to figure that out. If you figure it out let me know. Beware of anyone that tries to tell you they know what God's will is for your life, i.e. what job you should take, who you should date, or any other big life decisions. I've seen people in 12-step programs start dictating other people's lives just because they had been longer without a drink. Personally, I just believed that some general principles should be used as bumpers in one's life to live within. My sponsees that did take my personal program suggestions seemed to like it, they even suggested I write a book. I wasn't trying to reinvent the wheel; I was just passing along bits and pieces of info and direction other people had taught me along the way. I knew they were practical and good general guidelines for life that almost seems like common sense now. It wasn't until I strayed off the path of my own program that I would realize how effective it was.

ANTHONY BOURDAIN

Sometimes in order to see something clearly you have to step away for a bit. While I didn't relapse, I did fall back into a diseased mindset. My disease of MORElaria manifested in the form of "hustle culture." An ailment based solely upon how you look and what others think. It's Self-consciousness on steroids. Work more to make more money, to buy more things, to look like you have more than others. You crave more money and clout and will do whatever it takes to get it and make it known. We see this now more than ever with social media.

My financial losses put a crack in my self-esteem, but even when I had enough money to buy almost anything I wanted I was still depressed- because I was tying my self-worth to the material world. Pretty amazing and at the same time sad how a few numbers changing on the screen of your phone can completely alter your life. Good and bad. Especially the zeros. If more zeros are added to your numbers, you get happy, if your account reaches zero you get sad. Very sad.

The fear of "losing it all" was no longer just a fear. It happened. I was now in full-on panic attack. Prior, my wife would tell me "things always work out." *Yeah right...* She'll never be on the street because she has family. I on the other hand land smack on the concrete with no cushion. Everyone has a fear of losing everything, but very few actually do. I had already been homeless and lost everything before, so I knew it wasn't some far-out fear. Some people have so much parental support and are so stabilized in their family that it would be impossible to become homeless. I have a friend that has been a heroin addict over 20 years; no matter how bad he messes up and how much money he blows he can always live in the back of his parents' house. They also feed and give him small amounts of money here and there. He'll never be homeless while they're alive. Which in my opinion is keeping him sick. As funny as it sounds, I've met a few people on the streets that for some reason chose to be homeless, even though their family was begging for them to come home. Me and my friend Brandon chased a young couple out of Hollywood once. We heard the girl's parents crying for her to come home. She was on the phone with her mother demanding mom send money. The mother was crying and the dad was jumping on and off the call. They were begging and pleading with their daughter who was maybe 17 to come home. Brandon and I looked at each other and said " Wait your parents want you home?" The girl responded with something like: *Yeah but fuck them they don't understand me.* My friend and I wished in our hearts our family would want us back. We couldn't believe these kids were out here by choice. Brandon being a huge intimidating dude started screaming at the couple to get the fuck out of Hollywood and go home. He said if they ever came back he would kill them. He was so intense it started to scare me. They left in a hurry.

Whether a fear is a reasonable one or not it's like an infection, you have to kill it immediately before it starts spreading. Once it's got you in its grips it's hard to make sound decisions. If you've ever played the game of Tetris I'm sure you've had the experience of messing up the placement of a piece. Once distracted, another one slips through to the wrong place. You start to panic and put yet another piece in a bad spot, then the pieces pile up and you start just putting them anywhere. Next thing you know they've stacked to the top and you lost the game. Now if you would have stayed calm and ignored that first blunder, you'd have been fine. Instead fear took the wheel and drove you straight into a tree. That's pretty much what happened in my life but unlike Tetris I couldn't just hit NEW GAME. This was no game, my kids just lost everything too. All my properties, businesses, investments and even my wife were all gone within 18 months. I fucked up big time. It was like quicksand, the more I struggled to save myself the faster I sunk. Sometimes I'd wake up and for a few seconds thinking it was just a bad dream, but it wasn't. Not just the money, I could always get money again, but my life as I knew it was gone. Fifteen years' worth of work, POOF, back to square one. When I started, I had no responsibilities and all the time in the world to make mistakes. If all I ate was instant noodles and protein shakes for a while so what. This was different, now I had five kids and an ex-wife relying on me for food, clothing, quality time and respectable living standards. I hardly had time to watch a movie let alone build a new life with absolutely no type of existing structure or support. I was on my own. Every dude likes to think of himself as "the lone wolf" from time to time. There's something stoic and mysterious about it I guess. The truth is the lone wolf dies off. Without the pack to pick up slack when times get tough the lone wolf perishes. That is why friends, family and community are so important.

Just as a nuclear bomb has radioactive fallout after the initial destruction, there was a fallout after I blew up my life. Once the dust cleared and the panic settled, I rolled smoothly into a debilitating depression that lasted a little over a year. Yes, an entire year. I'm not talking about rainy day blues either. I mean all I thought about was what a mammoth loser I was and how I let down my kids. In between those thoughts were the ones on how I could get out of this life. After my Papa died my Nana used to always say to me "Honey, I wish the good lord would take me already." I found myself saying the same thing to my ex-wife. She was safe no matter what, her parents were good people that had her back and bought her a little flat in Barcelona and she kept the dance studio for income after the split. Thankfully we remained civil. We shared custody of our 2 toddlers and my 3 daughters from a previous relationship lived with me full time. My kids and the fact I didn't have life insurance money to leave them is all that kept me above ground. I held off giving the reaper a call till I could come up with a way to get them enough money to get a head start in life again. My teen daughters had nowhere to go if something happened to me they would end up in foster care since their mother was not doing well and no longer active in their lives. Not long ago my kids were set for life. I had properties for each of them and enough means to support whatever path they decided to take. Now they were eating oats for dinner.

In fact it was so bad in my head the only thing that

calmed my racing mind down enough to fall asleep at night was fantasies of dying. I would tell myself, in a month from now I'd be dead so none of it matters anyway. That would comfort me. Indulging these thoughts was my version of counting sheep. I hadn't been depressed before for more than a few hours here and there in the past 15 years. I didn't think it was possible for me to be stuck in this psychological purgatory for so long. I was miserable as a kid, but I really didn't have much of a gauge to compare it to, so it was a baseline for me. After being free from the gloom for so long this really hit me hard. The way I had been living my life before worked. It allowed me to surf the waves that life sent me. Until I stopped working it and wiped out. Now I was drowning and couldn't get back up. How do I get back to that? I didn't have the type of tools yet to get me out of such a deep malfunction.

GET BUSY LIVING OR GET BUSY DYING

Lying in bed dreading another sleepless night of tossing and turning, I clicked on a documentary about Bill Wilson the founder of AA. I normally have no interest in any AA material outside of the actual program itself. I typically like to doze off to horror or crime but clicked anyway because I was tired of scrolling. The documentary turned out to be fascinating, it mentioned that Bill Wilson the founder of a program that suggests total abstinence from mind altering substances was experimenting with LSD! While he was sober! "I found myself with a heightened color perception and an appreciation for beauty almost destroyed by my years of depression" WOW! Then he added "I am sure that LSD has helped me very much" and how the psychedelic helped him "eliminate barriers erected by the self, or ego, that stand in the way of one's direct experience of the cosmos and God." Holy shit, this was blowing my mind. First of all, I was shocked Bill W. had gone through a major depression, and even more shocked that it was LSD that helped him out of it. Another layer of surprise was the fact that he was able to use a mind-altering substance multiple times without a *relapse* back into alcoholism. Why was AA excluding this potentially lifesaving information from its members? Members that live and die by the words printed in that book and the teachings of Bill W. I had so many questions, so I started to do some research. What I found was amazing, the gist of which is: Most experts agree LSD as well as psilocybin are non-addictive and have been shown to have positive results in the treatment of depression, PTSD, anxiety and even addiction. Well, I was sold. I had nothing to lose and if it was good enough for Bill W. then it was good enough for me.

Remember I had been totally abstinent from any type of drug or alcohol for 18 years at that time, so it wasn't as easy a decision as a regular dude might have. I knew exactly what waited for me on the other end if I was to *relapse* back into addiction. I'd have a needle in my arm a crack pipe in my mouth and be back in handcuffs before I knew it. This time in front of my children. At this point though my depression was so great and my value for life was so feeble, I felt I had nothing to lose. Once again I said to myself, I'M DONE and took action right away. I called my lifelong friend Kevin to see if he could still get his hands on some LSD. As teens we both loved Psychedelics and had some great times. Fortunately his answer was: "Of course. I'll put together a little something for you. Pick it up tomorrow." He gave me a couple LSD tabs and some samples of other psychedelics free of charge (another simple but deeply appreciated act of kindness).

Next thing I did was book an Airbnb with a nice scenic view up in Joshua Tree California. LSD in hand, I headed out on the two hour drive to Joshua Tree for an experience that could make or break the next chapter of my life.

I timed my arrival perfectly. I settled in the eclectic little cabin and took seat outside just as the sun began to set. I popped the LSD tab (Black pyramid for those that care) in my mouth and lit up a cigar with Grateful Dead and Pink Floyd playing in my AirPods. Right about the time the cigar was coming to an end the LSD was starting to kick in. The vivid blue, pink, and gold sky was mesmerizing (As I'm writing this I just watched the video I took of the sky at that moment). The music playing was starting to have a strong effect on my body and mind. The glowing sky was starting to overwhelm me. I started getting a little scared. "Deep breaths, relax It's gonna be alright." I kept saying to myself. I would love to give you an accurate description of that night but my experience was beyond the reach of language. My little mind couldn't really comprehend everything or hold onto it. Almost like when you wake up from an intense dream that you can't remember the details about, even though it just happened. I've tried to explain it in conversations, but I just end up sounding like a loon. It was like I went to another state of mind where time doesn't exist. It felt like I was gone for a thousand years. Then, I slowly, bit by bit came back to reality. I remember thinking: *I'm Ok. I'm in Joshua Tree.* A moment later *Ok I have kids. I live in LA. My name is Richard.* It was like my mind was rebooting. I came back with an awkward almost embarrassing view of the way I had been living my life. I believe this was the killing of my ego (though it seems to have 9 lives). I know those are weak descriptions, but it would get even weirder if I tried to go into deeper detail, so I'll leave it at that.

I didn't get much sleep at all but I woke up as if I had the first real restful night's sleep in almost a year. I woke up feeling great. The most significant after effect was it brought me back to the beauty of the real things in my life. The simple things. My kids, my health, my strengths, the struggles I had overcome. The things that made me, Me. Sounds cheesy but these valuables were brought back to the forefront of my mind from way in the back row where they had drifted to.

It was like my brain was a glitching computer that got stuck in a loop of regretting the past and fearing the future. The LSD gave me a hard reset and restored my brain to optimal function. I couldn't believe it. I was scared that it was too good to be true. After all I just spent a year straight in a deep depression. Was I finally out? Best of all, there was no phenomenon of craving or urge to use other drugs. No guilt or feeling of losing my sobriety or recovery. In fact I felt the opposite, like I had restored my gratitude and could better continue on my recovery and help people even more now. I have another tool in my bucket; one that can get people out of a deep depression. I felt as if I had discovered gold. Why hasn't everyone been doing this?

Well for one there's legality issues in most places. Two, there's a stigma still attached to psychedelics dating back to the hippie days. Three, LSD, is an extremely powerful psychedelic. If it has the power for such a drastic positive change, it must in turn have the power to do some real damage as well. People with any history of mental disorders or dysfunctions should steer clear. PLEASE DO YOUR RESEARCH. Fourth, as for people in a 12-step program total abstinence is driven down your throat with absolutely no exceptions. Which for the *real addicts* like me I agree total abstinence is your best bet, but also you have got to have common sense. There are rare occasions that certain substances may do some good without relapsing. For instance, I had a surgery that I had to be awake for. The doctor recommended nitrous gas for the procedure, or since I told them I was a recovering addict I could opt for local anaesthetics, but it wouldn't be for the lighthearted. What did I do? Did I tough it out to be a die-hard total abstinent? Hell no, I took the suggested anaesthesia and was fine. It wasn't a relapse; I wasn't doing it for fun to get off. One lady in AA even scolded me because I use mouth wash with alcohol in it. I didn't understand these types. I didn't get sober to live in fear. I got sober to be free. Being "Sober" wasn't my identity. I never felt any fear of relapsing, any urges to use or any wishes I could. I looked at my sober state of mind as a strength not a weakness. Total abstinence is a general rule, of course don't drink and do drugs. I won't be lighting up a blunt or doing lines of coke anytime soon, but you can still drink coffee and smoke cigarettes. Nicotine and tobacco are drugs as well. Don't be a fool, it's not an immutable law. In this case LSD brought me out of a depression and saved my sobriety. I'm not saying everyone with depression or in recovery should go out and drop acid or eat some psilocybin mushrooms. Again, some good judgement and common sense is needed. If you're in doubt, default should be to pass. Either way do your due diligence and research with an unbiased eye. The point is we don't wanna throw the baby out with the bathwater. We should always keep an open mind to progression and adding new tools to the kit whenever applicable. People like myself and countless others who are in service to those in need, require as many resources as possible to keep up with the never-ending demand. The book of AA in its conclusion says: "Our book is meant to be suggestive only. We realize we know only a little.." The program was meant to be built upon, not as a final word. Try telling that to old timers in AA though. I doubt you'll be met with open minds. Therein lies the problem. AA and the other 12-step recovery programs such as Narcotics Anonymous, Cocaine Anonymous, and Crystal Meth Anonymous are static programs, whose members fixed in dogmas prevent any growth or progression. Even the Catholic Church is starting to come into modern times and accept ideas that would've had you burning on a spit like a rotisserie chicken not too long ago. In the example of AA, the program has remained the same since 1935. Even though one of its key principles is OPEN-MINDEDNESS. The book itself admits to knowing "only a little" and invites growth and feedback. The founders knew what they had was great but it was just a start. So what can we do to improve upon their creation?

Part Two

THE ADDICT

I've spent years and years, working with addicts helping them get and stay sober. Sponsoring dudes, letting them stay in my home, dragging them around with me, hiring them, you name it. Always out of service and long before I ever owned any treatment centers. I'm no longer in that business and continue on. It's a passion of mine and I consider it my only obligation in life other than my children. I'll be helping addicts till I die. I'll just use the term *addict* so I don't have to keep doing this: Addict/Alcoholic. Plus, there's really no need to tack on the term alcoholic since alcohol is a drug too. So, if you are addicted to alcohol that would make you a drug addict as well, right? Saying you're an alcoholic not an addict is like saying: I'm a Pit Bull not a dog. Really who cares what it's called, they both equate to the same outcome regardless of the substance in particular. Often times I'll get a call from a person in dire straits. Maybe even their distraught mother, father, son, spouse, you name it. I would spend hours upon hours on the phone with the loved-one of the addict, listening to the gruesome details of the situation. Nearly all of them were at their wits' end willing to try anything to end the nightmare. Anyone that has had someone dear to them become an addict knows a *nightmare* is exactly what it is. Especially if your dream of raising a family has come true and you spent nearly the last two decades doing everything possible so that your kid can have a good life, only to have them end up strung out on meth looking like Nosferatu. What happened? One day they were a silly chubby baby and the light of your life. The next day they're punching holes in the wall cussing you out and selling your identity to scammers. Is it something you did? Is it something they were born with? How do you fix it? If your kid has a broken arm you take him to the doctor. The doctor fixes the arm, life goes on. Those dealing with an addict know the solution to their problem is not so clear-cut. A doctor can't fix a sick spirit. Again, I use the term "spirit" not in any religious sense, but as in the essence of oneself. I know of no better word to describe it. A doctor or therapist can't say "Here's a medication to stop Timmy from smoking meth. Here's another pill to stop the lying and stealing. We'll also put his legs in a bed sling for 3-6 months to keep him from running away, then he'll be good as new!" Nope.

The solution, if there is one, can be unbelievably complex and varies person to person. I say "if" there is a solution because the truth is, there are some so entranced with the drugs and lifestyle that they will meet their end before they get a chance at a new beginning. Many believe all the addict needs is love. While that sounds cool, it is often the "love" that kills them. Sometimes what the addict needs is seemingly dangerous and contradictory to all parental instincts. Try telling an upper middle-class mother that maybe she should stop paying for Chads food and motels. Let him sleep on the streets, might do him some good. "But he won't survive, he'll die out there!" Chad's 29, maybe it's the lack of confidence in him and unwillingness to let the kid become a man that got us here in the first place. Yes, cutting off an addict and letting them survive on the streets, go to jail and figure things out for themselves can be risky. However, in my opinion propping up their fentanyl habit is not only riskier, it's deadly. Also my opinion: it's never bad to let your kids learn to figure out their own life. On the other hand, sometimes the addict needs to be heard or forgiven, apologized to and loved. Sometimes you'll have a 40-year-old man still hurting from events that happened in childhood and all they need is to let go. A lot of the times there's nothing you can do but damage control till they hit a bottom. Again, there is no one-size-fits-all solution but there are a few effective ways to go about certain scenarios. I'll lay out a few examples and what seem to have been the most effective solutions for the addicts I've worked with.

GOD LEAVES THE ROOM WHEN YOU START DOING IT FOR MONEY

Want a place where the rent is free, and the girls are pretty? Feel like chilling by the pool and smoking some weed while being prescribed some of the best pharmaceuticals you can imagine? Want to put a few grand in your pocket just for doing all of this? If so, then it might be time you check into a private treatment center! Ever look through your kid's phone trying to find their drug connection? Forget about Chuey, Jamal and Brian. Look for the admissions coordinators for treatment centers, that's the real Plug.

I've heard parents say "I only want the best for my kid!" So they look online for rehabs with the nicest websites and most luxurious housing. "Wait I want to make sure they have as many of those (easily attainable) accreditations as possible." They love the head shots of wholesome looking celebrity-like doctors and staff featured on some TV show or (paid for) magazine article. "WOW this place has Yoga and meditation classes!" as they scroll through looking at stock images of people giving each other high fives. "Oooh look at the amenities." Tennis court, pool, art therapy, music therapy, brainwave therapy, ping pong table, hypnosis, frequent trips to the bowling alley. "Oh look honey, there's even a music studio you can work on your rap career!" "Maybe Chad just needs an outlet for his creativity?" Yeah maybe, since there are no successful musicians that are addicts right? I have yet to meet an amenity that had anything to do with a grown man or woman overcoming a soul wrenching addiction. "Look Clark, this place has a sauna! I wonder if that will help Chad stop performing oral sex on his dealer for meth and sharing needles with his HIV infected girlfriend?" I've seen mothers wail and cry after getting their children taken by child services. They come begging to get sober and get their kids back. Then work for months doing everything they possibly can to regain custody of their children. Only to pick up a crack pipe and go on a binge a few days before the kids would have been returned. Tragedy and addiction are brother and sister. Do you think that a fancier house or more outings to the theme park would've made a difference? If something is powerful enough to make a mother go against her maternal instincts and choose drugs over her own children; do you think the zip code of the rehab really matters? Do people pick churches or religions based on the aesthetic quality of their website? Matters of the spirit are much deeper. I do believe addiction is a spiritual as well as physical sickness. Yet still, people fork over anywhere between $5000-$60,000 a month for what they think is the "best of the best." Because their son deserves a facility with a graffiti mural of celebrity addicts in the lobby! Only to have their boy "AMA" (leave Against Medical Advice) or relapse a week later. The poor chap goes on a gnarly bender. His family manages to get him readmitted and forks over more dough. To no surprise, he does the same thing again next month. This is often repeated over and over until the family has exhausted all of their savings, retirement, home-equity, lines of credit, credit cards or cash. I've seen this exact scenario played out many times or I'm contacted just after this has taken place. I'm talking about people who spent a lifetime building up a nest-egg only to blow it all on treatment centers. Most of which just put the clients in groups all day. Groups often taught by people with no real experience. They were just able to get someone to sign off saying they did the required hours of training, then take the online test. BAM! Now Chad who was caught doing meth with a tranny last week can teach groups. I always had a few clients in my program that were doing groups for other facilities. The other treatment centers would get them certified and have them teaching groups in a couple days. I'm talking about people still relapsing, or newly sober, were teaching groups on "how to stay sober" at high end facilities. Why? Why do you think? The treatment center will bill the insurance company anywhere between $1500-$2500+ per person, per group. Maybe 12 people in a group, 2-5 groups a day, 5 days a week and then pay the facilitator (Chad) $150 to teach the group. I would be mystified when dudes I wouldn't trust to facilitate an UNO game would boast to me that they were facilitating groups at another program. Programs that people are trusting, praying their loved one will come home and stay sober. Once I even called the owner of another program to give them a heads up that the person they just hired was a client that our facility had just kicked out a few days prior for doing drugs and trying to blackmail me. The owner (who passed from an OD that year) just said OK and kept him on. Soon after I found out they were using him as a body broker and poacher. A "body broker" is someone that is using money or drugs to solicit addicts into a treatment center, so that the treatment center can bill their insurance. A "Poacher" is someone that entices clients to leave the program they are in, and go to the program that the poacher works with. When I left the treatment industry in 2022 I'd estimate about 60% of the clients in private treatment centers had no intentions on staying sober and were just using their insurance cards as a commodity going from facility to facility. One poor guy was getting passed around from broker to broker so much I had to call his dad. I heard what was going from other clients and saw texts to confirm. I called the dad suggesting he cancel the son's insurance policy. That's all the poachers are after, it's the golden ticket for the addict. Once you cancel their private insurance plan and put them on MediCal none of the crooked places want anything to do with them anymore. These places can't take MediCal so there's no money in it. If they want to get sober they have to do it at a real facility now. I'm speaking about Los Angeles treatment centers only, I don't know about any of the other states but I definitely know LA. On paper you would look at the situation and say: *No way I'd never fall for that, I would be able to tell if my kid was in one of those facilities.* This is happening in the facilities that look the most proper and have DHCS Licenses and JCAHO accreditations. In fact, all of the crooked facilities I'm speaking of are licensed and accredited. It's not just the treatment centers, the addicts are in on it too. It can't happen without their participation, so don't shed any tears for them just yet. At the very least the addict gets free room and board in nice accommodations as well as getting people off their back because they're "in rehab." They can even stay high switching from street drugs to the pharmaceutical version that the rehab prescribes under the guise that they're "weening off." The more seasoned addicts will be paid by the treatment centers for all this. All the treatment center requires is that the addict check in, stay, and attend groups (or at least appear to) so they can bill their insurance. I say this so that friends and family can be aware of the situation the addict may be getting into and will know the signs. Most are relieved and satisfied just knowing the addict is in treatment. They consider the problem as being dealt with; blind to what's going on and have no idea what their son or daughter is up to in treatment. They just know that he keeps leaving one facility and going to another for whatever reasons he conjures up. The addict is a master of manipulation; you very seldom can trust what they are telling you when it comes to matters dealing with their addiction or money. He or she may have had the best integrity and character of anyone you've ever met, till they became an addict. With addiction comes lies, it's nothing personal. The Addict knows exactly how to pull the heart strings and use their love or life as leverage to get what they want. Incidents like those described play out more frequently than you think. This is why every non addict and their cousin is opening a detox or IOP in LA right now, the drug treatment business is booming.

SHALLOW HAL

Another thing to note about the drug treatment world is; a better looking facility does not translate to your loved-one having a better chance of staying sober. It just means the facility owner has more money to throw at it. Sometimes I think people find rehabs with the same glasses they use to find hotels and resorts. Getting sober on its own doesn't make you rich and successful. It's not the case that the more sober you are the more money you make. In fact, the opposite is usually true, the people that are making the most difference in people's lives aren't receiving any money at all. I'd have to say the award for doing the most good goes to the sponsors in the 12-step meetings (which are free). Many private treatment centers are created and run by investors looking to make money whether your struggling addict stays sober or not. Now if we were talking about an internet start-up, car dealership or some commodity-based business, then that might be a great fit. However, treating addicts is a different beast. To mask this, they often hire a face man in recovery for better credibility. You may also hear some sob story of how the owner had a relative that was an addict and that inspired them to help. I've never seen any of those sob story folks out with us helping people stay sober for free though. Unless they're politicking, kissing babies and handing out turkeys for a paid publicity article. Yes most of the publicity you see is paid for. I'm not implying they are all malicious or greedy. After all everyone has to make a living, what better way than to help people get off drugs right? Well some positions in society can't just be handled by anyone looking for a new career. Would you let some greasy investor in a Gucci jumpsuit and Rolex (having no kids or experience) babysit your infant just because he "has a relative who has a kid"? Probably not. But you'd hand over your almost as vulnerable adult child to his mansion facility because he claims has a relative that was an addict? "He drives a Lambo he must be trustworthy!" A child's teacher is another good example of a role not just anyone can fill. One needs patience and passion for teaching kids, something that can't be bought or learned online. They have to come equipped with that already in their make-up. The same with cops. It takes a certain type of character to be a good police officer, they need to have that protector trait, along with bravery and respect for the law. I have a couple cop buddies that were just born protectors. Strong dudes with no coward in them at all. I've known them for years, they're exactly what every police officer should be like. LAPD should be proud. But then I've also had the unfortunate experience to cross paths with some bad apples in law enforcement in the county jail as I mentioned earlier. Sick men with complexes over-compensating for some inner weakness by acting tough and inflicting harm on inmates that can't legally fight back. When you hire people to fill positions that aren't fit for the role you get bad apples in any line of work. If the job is fast food or packing boxes it may not matter as much. What about politicians? Is that a career choice one should get into just to make a living? Some roles you kind of have to be born for. So maybe we should rethink how to go about finding help for an addict. The chances of our friends staying sober at the $60k a month rehab are pretty much the same as the free Skid Row rehab. Why? Because the outcome mostly relies upon the individual. Similar to someone getting in shape. Whether it be an expensive gym with gold dumbbells and cucumber water or a grungy dim lit basement with rusted iron weights, makes no difference. The outcome is based upon whether the individual is willing to put in the hard work, not the aesthetics.

DR. CONRAD MURRAY

The word *Ethical* in the treatment world doesn't mean: *doing what's morally right*. That may be the general world's use of it, but in treatment when you hear them use the word "Ethical" it usually translates to: *What we're doing isn't illegal, we do what we can within the confinements of the law- even if its morally wrong*. How can you tell a good facility from a rotten one? It's hard to give a short answer to that question, but there are a few indicators. Here were my litmus tests: If they allow marijuana, Benzodiazepines, Ambient, Adderall or similar pharmaceuticals. If they allow maintenance use of Suboxone or methadone without extreme circumstances. I've been to sober livings and detoxes where everyone was high out of their mind on pills and weed, but as long as their insurance was active, and they attended group it was all good. I hate to be the one to break it to you but anyone taking Adderall or Vyvanse (Amphetamines) and Suboxone or Methadone (Opiates) is STILL USING Amphetamines and opiates. You've just replaced the street drug with its pharmaceutical version. Healthcare providers and big pharmaceutical companies are your new dealer. They'll try to sell you on M.A.T (Medication Assisted Treatment) which used to be looked at as shady unless you were crippled. I'm not here to tell you whether that is good or bad in your situation but, that is the situation. I've heard countless addicts tell their people they've been clean and sober for 30, 60, 90 days but have been taking prescribed opiates and amphetamines the entire time. Just because they are legally prescribed by a doctor doesn't change the fact they are still addicted to a substance. Doctors were legally prescribing oxycontin to addicts all over the country kicking off the Opioid epidemic. They weren't any less addicted just because the doctor prescribed them, right? The legality of it doesn't matter either. Alcohol is legal, doesn't make being a raging alcoholic any more acceptable does it? It may be less dangerous and a better option than scoring street drugs, but you're still just jumping out of the frying pan into the fire. Actually I take that back, pharmaceuticals *are* just as dangerous. At least with street drugs there's no misinterpretations about what you're doing, you're buying drugs from a guy off the street. You know you have got to be careful. Whereas with pharmaceutical drugs people have this false sense of security, as if they are less likely to overdose and that they aren't really "addicts" because a smiling doctor prescribed it. People tend to be more reckless. "My doctor says I need it" is also a much easier narrative for addicts and their family to believe. Though it keeps them strung out longer.

Many treatment centers are more than happy to cosign the prescription pacification of addicts. "Sir, can you call my mom and tell her that I'm doing good and I'm not high. That the medication just makes me drowsy?" This keeps the addict happy and comfortable, which helps them stay put in the program while they're racking up billable days. The treatment center knows if they try to take the client off the medication (to actually get them sober) the client will just leave and find a rehab that will allow them to keep the prescription. I dealt with this issue almost every day. Addicts would call up asking if we allowed Vyvanse, Suboxone maintenance or Marijuana use, sometimes all of the above! When I would say No, they would just keep calling places till they found one that said Yes. That's where the body brokers help out. One of the lures brokers and poachers use to entice addicts into the program they are working for is they tell them they can smoke weed and take these meds. Remember not every person in treatment is there because *they* actually want to get sober. Many are there because *family* wants them to get sober. Maybe they messed up their life pretty bad and checked into to rehab as a default solution that will soothe scathing spouses and employers. Doesn't mean they are actually ready to give up ALL the drugs. So they wanna smoke a little weed or ride a Xanax wave through their rehab stint. Some just don't have anywhere to go and no money for drugs, but they have health insurance from their parent's job. The body brokers, poachers and treatment centers offer them a solution; a roof over their head, 3 meals a day and good free prescription drugs. Throw in trips to theme parks and a pool then you got a deal! These places can operate completely legally and seem super legit to the naked eye. In fact most of the staff can be completely unaware of what goes on between the owner and body brokers.

 Sometimes I'd ask the client *What program allowed you to take those meds?* I'd be surprised at some of the places they would tell me. Many of them were programs that go around boasting their ethicality. There's nothing ethical about taking in a client on narcotics, accepting money, then discharging them still dependent on narcotics. When I got sober in 2004 no rehab would even think of letting a client take Xanax, Aderrall or any narcotic med. Hell you were lucky if you got an aspirin. Now it's the norm for clients to be on heavy meds. The point of going to rehab is to come out sober. At least that's my aim when working with addicts; getting them sober. The point should be freedom from addiction. A client should come out the other end able to start a new life, stronger than ever, independent of ANY substances.

TO SERVE MAN- IT'S A COOK BOOK! OH NO WAIT, IT'S A JOB DESCRIPTION...

A good indicator of a facility whose aim is only to collect money, not get people sober, is when they don't take scholarships. Whenever other treatment centers would call me up wanting to network or collaborate, I would ask them; *How many scholarship beds do you allot?* If they said "Oh we don't do scholarships" I would tell them: *Then we're not in the same business.* If they said: " We usually have one or two." then we were good. I understand you have to pay the bills. We all do, but in my opinion any treatment center without a good dash of altruism is a scam. Anyone genuinely in the industry to help people would have no problem giving at least 1 out of 12 or however many beds, to someone who is eager to change their life but can't afford it. Especially if there are empty beds available. In fact, the *real ones* out to make a difference will tell you all their paid for beds are just there so they can afford to have the free ones.

Those are my people.

The owner of a treatment center is dealing with the lives of addicts, it isn't like running a gym or spa. If there's a temporary payment issue and someone has to miss the gym a few days, no big deal. But when you're dealing with someone's life you can't just say "There's an issue with your payment. Thats too bad, you were doing so good. Oh well back to the crack house you go!" In treatment there is a much deeper need for humanitarianism, devotion and compassion. Often times that means eating the cost to help someone. Even when my company was just starting out, not even making rent and operating at huge loss, we still took in a bunch of scholarships. Treatment centers shouldn't be run like hotels; The minute your insurance runs out they pull you from group and kick you out. Just like a police officer shouldn't be the same as a bouncer. Dealing with addicts successfully often means you're going to be putting in a lot of time and effort with no expectation of payment. It takes heart. A certain type of heart usually only another addict that has been through the same hell will possess. Not to say that a non-addict or "Normy" (as we call them) can't be effective. I've met plenty of treatment workers that love their job and do care. They are not the problem. It's the individuals that financially benefit from allowing actively using addicts in any form to remain in their facility.

Wait, weren't you just saying they shouldn't kick out addicts?

Addicts that are sober and willing to do whatever it takes, should not be kicked out for lack of finances. On the other hand any actively using addict is dangerous to himself and others and should be discharged ASAP. So what you'll have in many facilities are actively using addicts with money or good insurance policies kept in the program no matter what. While others whose insurance cut out or family can't afford it anymore are kicked out immediately.

You might think it's harsh to kick someone out with nowhere to go, just because they started using again. *Why not just give them another chance Richard? I thought your heart was in it.* The reason it's usually wise to kick an addict out after a relapse is because once the phenomenon of craving kicks in they will probably use again putting themselves and others in danger. *Well, what if the person only took one hit of weed or one sip of alcohol?* That's rarely what actually happens. Again, this is where the good judgement, expertise and keen eye for bullshit that comes well equipped in most former addicts is needed. When I first opened my sober livings, I was against throwing people out on the street just because they relapsed once. I learned the hard way why that was a bad policy after dealing with fist fights, sexual assaults, thefts, and fatal overdoses from people allowed to remain in the facility after a relapse. Relapsers are like a virus that infect those around them. More often than not, they've snuck drugs into the facility. Next thing you know their roommate is relapsing with them, then they get another friend high. Now you have three people to kick out instead of just that 1 you should have got rid of in the first place. You might as well have just participated in the ruin of the lives of those other two roommates. Also, a freshly relapsed addict often runs out of money fast and the first thing they do is steal from other clients in the facility. Those in charge owe it to the clients that are sober and trying hard, to keep them safe and out of the destructive path of active addicts. That's where the *heart* and ethics TRULY come into play. Will the treatment center choose the well-being and safety of sober clients over continued billing of the relapsers and active users? Remember we want these guys to hit a bottom - safe harbor from consequences usually only stunts their descent. The more painful their using experiences are the better, in my opinion.

Richard what made you so different? Look closely and you'll see that most treatment centers and sober livings are started by wannabe investors and/or freshly sober addicts trying to get in on the hustle. Both have no business being in charge of people's lives. Not all are like that but it's safe to say most. Now I'm no saint by any means, I made plenty of mistakes. I also like to make money as much as the next guy. What made me different in this situation? The opening of my first sober living came organically and as an extension of what I was already doing, which was helping addicts and real estate. I already had multiple streams of income and was living well, prior to doing anything in treatment. My interest was in doing something cool that would help people whether I made money or not. Like our Airbnb sober living, which again I believe was a first. That was actually a cool experience, we got sober people from all over the world. I didn't rely on my treatment center or sober livings for income. In fact, they were usually a loss. My objective was to keep people sober, I didn't care if I had to kick everyone out. I could make decisions based on what was right not what was going to make the most money. I didn't need to make any shady calls to stay afloat. I saw people take 6 figure loans from their families or invest everything they had and go all in on some huge fancy house. Only to find it wasn't the gold mine they thought. Inevitably they succumb to the dark side to make their payments. I saw it so many times I could write a separate book on the subject entitled: *How to turn yourself into a criminal in 2 easy steps: 1.*

Open a sober living or treatment center. 2. Depend on it to support your family.

CULTURE VULTURE

In my opinion, the X factor in an addict staying sober isn't in the facility, it's within the individual. As I mentioned earlier, I got sober in a facility called the Royal Palms. Don't let the fancy name fool you. It was an old converted hotel located in the drug and gang infested neighborhood off 6th and Alvarado. One block away from where I used to pawn my stolen goods and buy crack. Although that area has undergone heavy gentrification, at the time it was one of the most dangerous areas of Los Angeles. Everyone in there was straight out of prison, jail, or the gutter. My roommate was doing heroin in front of me. Then after he got kicked out, the next guy was smoking crack in the room. They got caught and kicked out on the spot. I remember the guy that was smoking crack was in the middle of getting his haircut when staff found him. He was cussing and yelling as they kicked him out looking ridiculous with his head only half shaved. It was hilarious. There was a zero tolerance for relapse, although with 80 people it was hard to manage. It was also one of the few programs where you were allowed to leave every day after groups from 5-10 pm and weekends. You had a lot of freedom to fuck things up. But guess what, I stayed sober. So did a hell of a lot of other people too. Why? Because even though there was no AC or heating, no massages or sound baths, they did have something that mattered even more; a culture of get sober or get the fuck out. It was a Medi-cal facility so there was no shortage of clients and no incentive for keeping anyone in the program that was fucking up. It was a social model program, all the work around the facility was done by the residents. The staff was former residents that had been there for years and hardly made anything but were doing what they loved. All these things amounted to something that you can't purchase or fake; a culture. And that takes time to establish. This culture allowed people that were serious to thrive, at the same time weeding out the bogies. The best part; it didn't cost me a dime. I was homeless with no money when I went in and was able to live there for free long enough to get back on my feet. It was covered by Medi-Cal. Treatment centers like many other things privatized with financial incentives for numbers rather than outcomes, just aren't the same.

IF YOU BABY'EM YOU BURY'EM

There's a saying in recovery: If you baby'em you bury'em. From what I've seen it seems to be a literal truth. Personally, I'd send my own children to a state-funded facilities before a private one any day of the week. After all, if someone has been out there on a bender maybe an ocean view and infinity pool isn't what they deserve. Your alcoholic sister gets a third Driving Under the Influence charge and her kids taken away. Now she gets to spend a month in a mansion treatment center with a private chef? Is that what she actually needs? Wouldn't a good helping of humble pie go farther than a luxurious personal sabbatical? What happens when you rob someone of consequences? I tend to think when we rob people of consequences, we disturb nature. The process for restoring harmony is disrupted and stalled. One surefire way to throw gasoline on a forest fire you're trying to put out; give an addict cash. Giving an addict cash is like putting bullets in their gun. Same goes for gift cards, valuables and anything they can sell or trade. Even once they have a little sobriety under their belt it robs them of ambition. These are grown men and women. Adults, that for whatever reason got thrown way off course for years, sometimes decades. Think of them as an athlete with a badly broken leg that needs time to heal and get stronger again, just to do basic things. Even though the leg may appear normal after short time, it's still not ready for action. It's a process, if you deviate you risk re-breaking the leg again and starting from scratch. Now, everyone is different. I'd say giving an addict one year to get a decent foundation of sobriety, recalibrate to life, and figure somethings out on their own, is a good start. After all, if they're adults and can't handle 1 year on their own; they're in trouble. What are they gonna do if something happens to you? Listen to me when I say this; I have witnessed unbelievable leaps in strength, confidence and self-sufficiency. I mean miraculous growth, when people are actually allowed to grow. I've had mothers tell me things like: *You don't know my son, he would starve to death if I didn't go to the store and cook for him. There's no way he's gonna figure things out without our help.* While this may have been true, at that time, with them, in a situation that nurtured their adolescence. Once they feel the exhilaration of being on their own, and the self-esteem from achieving even small feats, their confidence compounds. They start to become their own person. Only when you take the training wheels off can they really start learning to ride on their own.

Now here's the even harder question a parent or spouse has to ask themself: Is there something funny going on with me that wants to keep the addict dependent on me? That's a tough one to face. It's not always an addict with a Peter Pan mentality, the overbearing mother often plays a major part in the act as well. That's veering out of my lane a little though, but something to think about. Back to my forte: the addict.

Here's a tale of a half-baked cake taken out too early. I was working with a guy for about 2 months. He had been with us before but cut loose fast, this time I wrangled him in and had him on the right path. He came a long way in a short amount of time, the dude was on fire. He stopped smoking weed (a huge problem of his) got off his pills and was completely sober. I came in one morning and he couldn't wait to tell me about some girl he met at a meeting and how he got a sponsor. Not long after he was meeting with his sponsor and started working the steps. Not sure if he got the girl but he was definitely starting to get excited about life. Even started doing his chores around the facility. He was proud of himself and on just the right trajectory. Now desperate for a job, he was out searching every day and making inquiries on the *Indeed* app. His mother would often check in asking me how he was doing. I would gladly report that he was doing great. She would ask if he needed anything and I always told her the same thing, "Just your love. All of his basic needs are covered by us, don't worry."

The man excitedly told me had a job interview coming up. A few days later I show up to the facility a little after the interview was to happen, assuming he'd be back by then to tell me how it went. To my surprise when I got there he was still sleeping! I also noticed some Nike shoe boxes and McDonalds trash around his bed. I woke him up "Yo what the fuck dude did you sleep through your interview? What's all this shit?" He groggily came to " Oh man my bad... I must've over slept." He followed up by saying "My sister came by and gave me some money so I got some kicks and food." "Bro are you high?" I asked as I started to hint the smell of weed and a slight intoxication in his demeanour. "Nah, nah man, I'm just tired." I drug tested him and he came up positive for THC and blew positive on the breathalyzer as well. This was in sober living, so I had him pack his stuff and told him he can come back after he detoxed or had a month sober again. He ended up just going to a marijuana friendly sober living that allowed him to smoke weed all day. Yes they do exist. He went down hill from there. About a year later my manager called me up and said in a lovingly menacing way: "Guess who's sitting in the living room with me right now?" It was our friend, only now he looked like he had just got back from a tour in Iraq. We were all glad to see him and welcomed him back. The man that came back to us was no longer the same guy. He was darker and had deeper mental health problems flaring up that weren't active when he was with us prior. He couldn't stay sober a day now and had a chronic masturbation issue all of a sudden. This dude had been chewed by the drug world (which now includes sober livings and treatment) and was thrown up a pulp of a man. I've been meaning to call his mom to check in but I'm always afraid of the: "I'm sorry to say he passed." Which I've heard more than anyone needs to in a lifetime. Hopefully he is ok now.

    This was a man that had regained some drive and was working hard towards his goals. Then before he could get the self-esteem boost of fulfilling his goals (which often propels addicts into further positive action) someone with good intentions gave him a few hundred dollars. Not knowing that it would suck all the drive out of him and allow him to treat himself to goodies he didn't earn. Including some marijuana and alcohol. The man didn't need cash, he didn't need new Nikes, or clothes either. What he needed was a boost in his self-esteem, pride and confidence. The type of things you can't buy or gift someone. They need to be earned by the individual via hard work and esteem-able acts. The newly sober can be extremely fragile and the wrong kind of "help" can lead to a disaster. Sometimes it's best to cheer them on from the sidelines. Let them build up the strength to handle normal matters like handling cash. Hopefully by the time they do, you won't need to give them any.

TOUGH LOVE IS BETTER THAN LOST LOVE

When it comes to addicts getting in trouble with the law, my general rule is: Don't bail them out. Tell'em you love'em and they can call you but they have to deal with their own problems. Remember we don't want to rob anyone of consequences. Now I'm just talking about addicts. If your *normy* husband or wife gets locked up for some misunderstanding bail them out dude, c'mon.. But if your junky brother assaults a security guard, put a $20 on his books, tell him he's an idiot but you love him and hang up. We want to fan the flames of desperation, not put them out. The trick is to do it in a way where they still know you love them. You would be surprised the magic some time in jail or on the streets can work. Sometimes it's all that is needed to do the trick. Sometimes they end up loving it, in that case you can't do anything about it anyways. It has to run its course. No more than you can talk someone out of loving a person or a drug. The street life can have its own draw believe it or not. I loved it on the streets, at least at times. Don't worry though, it's a phase that will pass (crossing fingers). The harsh, unpopular truth is that they may *need* to go to prison. Keep in mind, every criminal has a family, and a backstory for the crime they committed but it's still a crime. Especially to the person on the other end of it. I know if you were a victim, you would probably want the offender to rot in jail. Your loved one is the offender, regardless if "Chad is a sweet boy at heart." Let Chad learn what happens when you commit crimes and what it's like to be with other criminals. They can decide if that's the life they want to live. Sheltering them from consequences doesn't help. In fact I've heard quite a few recovered addicts say prison saved their lives. Go to an NA meeting you'll find some recovered convicts. Ask them if they would take back their prison sentence. You'll get mixed reviews but there's definitely a bunch that will tell you it saved their life.

Would you rather your brother go to prison for 3 years, learn some discipline, get out clean and become a productive member of society? Or have him get rescued from every debacle, continuing to be a nuisance to everyone for the rest of his life relying on family for money? I've had clients in their late 60's screaming at their 90-year-old mother that she needs to pay his rent and send money for food. The man was an Ivy League educated attorney before alcohol got him believe it or not. I spoke to the mother quite often and she was in the same situation most enabling parents end up in. She was a hostage. This had been going on for over 20 years. A classic case of co-dependency. She wasn't helping her fully grown man child and she knew it, but was afraid to set boundaries and cut him off. She knew she was in her last days and didn't want to be disowned by her son and die alone. She told me this. The time to have cut him off was 20 years ago, now it was pretty much too late. He was in control. Don't let this happen to you. Human beings are capable of remarkable things when put in situations of survival. I've never seen an addict who was cut off by their family die of starvation or exposure. But I have seen quite a few addicts being financially supported by their parents die of overdoses. I have an album in my pictures app that was originally called The Hall of Shame. It started out as just funny pictures and videos of antics and shenanigans that went on in the treatment houses. Then people in the pictures started dying. I started adding obituaries, missing persons, wanted posters, and RIP posts. It's a much bigger album than it should be. I look through the pictures and remember these people whenever me or a client needs a reminder that this is life or death. I said this before but it's worth mentioning again GIVING ADDICTS MONEY IS PUTTING BULLETS IN THE GUN. Same goes for paying their basic living expenses. This allows them to use the money they do have on drugs, and not bills. Even though they may tell you they are dead broke they almost always have some hustle they are getting money from, most likely one of those hustles is YOU.

 When I say cut them off, I mean financially or anything that is helping them maintain their lifestyle as an addict. I do not mean cut them off from your loving support and affection. They need to know now more than ever that they are loved. Addicts like me who had no financial support or help from family tend to seek the help they need faster because there was no other choice. It was heartbreaking for me at the time for my mom and dad to both slam the door in my face, allowing me to go to jails, mental institutions, and stay homeless till I figured it all out. But it turned out to be the best thing they could have done. If family would've helped me any of the times I begged them to they would have just robbed me of either consequences or ambition. I saw so many people in treatment call their family begging, guilt-tripping, arguing, and crying for money that they "needed." What did they use the desperately needed money for when they got it? Usually it was spent on Uber eats, fast food, and vape or cigarettes. Or maybe they went to buy some drugs. Sometimes they would use it all on designer clothes and shoes. Gotta look cool when you're in rehab of course... Either way, nine out of ten times it's wasted. The ones that didn't have money to partake were always more eager to get their life together. If the addict was not in treatment, the money was almost always used on drugs. They used the parents' money to buy drugs, then try to hustle up rent later on and just pay the bills late (if at all).

When it comes to jobs, most parents think if he or she "just gets a job they'll be OK". Or they just need to "stay busy." If that were true, there would be no addicts in the workforce would there? Everyone busy or with a job would be sober. Same goes for money. "If I was successful and had more money, I could stay sober." Then there would be no rich addicts, right? "He just needs to get on his feet to stay sober." I disagree. They won't get on their feet *until* they stay sober. Of course they do need to get a job or go back to work at some point, but you don't want to take the turkey out of the oven too soon. It could still be raw in the middle. If they are in treatment it's probably best to complete the program first. If they are not in treatment and fresh off the pipe then all of a sudden get "the job opportunity of a lifetime" as they always say, they will lose it most eventfully anyway if they relapse. Which they most likely will. The best bet would be to politely decline the job or defer. At least, if they defer or decline, they will not tarnish their reputation or burn any bridges like they will if they take the job prematurely and relapse. Naturally there are those easy cases that get clean after they scrape a knee or forgot to feed their cat. My guess is if you're reading this, you're not dealing with an easy category. Keep in mind these are just my opinions and experiences based on the addicts I have worked with. There are plenty of other schools of thought, as there needs to be. Find what works for you, don't just keep repeating things that aren't working.

Here's another rough one; when the addict gets their kids taken. Getting kids taken away is a tragic event for everyone involved. So is hearing a 6-year-old screaming and crying locked in a room thinking they're trapped forever. I've seen a father lock his son in the backroom while he went to go score heroin. My old friends reading this will know who I'm talking about. Dad left the boy watching cartoons and thought he'd be back quick. Unfortunately the connection was hours late. Dad started getting sick, so when he finally did receive the heroin he shot it up right away instead of waiting till he got home. Dad and everyone he was with passed out for another couple hours. I know because I was one of the people that Dad picked up to pitch in on the gram of heroin. We didn't know he had padlocked his kid in the basement room till we got back to his house. Right as we walked in we could hear the kid screaming. It was heart-wrenching even to us wannabe thugged out druggies. I've also witnessed a toddler take a hit from a bong as tall as him. This kid's mother would blow marijuana smoke in his face and give him sips of whatever alcohol was laying around. This kid was also present during nasty fist fights, police raids and guns were always somewhere within reach. The kid loved to throw up gang signs and the middle finger to make everyone laugh. This was happening when I was in 7th and 8th grade. I often wonder what came about of that kid. I can't count how many single mothers I've encountered in my drug selling/using/treating that were prostituting or dealing or both with kids in the house. I had a woman in our facility who previously lived with her sister and nephew while she was doing and selling drugs. The nephew somehow got hold of her pills one day and overdosed. Shortly after the boy passed away, it was all over the news. Like I say, tragedy and addiction are brother and sister.

I have 5 daughters, fortunately they were born after I got sober. I love them more than anything on earth, nearly every parent feels that way. But once drug addiction comes into play all bets are off. As well intentioned as a parent can be, it only takes that one: *I'll just be gone 5 minutes* or *The baby's sleeping she won't know,* to put a child's life in serious danger. If I ever start smoking crack or doing heroin someone better take my kids from me, I will no longer be in control. The drugs will have me doing god knows what. Let me be clear, I am not saying you should call child services on every parent using. Each circumstance is different, but, in many cases something does need to happen. Maybe the kid can live with a relative till the parent gets help. I believe every adult, should be looking out for the well-being of every child in their circle when needed. I know child services is a last resort, but if you've seen some of the things I have, you'd know a drug addict parent can be the worst scenario possible. I have a few friends that came up in foster care and placement homes, each has a different take on it. Some good, some not. I also know people that were really fucked up from living with alcoholic/addict parents, so it's not always the better option. I'm glad I'm not in charge of deciding whether a child should be taken from a parent.

Sometimes it's glaringly obvious and sometimes it's not. That's not my call though. I just know that it does happen often and in some cases I can't disagree with the courts for their decision to take the kids. The chances of the kid dying or growing up warped were much higher with the addict parent than the system. Best case scenario is the kids go stay with a grandparent or trusted family member. A recovered addict often becomes an amazing parent once they turn their life around. Keep in mind my first daughter was conceived while I was still in rehab and homeless without a job or any prospects. I could've easily become like one of the previously mentioned parents. I happened to be lucky that the birth of my child hit me hard enough to propel me foreword and give me momentum to do right.

Part Three

THE ADDICT MUST DIE

You have to die a few times before you can really live- Charles Bukowski.

... AND THEN YOU WOKE UP

I looked down at the palm of my hand and saw a few generic versions of Klonopin pills. A couple *R 35's* a couple with an *-M-* on it; about six or seven in total-but who's counting. I pop'em in my mouth, there's a faint minty flavor, as I chew them up and jump on the bus. I show the bus driver my day pass and turn up the volume on my red CD walkman I stole from Target a while back. I only have 3 CD's: Tupac's- *R U still down* album (my favorite), Eminem's- *The Marshal Mathers LP,* and Art Laboe's- *Dedicated to you Vol.2*. It's about a 20 or 30 minute bus ride from downtown LA to the K-Mart on San Fernando Rd. in Glassell Park that I'm headed to. There's a McDonald's there so I can stop and get high at first. The pills should kick in right about the time I get there, then when I do my dope it'll hit twice as hard. "DING" here's my stop. I jump off the bus and head into the McDonald's straight to the bathroom.

I can feel the pills starting to kick in as I rip open a balloon and pull out the chunk of dry brown heroin. I put it on my little piece of already burnt crumpled up foil. Right next to that piece of heroin, I lay down a $10 chunk of crack cocaine. We used to call this combo of smoking crack with heroin a "Belushi." I grab my lighter 'n straw and fire away. The crack and heroin start sizzling and melt together as I vacuum the smoke up through my 1/4 of a McDonalds straw. Ooh-weeeee... that's good. I stagger out of the McDonald's and step out to the street-I look both ways and as I'm about to cross... *I'm feeling pretty dizzy... the worlds fading*-everything turns to black...

Hmmmm... this is uncomfortable. I'm thirsty. Why can't I move my hands? Wiggling my feet I notice I can't move my legs either. My eyes are still closed, but I'm not quite fully awake. *Am I dreaming?* As I continue to try and gain control of my limbs-the voices in the room become audible. -OK now I'm starting to panic- *What the fuck!* -I open my eyes- *What the fuck! Where the fuck am I?* As my eyes adjust the brightness I see a large female black nurse looking at me. "Settle down honey settle down." *What the fuck where am I? What is this?* She explains to me where I'm at- I'm in a psych hospital. I don't remember her explanation, but what I remember next is asking: *How long have I been here?* "Honey you've been out three days," she replied. *What the fuck?* I don't remember anything else after that. The next memory is sitting in a car with my mother driving on the freeway. I don't remember anything else from that incident. It wasn't until about 10 or 12 years later that I would ask my mom: *Hey, I'm not sure if this was a dream or not; but I feel like I remember waking up strapped down in a psych ward?* -I wasn't sure if she'd even know what I was talking about-

But she immediately gave a gruff reply: "Yeah that's not a dream. You went fucking insane. I don't really want to talk about this."

Wait, what? Really? What happened? I was surprised she remembered and dying to know details. My mother (now visibly irritated to have to recall another shitty incident I put her through) tells me: "I got a call that the police had picked you up at a Del Taco trying to start fights with customers. The officer said you were acting so bizarre that they took you to the psych hospital instead of jail. I had to drive all the way down to Cerritos and when I got there you were trying to swat imaginary flies that weren't there. Then you didn't recognize me and started to get aggressive, so they had to restrain you."

-I couldn't help but start laughing- My mother, however, didn't think it was funny at all. I couldn't get much more out of her other than that. I always wonder what else I've forgotten. So many people have told me stories of things I must've done while I was high, because I have no memory of doing them whatsoever. So many fuzzy partial memories as well. I have a few other really odd recollections in my mind that I can't confirm, I don't know whether they are actual memories or were some sort of dream. Most are typical junkie activities of no consequence, others I like to hope are just bad dreams.

ONLY FEAR OF DEATH

This is just my opinion, but I think most addicts have some form of death wish. Whether it be a literal death or just the death of life as they know it. Something's got to give. Until then its bottles to oblivion. Sort of like a suicide on the installment plan. For some reason or another life just didn't seem to fit. Maybe there's something better on the other end? Was it that we were we born into the wrong life? Wrong family? Wrong time period? Wrong country? Why was regular life so intolerable? Everyone else seemed to be getting along just fine. Maybe like the caterpillar we were born into a form that wasn't meant to be permanent. We had to go through our caterpillar phase just to do away with it, so we can become our true form. The butterfly.

Throughout my life as far back as I can remember I've always thought about my own death, not always in a bad way. Sometimes just about a cool way I'd like to die i.e., shark attack or heroic gun battle. Death has never held much weight, I've always kind of been indifferent to it. Most other kids and people around me, then, and now seem to fear it. To me, life has always been the scarier of the two. The earliest memory of wanting to die was in about 3rd or 4th grade. Nothing huge, I was just peaking around the doorway, watching my mother and her boyfriend eating Taco Bell for dinner in the living room. I watched as they loudly opened the crinkling bags and wrappers. Handing each other tacos, passing napkins, and different hot sauces. Soft tacos were my favorite food at the time. Hungry and hoping they'd offer me some (which they didn't) I remember thinking; I wish I could just drop dead right in front of them and see how they'd feel. As a kid my mother and I would get into these heated arguments spewing hate at each other. Saying things like; "I hate you" and "I wish you were dead." But I never really wanted her dead. I was the one that didn't belong, not her. At least that's how I thought at the time. Maybe I was more interested in wanting to know how my death would affect her. Would she regret those words or would she feel some sense of relief that she would no longer have to deal with me?

Flash forwards to a few years later, down town L.A. Sitting in a graffiti covered bathroom stall at Union Station about to inject triple my regular dose of heroin. That was as much as I could fit in the needle. The plunger was pulled out so far it was almost dangling off the back of the syringe. You can't shoot up one full needle of heroin then shoot up another, you'd pass out off the first one. I thought about trying to make a denser liquid but any thicker than what I was about to do would just clog the needle. Turns out there was more logistics to this than I thought there would be. All my accidental overdoses were so effortless. I'd just shoot up. Then wake up to someone slapping my face or soaking wet from having cold water poured on me. Oh well let's get on with this. *Wait, last but not least I better pull up my pants.* Being found on the toilet with my ass and junk hanging out wouldn't be very cool. I didn't want embarrassing crime-scene photos. Yeah, even in those moments I worried about what people thought. I also remember not feeling any kind of sadness or pity. Nothing like that. I was thinking more along the lines of *Fuck you, I'm outta here!* Almost in an excitement. Like I was a kid getting to leave school early or finally getting off a long hard miserable day's work. Adios muchachos.

I slid the needle into the scabbed up shot out vein of my

inner right arm. I start moving the needle around a little trying to register the vein. *Come on fucker! Where are you?* Digging around inside your vein looking for blood is no fun. *Mother fucker! The needle is clogged!* Maybe I did make it too thick after all. No problem I'll just lick it with the flame of the lighter to melt the clog and try again. Doesn't work. I tried a couple other little dope fiend tricks but ended up breaking the needle! *FUCK!* I start to panic. Not like I can get another needle delivered to the toilet. This one is toast and now the anxiety is kicking in full effect. Why didn't I bring a spare? I'm starting to feel withdrawal now. I still need to shoot this up before I get sick.

Anxiety brings on dope sickness twice as fast for some reason. If you've ever been addicted to heroin you know the feeling. It's the mental aspect of it I guess. Well this dope is going in me one way or another so I end up snorting it as a last ditch effort. Snorting doesn't hit you as hard or fast as injection obviously, but it was worth a shot. I popped the needle attachment off the tip of the syringe and squirted it up my nose. Eww... I almost gagged as it trickled down the back of my throat. Then... Black out... I must've nodded off as I was cleaning up. Sometime later I came to... still in that stall... still alive... not even that high. I remember vividly my first thoughts after realizing I was still alive: *Fuck you God!* Not only was I pissed off cursing God with a crying frustration that makes me punch my legs, but now I don't have any money or dope. I didn't plan on leaving that toilet alive. My escape attempt failed, there I was sucked back into the abyss.

I've told that story a few times to people and I always get the same response: "It wasn't your time to go" or "God had bigger plans for you!" "It was the loving hand of God." I used to think; if there was a god he wasn't saving me out of love. He was probably a sadist pulling me back into the torture chamber. *You're not getting off that easy kid! HA HA HA!* Whether it was a malicious god or just bad planning, that dose should've killed me and didn't. I'm still alive sitting here in Spain, writing this feeling like it's about time for another coffee. Here's the funny thing, something in me did die that day. A part of me that had hope. Hope that there was a way out, to bow out of this mess. Hope that this life wasn't a reality that I was going to have to face. The door I ran to was locked, I guess I'm stuck here. Maybe that's what needed to happen? I needed to burn the escape ships and fight the war. Whatever it did to me, the result wasn't a new bright outlook on life like you see in the movies. All my morale for life had been snuffed out. Things would get much worse before they got better. I think maybe Richard did die that day after all. The previous "Richard" then a new updated version of Richard was left. How many different "Richards" has there been? This new version was even more lost and confused than the last. Reborn into loneliness, not sure what to do or where to go next. Maybe that's what a "rebirth" is supposed to feel like? These "Death of self" moments followed by "rebirths" seem to happen frequently in my life. Sometimes it feels like the death part happened, but the rebirth part hasn't yet, so there's this weird period of feeling lost. The lucky ones have a death and rebirth occur at the same time, I guess. When I first started drinking was that not the death of an old *Richard* and the birth of a new one? When I got sober did I not kill off an old *me*? When my first daughter was born, was that not also the birth of *Richard* as a father? I became a completely different man each time. Different perspective on life, different set of goals. A completely new purpose. If we want a new life, a new start, a new purpose, the addict must die. We cannot stay sober in the addict version of ourselves. It's too dark in there. What's the best way to pull someone out of the darkness? By first turning on the lights of course.

TIME TO SCORE
(Surrender. Commit. Overview. Repair. Evolve)

After nearly 20 years of working the 12-steps myself, and taking others through the work; I've formed a decent understanding and deep appreciation for the fundamentals of recovery. I say *decent* not to be modest but because working with addicts in recovery on the front and back lines is almost like a discipline or art-form that one can spend an entire life practicing and still feel like a student. Just like any other art form I have great admiration for the legends that paved the way, influencing and inspiring me to follow in their footsteps. Now I've formed my own interpretations and style of a recovery process. Much like the way that Bill Wilson improved upon the program of The Oxford Group and created the 12-steps.

My goal with the SCORE Program was to distil the 12 Steps down to its very essence burning off any dogmas, subjective beliefs and create a simple straight-forward recovery process based on action not belief. I've also infused principles for your physical and mental health along with aspects for one's spirit as well. Remember, when it's all said and done, the better we feel sober, the easier it is to stay that way. Rather than go too much into details I'd rather get straight into the process. I'll explain as we go. Read through a section first then go back and start the work. Don't overthink it, just start.

SURRENDER

We'll start off with a few questions to deeply contemplate. First ask yourself: What is my problem?

Whether it be using, gambling, living an unhealthy lifestyle or maybe it's just living in a way that feels untrue to who you want to become. Maybe it's all of the above, either way identify it and write it down on a piece of paper. It could be a napkin, doesn't matter, there's a power in putting pen to paper. Write all the questions and answers down. Even just something as simple as these: I'm an alcoholic. I'm a fat ass. I can't stop cheating. I'm addicted to pain pills. I've got to stop smoking. I'm mean to my wife and kids. I let people walk all over me. I'm a junky. I feel like a loser. My life is ok I just want a new experience. My life is shit.

Now ask yourself: How has my problem negatively affected me? Could be a ruined relationship, loss of finances, resentful family, low self-esteem etc.

How is my problem negatively affecting others? As in: I let down my partner, I let down my mother (don't group people together name them individually), I'm missing out time with my kid, I caused this person harm or financial loss etc.

Whatever it is, don't be afraid to be brutally honest. Remember this is only for your eyes and should be written in your voice. Normally you probably wouldn't want to talk negatively about yourself, to yourself, but this is an exception. We are going to get to work immediately on ridding ourselves of these issues. We do this by identifying the issues and acknowledging their power over us. We're stuck, we're fucked, we are surrendering, but we aren't giving up. We are just tired and frustrated from not getting any results. So we stop, take a breath and regroup. We are ready to go about the solution from a different angle. If you're lost in a foreign country driving around like dummy, there's no need to waste any more time or go further astray. Especially if you got loved ones in your car depending on you. Stop and find a local that speaks your language, knows his way around the area and can guide you out. Consider this book your friendly local guide to direct you out of the muck. I've been in and out of where you're at a few times. I know the area well. I am 100% confident I can get you out. C'mon follow me.

 Time to get brutally honest. This is a Must. Everything else afterwards is resting on this principle as a foundation. Dig deep. Get honest. Being honest with yourself is vital in all of this. I'm not saying stop telling fibs and lies to people, although that might be a good idea. I'm talking about being candid with *yourself* and the issues negatively affecting your life. That's the first honesty you must tackle before you try to get those other forms down. In AA, Honesty is the principle of the first step. Most people seem to be confused though, they think it means you have got to go around being literally honest. That's not what they mean. They mean getting honest with yourself surrounding your drinking problem.

 WARNING: Do not go telling your mom she looks fat in that dress! Or tell your wife that, yes, you think her sister is hot. You don't have to go around telling kids Santa Clause doesn't exist either. As the author Robert Greene puts it in his book *The 48 Laws of Power*: "Honesty is actually a blunt instrument, which bloodies more than it cuts." Let's just concentrate on honesty within self for now, deal with George Washington honesty once you're done with this book. Once you are done with this process you will find it much easier to be more of an honest person in general.

Whatever it is that you want to change, the first requirement is: You must be ready and willing to go to any lengths. There is no helping someone that is not ready AND willing.

Now that you have identified your problem and written it down on a piece of paper, ask yourself: Am I done?

Think on it a few minutes. If your first thought is: I'll start next week or just one more; you're probably not done. That's ok, finish reading the book and try again when you are. Either way do this; picture all the trouble your issues have caused. Recall the pain you've caused yourself and people that you love.

What are the three most painful experiences caused by your problem? I.e., I lost my relationship, I lost my job, I embarrassed myself in a situation. Write them down, be detailed. Talk to text in your phone if you have to, get it down somewhere.

Can I safely continue in any form at all? As in: can you still do this without consequence once a week, once a month, on occasion? Do I have control? Have I ever tried to stop but couldn't? Can I stop completely? If so why haven't I?

What do you think the solution is? Whatever it is why haven't you done it?

Now imagine what life would be like if your problem was gone. How much of an improvement would it bring? Picture how proud you would be of yourself. I'm sure there's someone that holds a special place in your heart that has been affected by your issues. Picture how proud they would be if you overcame your struggles. See them smiling upon you proudly, even if it's from up above. If this exercise doesn't bring you to tears or call upon intense emotions, try it again later. Make sure you are in the right mood and place to be able to focus and recall with sufficient force. It may take a few times to get in there deep, but that's where you need to go.

Next, we have to find out how willing you are to solve your problem. You must be willing to do whatever it takes. Not only willing to take the actions but willing to endure what comes with it. This usually comes in the form of discomfort, discomfort in the change itself and discomfort in how people react to your change. You may lose some friends, you may feel embarrassed, you may piss people off. Fuck them. You'll never get anywhere worrying about what other people are going to think. They'll get over it. You've got to be willing, and you have to be desperate. Desperation is the key ingredient when cooking up a new chapter in life. In the book of Alcoholics Anonymous they say an alcoholic must have "the desperation of a drowning man."
Are you willing to go to any lengths?

(Identifying the problem)

Directions:
-Write out your problem or problems
-Next to the problem write out how it negatively affects your life.
-Next ask yourself how it affects others

-What are you 3 most painful experiences caused by your problem?

-Ask yourself: Can I safely use/continue in any form at all? Do I have control? Can I stop completely? If so why haven't I?

-What is the solution?

-When you're done grab your list and head into the bathroom or some private place with a mirror. Don't chicken out, do this. Really. Picture how much better your life will be once the problem is gone. Picture how proud you and others will be. Call upon all your emotions. Look yourself in the eye and say: I have had no control over _____ It has beaten me, but today that changes. I am willing to do anything and everything I need to do to kill my problems and accomplish my goals.

You can word it how you want, just make sure it is effective and sincere. The objective is to truly admit to yourself deep down that this problem has beaten you down. This issue beat you, till now. Now is your comeback. Once again this may take a few attempts, you need to be able to dig deep down into your core and truly acknowledge the problem, then you can draw upon the spectacular strength of the power that is within us all. Call it God, call it human will. Whatever your name for it is, it's there, and it's in you too.

COMMIT
(Goals and prayers)

GOALS

Now that you've established the problems and are ready to tackle them, let's talk about solutions. To get anywhere, first you need to know where you are at, what your destination is, then figure out the path to get there. Ok so we know where we're at (our problems), now let's decide where we want to end up (Goals). Time to pick a destination and start walking towards it. It's easy to get there when you break it down into small daily steps in the correct direction. Just keep doing the next right thing.

One of the most influential tools I picked up in life, was from Napoleon Hills *Think And Grow Rich*: Writing down your goals and reading them in the morning and night. Not only financial goals but things like staying sober, being confident or being a good parent. While this may have always been familiar to you, it was brand new and a revelation to me. Not just to write your goals down, but to keep impressing them upon your mind throughout the day, everyday, till they are actualized. I think it's vital, and I treat saturating my brain with my goals as a daily necessity like brushing my teeth and taking a shower. I teach my kids the same, in fact I share with them everything I learn along the way. As a child I was fed, given shelter, and clothed but never really talked to about LIFE and how to navigate it. Other than "Keep it up you're gonna end up dead or in jail." Not to say I didn't learn anything from my parents, each one taught me something crucial to my life.

My mom gave me freedom growing up and let me deal with my own mistakes. I was never coddled. I learned to take care of myself early on.

My step-dad drilled into me something so simple but so very important in life: ALWAYS BE EARLY, NEVER EVER BE LATE. I can't tell you how many times this has saved my ass and gave me a leg up on people much more qualified than me just because I'm reliable. Always be early and you'll never be late. That alone was a priceless gift. My dad taught me the old school Mexican hard work ethics. He used to say: "If other guys are carrying one log, you carry two. If they are carrying four bricks, you carry eight. Never let someone out work you." He'd wake me up at the crack of dawn take me outside and put a shovel or rake in my hand. My step-mom taught me to be confident and fearless in speaking my mind. As a kid I had a naturally quiet disposition, so she helped me balance out keeping my mouth shut when I should, but speaking up when needed. My Nana & Papa taught me the most crucial necessity in life: How to love someone through good and bad. When times got rough everyone turned their back on me, except them. Their love kept my pilot light of hope lit.

Throughout my life whenever I observe a certain strength of character that I admire in someone, I make it a goal of mine to develop that trait within myself. I'm like that X-Men character Rogue that absorbs people's special powers when she touches them. My goals as a parent is to pass on the essentials I've learned in life to my children. That was a primary inspiration for writing this book (for you girls, even if nobody else reads this, you'll still have it. Otherwise all life lessons can be learned from watching *The Simpsons* and *The Twilight Zone*...).

As soon as I wake up in the mornings I sit up, grab my bottle of water and as I'm chugging I read my goals and take a second to picture them in my mind. There are many methods on how to write out your goals, mine is simple. My goals are much different now, but here's an example of one of my past life goals I still had in my old notes: "I will become a millionaire real estate investor. I will live comfortably off the income from my rentals and businesses. I will quit the television industry and travel the world with my family whenever I want. I will be in the best shape of my life. I will do this by dec 2018."

    I choose not to get too into details with my life goals just as a personal preference. I used to do it but reading and trying to visualize a goal list that is three pages long was a little too much each morning to wrap my head around. Try a detailed goal list one day and try a simplified version another, see which you comprehend best and stick with that. The important thing is not to just read it off mindlessly, but to visualize the situation. For instance I used to picture myself walking into work saying "It's my last day fellas, I'm out of here. See ya, wouldn't want to be ya!" Saying goodbye to everyone shaking hands and giving hugs on my way out. Picturing some congratulating me and others dying inside. Picture yourself posting a "JUST GOT THE KEYS TO OUR NEW HOUSE!" Picture on social media. Or a TMZ post SUPER MODEL HOOKS UP WITH RANDOM NOBODY RICHARD GALVAN!

    Whatever it is get the visual in your mind's eye. Don't just do it when you wake up or before sleepy time, visualize and daydream through your day. If you get frustrated at work don't dwell on resentment, picture your future life instead. Talk about it with your friends and co-workers, keep your dreams in the forefront of your mind. I remember telling my friend at work as we were unloading a truck pushing cases into the studio: "by this time next year I'll out of this business traveling and just chilling with the fam." He told me: "Yeah right you're gonna be right here with me unloading trucks just like we are now." The following year I did quit that business and was traveling around with my family at my leisure. I also love blasting music while I'm at the gym, super-caffeinated thinking of living out whatever goals I have at the time. I used to picture myself having guests over at my new house on the beach admiring the view with my beautiful wife and children and watching friends take videos and tagging me in pics telling me how lucky I am. Yes, I may be a little shallow, but it worked. I accomplished those goals and many others, noble and shallow. I'll leave the goal and visualizations of world peace and living like a monk to you.

We also want to have a goal list for the day/week. This is just as important. These are the small things that bring you closer to your life goals, as well as the day-to-day errands. A simple to do/check list, to knock out as you go about your day.

Example: Read twenty minutes (of real estate book). Compliment three new people. Grab bananas and hummus. Gym. Renew passport. Make an appointment to see the house on PCH. Make eye doctor appointment. Introduce yourself to that investor dude at the gym. Check in with three agents say hi and see if they have any interesting deals. Watch one 'how to real estate' Youtube video.

An empty goal list is a good feeling at the end of the day. That makes you one step closer. Then add back the usuals and whatever else is needed for the next day.

PRAYERS

If you pray, of course make sure to keep your prayers in there. Make them separate from your goals. Maybe try to keep your personal prayers unselfish and for the power to do good and serve. Example: God please help me to be the best father I could be and the best husband I could be. Please keep me sharp and give me the energy to be the hardest worker I can possibly be and bring the most to the table at work. Please give me the drive to work on my goals so that to accomplish them I can be a better example and of service to my fellows. Help me to be bring some good to everyone I encounter today, Amen

At the end of the day give thanks.

For those that don't believe in gods or just don't pray, no problem. You can skip over the prayer part. Honestly though, even if you weren't saying these things in the form of a prayer to a god, but rather in an affirmation to yourself instead, it definitely couldn't hurt. Or don't, all are welcome.

Directions:

Write out your life goals. Read them morning and night. Visualize.

Make a separate daily goal list of whatever the next small step is to get you closer to your major goals as well as your basic errands for the day.

If you pray, say your prayers. Keep it unselfish. Alternative: If you don't pray maybe try something in the form of an affirmation.

Have them written on a piece of paper by your bedside to be read immediately upon awakening and before you go to sleep. Also have this on your phone notes to be read at least 3-5 times throughout the day. Even if it's just every bathroom break. The idea is to saturate your subconscious with its instructions and keep you aimed in the right direction. My daily goals and errands I like to keep in my

Reminders app to alert me at the proper time.

Once you've accomplished a goal, update accordingly. Keep knocking them out one by one.

COMPLETE ABSTINENCE OR MODERATION?

Whether or not you should choose complete abstinence is up to you. I would highly recommend it. Not only is it the safer, healthier option but also for the sharpness of mind and countless other benefits. On paper it's a no brainer which option is best for your health and productivity. You might take a hit on the easy bonding alcohol provides, but you are freed from all the dumb decisions you'd make while under the influence. You will definitely see a huge improvement in your life with complete abstinence. I can't promise the same if you go the moderation route, it could be ok or it could get worse. Chances are if you've found yourself reading a book called *The Addict* you might have an issue. Maybe even the allergy Dr. Silkworth talks about. It might just be in the early stages and could grow worse if you don't completely abstain. Or maybe not. Only you know your experiences. I highly suggest you read *The Doctors Opinion* in the book of *Alcoholics Anonymous* before making your decision. It's definitely worth the 20-minute read. Evaluate your past experiences and make the best decision for your future. To each his own. When in doubt, go without. Sure, it's not the easiest thing at first but you know what they say: Easy choices, hard life, hard choices, easy life. Or my favorite: The lazy man works twice as hard. Better to deal with the small pains of sobriety now than the huge pains of using later. Once you get over the initial hump it gets better. I haven't had a craving or missed alcohol or drugs at all since my first few months in 2004. It's not even a thought any more when you stay on the path of continual growth.

    I used to see sober people as weak. (In a high voice) "Oh no thank you, I don't drink I'm a recovering alcoholic." I would think: *What a bitch!* As if drinking made me stronger or cool somehow. Plus I felt stronger and more confident sober than I ever had felt using. A real confidence, not a temporary liquid courage. I also didn't go around telling people I was in recovery, sober, or AA. I believed in anonymity. After all it's called Alcoholics ANONYMOUS. I never understood people announcing to the world that they were a recovering addict. You never know what bad experiences others have had with addicts. They could have had a family member killed by an alcoholic drunk driver. They could have had an abusive alcoholic parent. Possibly even an uncle that molested them and happened to be an addict, but now they're "in recovery." Addicts and alcoholics don't exactly have the best reputation or credibility. I've always chosen to keep my recovery to myself, even when it came to family and friends. Not out of shame, just because it was something that is personal to me and really no one else's business. When people would offer me alcohol or drugs I'd just say "No I'm good." Simple. If they pried more and asked why; I'd just say with a little more conviction "Because I don't drink." If I was at a bar or club, I'd just keep a glass of cranberry juice or sugar free Redbull in hand to blend in. I kept it full so if people did offer, I'd show them I was already working on a drink. I have yet to lose anyone I care about by staying sober. When you look people in the eye and say things with a little conviction most will respect you for that choice. It's all in your confidence and how you wear it.

My last drink and sobriety date is 10/11/04. As I mentioned earlier in the book this happened while I was in rehab out on a day pass. I'll touch on it a little more because it was significant in that it changed my thinking. I used to think I just had to stop doing hard drugs but could still drink, maybe even smoke some weed. That last drink made me realize I can't drink or use any type of addicting substance at all anymore. It was in that last drink that I realized the difference between a "Real addict" versus someone that just has a problem with drugs or alcohol.

I went to visit my friend Steve who was still active in his addiction. I had absolutely no desire to use or go back to that lifestyle. Keep in mind I just spent 6 weeks kicking in LA county jail after years of living on the street and had a little over a month of rehab under my belt. I was doing good and promised myself I wouldn't drink, even though I didn't think alcohol was really a problem for me. I had stopped drinking years ago when I started doing heroin. I just didn't like alcohol anymore, and especially didn't want to get kicked out of the rehab and be homeless over it. In spite of that I drank a tall can of beer the week prior and knew it was a stupid move. I didn't even really know why I did it, I just knew I wouldn't mess up again this pass.

Despite all my resolutions, I couldn't have been with Steve for more than an hour and already had a 32 oz. of Corona in my hand. *Oh well... fuck it!* You know the feeling. Then something happened about halfway through the bottle, something that doesn't happen to the normal person and only occurs in what we call "addicts" or "alcoholics." I started getting this sensation in my chest. Not a pleasant sensation like butterflies in my stomach but like a panic that needed to be calmed. Like an adrenaline rush filled with excitement, anxiety and urgency. My heart started pumping and the intensity was starting to build. HOLY SHIT! I recognized immediately what was happening and now I had a name for it. It was the phenomenon of craving. This is what they had been talking about in the AA book and those boring groups at rehab. "The Doctors opinion" written by William D. Silkworth M.D in the AA book describes alcoholics as having an allergy of the body. "We believe, and so suggested a few years ago, that the action of alcohol on these chronic alcoholics is a manifestation of an allergy: that the phenomenon of craving is limited to this class and never occur in the average temperate drinker. These allergic types can never safely use alcohol in any form at all.." In the meetings they said things like "I take a drink then the drink takes me" and "One is too many and a thousand is never enough" and that once an addict starts to drink or use again the phenomenon of craving kicks in, maybe not every single time, but eventually. Once the phenomenon of craving has hold of you, off on a spree you go and there's no telling when you can stop. They were right! This is what was about to go down with me. Fortunately, I must've caught it at the very slightest onset before it was able fully kick in. I know it was the phenomenon of craving because I've had this happen to me so many times before but didn't have a name or explanation for it. Each time I would come out of some type of incarceration, institution or rehab sober, I always had a resolve to stay off heroin and the "harder drugs." *I'll just have a few drinks like a normal person or smoke a little weed.* The problem with that is; I'm not a normal person. I start to drink or smoke a little weed, then that craving hits me. Unlike an alcoholic I don't drink more, I end up snorting some meth or heading downtown to score some crack and heroin. Then I'm off and running, strung out again. Nothing short of a pair of hand cuffs or a bullet can stop me. The realization of what was going on in my body and what was about to happen frightened me to my core. I mean a real fear, a fear worse than death for me. I put the bottle down and told Steve I had to go. I got the hell out of there and jumped on the bus back to the rehab. The minute I stepped out of his house I was praying and apologizing, pleading with whatever was out there to stop this craving from getting me. I arrived back to the rehab without getting caught and felt immensely relieved as I fell back on my bed. Grateful to be safe and having narrowly dodged that craving, I went to the in-house AA meeting willingly for the first time. The next morning, I went to another and got a sponsor.

Previously I had always avoided AA like the plague. It just seemed so boring and corny. *What's wrong with these people?* I thought it was a cult or weird church, but I was desperate. Even though I didn't consider myself a "drinker" Alcoholics Anonymous was all that was available in the rehab. I also saw that I fit the description of what they describe in AA as "The real alcoholic" (pg.21-22) "As matters grow worse he begins to use a combination of high powered sedatives and liquor to quiet his nerves so he can go to work." Then it goes on to say "Perhaps he goes to a doctor who gives him morphine or some sedative with which to taper off. Then he begins to appear at hospitals and sanitaria."

That basically described me. I went from drinking, to drinking with other drugs, then to "high powered sedatives" that's when things really got bad and I started ending up in jails and institutions. Everything in AA started to make sense, the book, the meetings and even the strange people. They were just grateful having escaped a situation similar to mine. I listened with an open mind to these people's stories and believed that they shared the same trait I had. Most importantly that they had discovered a solution. Their solution was complete abstinence, to work the 12-steps, and then take others though the work. It wasn't exactly the coolest solution, in fact it didn't sound very appealing at all. I was still reeling from that scare at Steve's house and would do anything to not go back to what I came from.

So, I made the decision to stay sober, get a sponsor and work the steps. It's still the best decision I've ever made in my life. I had come a long way from when I first arrived at the rehab. I remember I had told myself: *As soon as I can get $10 I'm gonna head downtown, buy a $4 heroin balloon, $1 needle, $1 for a Klonopin, $3 for a crack rock and $1 for 4 cigarettes, fuck this rehab.* Now I was doing AA... The first few months of sobriety was definitely awkward for me. Maybe even the first year. I had to get used to being in social situations without substances to calm my nerves. It was really hard at first to "just be myself" without drugs or alcohol. I didn't even know who the hell I was supposed to be anymore. I felt lost. Eventually your brain recalibrates, your social skills come back, and you start to get more comfortable in your own skin again. Assuming you put in the effort to grow that is. I found that I can be confident and have fun in any situation without drugs. I loved it (still do). During this re-acclimation to life sober, I saw that it seemed many people just used alcohol as a crutch. I noticed friends couldn't talk to girls, dance or be comfortable without some sort of social lubrication. They were using alcohol and drugs to relieve their own social anxieties. This gave me some comfort. I had always thought I was the only one to not have the world figured out. I realize now that nobody has it figured out. Everything everyone does, at some level, is done so they can be accepted by their peers. No one wants to be alone. I didn't look at not drinking any more as a loss, I saw it as a strength. I no longer needed help from any substances to be comfortable or give me confidence. Now all I need for confidence is massive amounts of caffeine!

ON THE MIND

The Roman Circus

Somewhere in my early 30's I had begun to settle into my new sober "regular guy" lifestyle. I had a house, wife, kid, dogs, cars, career; all the things I had dreamed of on the street. Nothing wrong with that of course. When I was about nineteen, I remember coming back from a walk to the liquor store after almost getting jumped by some dudes; this is a few days after some other guys out looking for me, beat up my girlfriend instead. *I can't even walk to the fucking store!* I was so angry and frustrated with my life. I told my friend that day I'd give anything just to have a normal person's life. A little job and family far from this shit. Be able to do simple things like go buy a bag of chips in peace without worrying about getting attacked, robbed or arrested. Well, I had arrived, but was this it? I almost felt like one of those soldiers back from Vietnam with my brain still wired for chaos. The stillness was too much for me, the comfort made me uncomfortable. The people at work, the parents of other kids, my own family; they all seemed to be from a different planet. The only place I felt at home was when I was amongst others like me. There were only two places to find these people: the streets or a meeting.

Before you read further keep in mind: I'm talking to my people with the troubled lives needing a change, not the normal people enjoying their lives. So, relax if you're reading this for someone else.

What do I do now? It's too stuffy in here. Thirty more years of living basically the same days, weeks and years over and over till I die? Was the couch and TV my final destination? Only looking forward to a two-week Hawaiian vacation once every few years? Do I take up golfing now? Or even worse; do I have to get supplemental excitement and accomplishments by proxy from watching sports and reality shows? Even though I loved playing sports as a kid, I never understood sitting at home for hours watching a bunch of strangers play the sport on TV. In an event maybe, but to me their goals had absolutely no effect on my life. I couldn't see how my friends would get so sad when their team lost. Like actually sad, as if they themselves had lost. Even crazier to me, was when those men they never met weren't playing a game, they would watch another group of strangers they never met on ESPN talk about the game. All day. If you're involved with sports and studying to improve your own skills that's different. For the non-sports star I always felt like there was so many better things to do with my time. I love weightlifting, been doing it my whole life; but you're not going to catch me devoting massive blocks of my life to watching it on a screen. I'd rather just go to the gym.

(High voice) *But Richard everyone else is doing it!*

Yeah, some people eat dogs too. As of the writing of this book 2.9 billion people on earth still have never used the internet. 70% of the world doesn't use toilet paper and over 700 million people can't read or write. Now I'm not implying any of these things are wrong or right, I'm just saying just because it seems everybody else is doing it... I'm assuming if you're reading this you want to be as productive as possible with your time. Of course, there's nothing wrong with being into sports but see it for what it is, entertainment. The excitement you feel is from a false sense of goal fulfilment, and a narrow camaraderie from sharing similar likes with others. I had a co-worker once who admitted to me that he only kept up with sports to keep up with the conversation. I was like: *Wait, what? Really, why? What if everybody else was also not very interested, but just going along with it because everyone else is? You guys would all just be wasting your time talking about something no one cared about and not even know it!* I too appreciate and marvel when I see humans with unbelievable skills in action. Do you really want to devote such a high percentage of your time and mental energy to watching others do things? I like live events and watching a match sometimes too, nothing wrong with entertainment. It's the faux quenching of accomplishments and thrill that is the real killer of ambitions. Not to mention the mass consumptions of your time. We need accomplishment in real form, and that takes a good deal of time. Time that a lot of people are using watching sports or TV. Both should be seen as a treat, like a candy or doughnut. A sports team probably shouldn't become part of your identity unless you're on the team. Sure, you might see Leonardo DiCaprio, Spike Lee, Drake and Jack Nicholson court side at basketball games. But these people all have major accomplishments of their own. It's a different circumstance than the couch potato that sells half of his day off to work, only to come home and turn on the TV to get some stimulation through watching other people's success and failures. You'll have plenty of time in your 70's to relax and watch sports after you lived a full life. Use your most productive years wisely.

"But Richard I love sports" OK, join a local league.

"But I'm out of shape, I'll get injured" OK, that needs to be fixed, probably should get back in shape then. Maybe start out with stretching and walking or find some other people of similar age and go super easy when playing. Get creative. If you really love the sport that much, you'll find a way.

"But I don't have the time" If you have time to sit there for hours watching sports you have time to get out and play. I told my friend once if he swapped out the countless hours he spends watching sports and learning about other men's stats; with learning some new skill, he'd be a master in a year. He probably could have become a doctor and a lawyer with all the hours he's spent watching football and basketball over the decades. With all the energy some people put into watching sports they probably could've solved world hunger or created a time machine by now. Plus, if you don't have time to do the things you love something is wrong and needs to be changed.

"But I'm too old or have a disability." Then disregard, or maybe find a suitable activity like walking groups, stretching or yoga. There's even the option of volunteering to coach kids or contributing in another way. The point is get out and do something in real life, digital screens trick your brain into a false sense of drama and accomplishment. When you are watching a romance or something exciting on the screen, your brain thinks you are experiencing that. We don't need to watch other people live life on social media or TV, we need the real thing. Look, I'm not above it either. My kids call me out too. For me it's movies. I rationalize by telling myself a movie is a story. A good story can inspire you in so many ways. Humans are storytelling creatures (although you can say the same for competition sports). Plus, it's over in 2 hours, done. There's no need to follow the people's statistics and lives. I am pretty good at unplugging though, and I know I've got to get out there and make things happen in the real world.

Create your own accomplishments and *real*-life excitement. But how? Maybe you are like how I was- stuck in a career I didn't enjoy, working my kids' childhood away to accomplish the goals of my boss and the company owner, not mine; I was trapped, dependent on that pay check every week. A perfect storm of monotony and fear to keep me in my place. Life doesn't have to be like that. Don't worry I'm not here to be your financial guru. You don't want financial advice from me, I choose experience over money every time now. This isn't about the money. What does any of this have to do with recovery? Well, it's much harder to stay sober if you are living a life you do not enjoy. There's nothing wrong with struggle, there's nothing wrong with trying to make more money, there's nothing wrong with being far from where you want to be. As long as you find a sense of accomplishment and satisfaction in your journey. If you hate the way you're spending the majority of the hours of your life- of course you're going to want to get loaded, if that's the only time you're happy. We all need a purpose to be fulfilled. When you're unfulfilled there's a void. What do addicts fill their voids with? Do you what you love and the money will follow. Even if it doesn't, you're still more likely to be happy. Besides, there's no guarantee that if you do - *what you don't want to do-* just for money, that you'll be rich either. There's plenty of proof of that, look around. If you *are* doing what you love, you're much more likely to excel in your field, and good fortune along with personal satisfaction is more likely to follow.

Maybe it's time to shake things up.

The only way to do great work is to do what you love- Steve Jobs

KEEP CHANGING THE DIAL TILL YOU FIND YOUR STATION

Everything matters. Having a sober, clear mind means you will be experiencing everything around you exactly how it is, there is no more drowning out the low spots with alcohol or drugs. Everything must be walked through with open eyes and dealt with. This can be overwhelming at first, even just the thought of it. I know, I dealt with it too, but it has to be done, so get over it. Think of your life as your home. If your home is dirty you have got to clean it. It's hard work at first and can seem impossible, but that's ok, just handle one room at a time. You will uncover the things you need to deal with as you go. It may be the hardest thing you've ever done, but you will feel infinitely better afterwards. From then on issues will be much easier to tackle individually as things come along. You will find that as the clutter is discarded from your house so goes the anxiety and darkness. When the house is clean open the windows and let in some fresh air and sun, take a deep breath and relax. Remember your mind is where you live and you're at home 24/7. Make sure you know who and what it's being occupied with, get rid of the junk and kick out the squatters. Cleaning house and fixing any misalignment of purpose and direction in one's life goes a very long way. So where do we even start? I'll hand you the mop and broom a little later in the book. Once again let us first feel out the situation. Forget about the drug problem or whatever vices are troubling you, what's life like outside of that? Where are you going to land once sober? Back to work, school, home life, the streets? Ask yourself: Do I like where my life is headed? Do I have a plan? What's the best case scenario if I stay on this track five, ten, or twenty years from now? Do I want to do this for the next twenty or thirty years? It happens, time flies and people can get used to anything. Look at the people that do decades in prison and don't want to leave. Humans can adapt and get comfortable in any situation given enough time.

 While I was living at the Royal Palms in 2004-2005 California governor Arnold Schwarzenegger started paroling a bunch of prisoners that had life sentences. A few of which ended up at the Royal Palms with me. I got to know a couple guys and heard what they had to say about their "All day" experiences in prison. Not everyone was glad to be out, they were institutionalized. One guy kept talking about how guilty he felt, like he abandoned his friends back in the pen. Some made decisions to do things to go back, some went on to adapt and do pretty good. My buddy Pete, I'm still friends with to this day, he also is in recovery and works in treatment; he is a shining example for change. All the guys I met had been rewired to adapt to life in prison. Once given the opportunity for a second chance, some chose to go back to prison rather than taking on the monumental task of tackling a new way of life. Which route will you take?

Ask yourself: Did I choose the route I'm on? Or did I fall into this by default via the influence of a family member or friend? Or even just because of where you live. I got into the television industry because my step-dad was in it, he was prone to work in TV because we lived in LA. I'm sure if we lived in West Virginia, we may have been coal miners. In Wisconsin maybe we'd be in the cheese business. Are you in an industry by default because of where you live? If you love what you do, great. These questions will just re-affirm it. Still ask them either way, especially if you are afraid to.

Don't get me wrong I was grateful for that industry, I just grew out of it. That happens. My stepdad gave me a second chance to work for him while I was in rehab. I was broke, couldn't find a job and had a baby on the way. I had humiliated him already the previous time he hired me. I was working as a spotlight on a stand-up comedy show. You know me by now, of course I shot some dope in the bathroom before I went up to work the light. The spotlight was on top of a two-story scaffolding overlooking the audience and stage. In the middle of the show, I nodded out while sitting on top of the railing of the scaffolding. I came-to because I heard a commotion and people yelling. I opened my eyes to see what was going on and saw that the entire audience and crew including the comedian on stage was staring at me and had been yelling trying to wake me up so I wouldn't fall backwards off the rail. Yeah, as you can guess, they fired me for that.

I fumbled a job with my father as a construction worker too. I shot some dope in a Port'o'Potty on a bridge building job, borrowed some money from one of his co-worker friends and basically fell out with heat stroke. He didn't give me a second chance though. I'll always be grateful to my stepdad for going out on a limb giving me another opportunity. I had to work for free or for cheap and with mostly other people for a long time to learn the trade. I ended up raising my first daughter, bought my first house and built the foundation for my new life off that career. So it was no easy choice ditching set lighting after it got me out of the gutter, but it just wasn't for me anymore. The careers my father and stepfather loved was their love, not mine. I was there for money. It was time to make the call. That's where the boys are separated from the men (or girls from women) it takes balls to make major moves in your life. People are going to be upset and doubt you, even tease you or say you're quitting. Other people will always think they know what's best for you but it's up to you to make your own choices and deal with the blow back. I loved the guys I worked with and had some fun days, but it was time to call it a day.

Are you one of the fortunate people to be in a job they love so much they live and breathe it? If so, good. Or are you like me, the guy that was just there for the money? If it's just for the money it may be time to find your real purpose, which might even lead to better money because you'll be more likely to give it your all and do it well. Even if you live and breathe your industry maybe it's time you switch companies or go into business for yourself. Maybe your purpose is outside of your job, like your family or something you do in your free time. Obviously, some situations will be much more complicated than others. I'm just trying to get you thinking.

For myself, I realized I had to change things after a conversation I had with a new guy at work. This guy had just got into our union IATSE Local 728 in Hollywood. He was excited and proud to be a member. That union is hard to get into, it took me about five years, and it costs thousands in entry fees. So, he was jazzed to have finally made it, he must've been about 25 years old. I congratulated the man and listened to him go on about how glad he was to be on a union job. Then I said to him: "Good I hope you like it because retirement is sixty-five. This is what you'll be doing for the next 40 YEARS!" That statement hit us both in the gut. I had never really thought about it like that either till I spoke those words. We both looked at each other stunned for a second, then started cracking up. It was funny, but at the same time it wasn't. I thought about what I had said all that night. *Man... I still got 30 plus years left.* There was no way I was going to be able to keep doing it that long. Then on another job a week or so later a co-worker pointed out that the only way to make more money (which I was hoping to do) in this business is to WORK MORE. I was already working 70-hour weeks. I wanted more money, but I didn't want to sell any more of my time. I wanted to spend more time with my wife and kid, any more time away I might as well pack my stuff and move out. I saw a lot of the guys getting divorces. They were either never home, exhausted when they were, or drinking heavy. Or all of the above.

2001: A SPACE ODYSSEY

Fortunately I had a friend at work named Anthony, who was on the same page as me trying to "make a jump off the slave ship" as we'd say. He had travelled a lot, which was fascinating to me. At that time I had never even been on a plane. He also liked to read, and my first reaction was to call him a nerd when he had a book in his hand. Shows you where my head was at. Another interest he had was Real estate, he owned a few houses, which again at the time blew my mind. I had never met anybody that had owned more than one house. I started asking him all kinds of questions like where he learned how to do all this and what I could do to get to get where he was. This is around 2012-ish before you could just pick one of a million social media influencers to follow and learn tips. He recommended Robert Kiyosaki's book called *Rich Dad Poor Dad*. I wasn't a very good reader at the time, so I bought the audio book version on Audible.

I listened to it on my way to and from work, long LA traffic let me get a lot of time in. I got so much information and inspiration out of that audio book that I ordered another, and then another. The audible app has been a game changer in my life. As of this writing I have over 130 books in my library, many I've listened to over and over. It also helped me get more comfortable reading real books as well, I had never really read a book before. I had read most of Arnold Schwarzenegger's *Encyclopedia of Body Building*, and chunks of The Bible, but nothing other than that in 30 years. Not even in school had I ever read any of the books I was supposed to.

I also started watching real estate investing videos on YouTube and listening to pod casts like *Bigger Pockets*. Meanwhile my co-workers were watching sports and sitcoms. I became obsessed. I saved and hustled up any money I could to make my goal of buying one property per year.

I talked with everyone I could to find ways to fund properties, get loans, get around issues like debt to income, get tips on renovations etc. I tried to soak up all the knowledge I could. When you put out that much action and focus into something you eventually meet the right people and it bears fruit. For me that person ended up being my mortgage broker Gloria. She walked me through everything I needed to know in real estate and helped me meet my goals and then some. My entire life changed.

My wife at the time and I opened up our first business, which was a dance studio called 101 Dance Center. I also moved all of us out of our house, put it up for rent, and moved into a tiny cheap one-bedroom apartment. I traded in my BMW for a little used Fiat too. I did all this to pay down debt and save up to buy another house. My friends and co-workers clowned me every time I pulled up in the Fiat. Even my own family laughed at me. My dad came by the apartment once and said to me "I'm sorry you're going through this," while looking around in pity with my step-mom and sister giggling in the background. I tried to explain to him and everyone else mocking me that sometimes you have to take a step back to go farther forward. Oh well...

Little by little I was gaining more income from my other ventures. I was working less and traveling more. Eventually after a few years of slow progress I had enough income and equity to quit my job and start a business that involved two of the things I loved most; working with addicts and real estate. I opened up a sober living. That would be followed by a few more, then an outpatient program and eventually a detox/residential.

Now when you start making big changes in your life get ready for the doubters and haters. Don't be surprised when your biggest haters are the people closest to you. Meanwhile acquaintances you hardly know are your biggest supporters. I'm with Grant Cardone when he said in his book *10X* "If you got 10 haters get you 20. If you got 20 get you 40. If you don't got haters you ain't doing enough..." I love that way of looking at things.

I'm in Lake Como Italy right now as I'm typing this section on doubters out. I just got a FaceTime video call from my old co-workers who I'm still friends with as I was brushing my teeth about to hit the hay. I answered it and they were all gathered around the phone laughing at me saying "LAKE HOMO! Stop trying to act rich!" I just started laughing, kept brushing my teeth, then hung up. Ahh I love those guys... They were the same guys that laughed when we opened the dance studio. They said things like: "You'll be right here with me doing the same shit twenty years from now" when I talked about my plans to get out of that business. My family was even worse. I say all this to let you know that it's just something that comes with the territory. You've got to learn to follow your instinct and drown out the doubters. Just stick to the script.

I won't speak on other minorities but I know with Mexicans you may hear things like: "Stop trying to act white," "You're selling out," "Keep it real," "Man you changed!" You may even start to be left out of things as you become more successful. It flares up people's insecurities and makes them uncomfortable. Even when I became vegan, I had friends that were grossly out of shape giving me shit trying to tell me how unhealthy it was. People that were living off of Tacos, hot Cheetos, soda and Popeyes chicken. If you've been listening to other people and letting them run your life, the pull of your instinct might have weakened to a little baby puppy that cowers any time someone questions it. We all do it, everyone is afraid to be turned on by the crowd. Start to follow your instinct again and it'll grow stronger little by little till it's like a vicious pit bull with a jaw of steel. You've got to be able to hold on tight, even when people start giving you all the negative stats. How many businesses fail each year, or they always have a friend that "lost it all." Or that the line of business you are getting into is too saturated, there's no demand, the economy is bad, you name it I heard it all.

One hot summer day at a park festival, my cousin Elvis and I were buying a raspado (a Mexican snow cone). We sparked up a conversation with the raspado vendor. We were talking to the man about how he got into the raspado game. I mentioned a business idea I had about Paletas (Mexican popsicles) to which he replied: "Too many people are doing that nowadays, it's not original. It's kinda like copying. You shouldn't copy other people." *Whatever bro, give me my raspado.* As I was walking away eating my raspado still stinging from the dickhead comment, I told my cousin: "Wait a minute fuck that guy! He wasn't the first person to start selling raspados at the park! He didn't invent the raspado he's copying too!" We had a good laugh and realized almost everything is a copy or improvement on something already done. *Burger King* and *Jack And The Box* aren't the first to sell burgers and fries. What if people stopped making cars after Henry Ford's *Model T* because they didn't want to "copy"? Elon Musk didn't get deterred from making rockets just because NASA was already doing it, same with electric cars and Tesla. Imagine if Steve Jobs didn't create the Ipod and change the music industry just because there was already someone making an MP3 player. Same with the personal computer and iPhone. There is always plenty of room for your ideas and dreams too!

The world isn't run by the smartest people or the most cautious, it's run by the charismatic and the action takers. You don't have to reinvent the wheel to be successful. Persistence, fearlessness and patience will take you far. In other words, your heart has to be in it. That's the only way you're going to be able to survive the struggles. Sometimes you might lose everything and have to start over. You might relapse a few times before you stay sober for good. You're probably going to date lots of duds before you find the right one. Can you hang in there or will you give up and settle for "as is" halfway through? Sometimes it's not till you get to the very bottom, that things start to get better. Think of the movies *ROCKY* or *RUDY*. Here's an example, I brought on a friend who had been begging me to let him join in on a venture as I was starting it up. I didn't want to ruin our friendship, so I kept turning him down, after a few months I caved and gave in. I brought him in under the condition he accept that we might not make any money at all for at least a year conservatively. I told him to give me one year of struggle and hard times. He accepted and said he was "All in. Ride or die." Within a month or two of all the stresses we were going through he was bitter and didn't like that the little money that did come in all went to keep the business afloat. He basically gave up doing his duties and eventually quit within six months. As upset as I was for him bailing and leaving me in a bad position, I still paid him out for his time. I paid him out of my own money just to try to keep our friendship. He was beyond disgruntled though, and thought he was owed more and had wasted his time. I was pretty discouraged myself at that point, everything seemed to be going wrong. I was haemorrhaging money and had just lost one of my best friends. My family life was taking a hit too. I felt like quitting at times, but unlike him, I didn't have that luxury. My heart was still in it and all my chips were on the table.

Fast forward to almost exactly one month after he quit; I opened the mailbox to find one of those big document envelopes thick as the bible. I figured it was an insurance company sending me a big welcome packet of disclosures and terms. I left it in the car and went about my day, almost threw it out when I got home. Eventually I opened it (I think it was the following evening) it turned out to be a giant stack of payout checks! Each one in the thousands, it saved my ass. I couldn't believe it, finally! Just when my gas tank was on empty about to putter out BAM! Hope. I couldn't help but laugh to myself at my boy quitting right before the money came in and right around the time I said it would. Funny how things happen like that, life has a way of testing your commitment to see if you're all in.

LIKE MIKE

"The cowards never started and the weak died along the way, that leaves us"- Phil Knight- *Shoe Dog*.

You may or may not know what new big life change you need to make, or if you need to make any at all, but either way it may be a good idea to start reading up on legends for inspiration. Books like the biography of Steve Jobs by Walter Isaacson (Isaacson's biography on Benjamin Franklin, DaVinci and Elon Musk are great as well). Benjamin Franklin's autobiography is one of my favorites. *Total*

Recall by Arnold Schwarzenegger, also *Pour Your Heart Into It* by Howard Schultz. You have a wealth of knowledge and experience from the most successful people on earth right at your fingertips. Never before in the history of man has there been so much knowledge accessible to anyone, anywhere, anytime. You don't have to go on a journey to the Alexandria library or consult any oracles, you have the internet.

    Jim Rohn said "Show me your five friends and I'll show you your future." I disagree. All my friends at the time were either criminals, broke or had a life I didn't want. I drew all my influence from the people I read about. David Goggins, Grant Cardone, Napoleon Hill, Robert Greene and Richard Branson were my imaginary friends. I planted their voices in my head. I'd picture David Goggins shouting at me when I wanted to quit or Grant Cordon telling me: don't make 10 calls today make 100 calls! Most of my friends were only concerned about going clubbing every weekend and spending their entire check on bottle service. The ones with families were buying fancy cars, ATV's and boats for the river. Meanwhile I was saving up for real estate, maxing out credit cards and taking personal loans out for my businesses. If you're not a book person don't be discouraged neither was I. Remember I hadn't read a real book till I was in my early 30's. A lot of the books I mention I listened to on *Audible,* then if I liked it I would read the actual book as well. I found it easier that way as a beginner. Books like *Sapiens* by Yuval Noah Harari I listened to then read, then listened to, I've probably been through that book six times at least. Another option you can try is what I used to do with bigger books like the biography of Steve Jobs and *Tools For Titans* by Tim Ferris, I would just read either 10 pages or 10 minutes in the morning and again at night if I could till I finished. The more you read the faster and better you get at it. Wake up, study your goals, then read for 10 minutes. I found this method also helps you to start and end your day in the proper mindset.

YOU ARE WHAT YOU THINK

You are the sum of all your experiences and all that has been collected in your mind. "Man's mind may be likened to a garden, which may be intelligently cultivated or allowed to run wild; but whether cultivated or neglected, it must, and will, bring forth" one of my favorite quotes from one of my favorite books *As a Man Thinketh* by William James. Your thoughts are the seeds of your actions. Your actions plant the seeds of your life. Productive actions bring forth fruits, destructive actions bring forth poisonous berries. Lack of any action results in a garden full of weeds. No matter what you do, or don't do, you will get a result, so might as well be proactive on the front end.

Remember our little saying: the lazy man works twice as hard. Therefore the best place we can start to clean up our lives is with cleaning up our minds. I share with you this not as a person who always has a clean house, but as a person whose house needs constant cleaning. Like commercial grade cleaning. The process in this book will help you I promise. Don't worry, doesn't have to be Sunday church mind. We mainly want to deal with getting rid of resentments and self-defeating thoughts. That alone will greatly improve your chances of staying sober, and make life so much easier. That's my only concern. Keep watching listening to death metal and watching porn for all I care, there are plenty of other people to turn you into Mr. Rogers (if that's what you want). I just want to keep you sober so you can make your own choices. Even once you are free of resentments, anger and guilt, you will still need to stay on top of trespassing thoughts. They're always trying to jump the fence and sneak in your head. We want to try and destroy self-defeating thoughts right away, replacing them with self-motivating thoughts. For me these don't really come naturally, I have to juice myself up sometimes. That can come in the form of: "Richard you're a fucking CHAMP (*Rocky* theme song in the background) you got this, you can do anything!" or it can look like this: "Richard you're a bitch if you don't do this! Just get off your ass and do it!" You can't think your way out of a crummy mindset, you're going to have to get up and act your way out. A triple shot espresso, little self-pep talk, and a quick gym session usually clears my head. Then I'm ready to tackle the world. Say or do whatever you have to as long as it gets the job done. Kill any loser thoughts immediately. I know it feels good to bathe in the mud of pity but the mud turns to concrete if you don't get out fast. If you find yourself wandering down a bad street in your mind, get out of there quick, stay where the grass is green. Whenever I'm stuck in the ghetto of my mind (outside gym hours) I grab my *As a Man Thinketh* book, and start reading, even if it's just a few pages. I have three copies floating around the house. Or I go on a walk and listen to a book or music. Cook, shave, ask someone about THEIR problems, whatever it is that clears your head, do it. Make a list of the things that get you out of a funk so you can refer to it when needed.

The mind works in the same way the body does, you are what you think, just as, you are what you eat. If you were to sit around and eat nothing but chips, candy and soda for a year, what do you think would happen to your body? Definitely wouldn't improve right? In fact you would probably look and feel like crap. When you look shitty, you feel shitty, can we all agree on that? The decline of our physical vessel, its appearance, and lack of physical energy will spill over into our psyche. Our mental energy then barrels downhill along with our confidence. OK, so we know that putting junk in our body will not only deteriorate us physically, but also mentally and emotionally as well. Great, now we are sad and feel like the biggest losers on earth, what do we do next? *Hi Chuey, it's Richard. Can I get an 8-Ball?* (Fast forward 2 weeks later) "Hi everyone my name is Richard I'm an alcoholic, I have 1 day sober." WELCOME RICHARD!!! Do you see the natural regression that takes place? This is why the physical matters also. Now let's do another hypothetical experiment, this time for the mind. What would happen if for one year all your mind consumed was 'reality shows' of people wealthier than you, social media, cat and prank videos, topped off with a daily affirmation of – *I am an ugly loser that nobody likes and I fail at everything*. Picture doing that for a year. How would you feel? What would your physical energy be like? Would it be easy to be productive? Would your mental or physical health improve? I doubt we would have to think too hard to come up with the answer. Our minds and our bodies are deeply intertwined, you can't just work on one, ignore the other, and expect to flourish.

When our mind clocks-out, so does our body. It becomes effortless to sit on the couch for hours at a time. We check our social media "real quick" and next thing you know we've been stuck sitting there for an hour. That's an hour of inactivity. Your body was also in a stasis of sorts. Now put both lifestyle experiments together, one year of nothing but junk food along with nothing but reality shows and social media focused on other people's lives, and clickbait. What do you get?

What would happen if this experiment occurred on a larger scale to include your family and friends? Imagine if it happened to an entire country?

ON THE BODY

"The groundwork for all happiness is health."- Leigh Hunt

As we've just touched on, mental and physical health go hand in hand, so let's talk about the little mechanism that is left out of 12-step programs: the body. Leaving physical health out of a personal recovery program is like teaching your kid to surf without teaching them to swim first. We live in our bodies and need them to perform all of our daily functions, if our bodies are screwed, we're screwed. Basic health may seem so basic to some. Yet you would be surprised how many addicts I have worked with that had absolutely no concept of upkeep on their body. I once worked with a dude that didn't drink water. Yeah, no water. He only drank apple juices (he thought was healthy), sodas and milk. Imagine sponsoring someone and taking them through the 12-steps with the goal of staying sober and some sort of spiritual progress. But then not addressing the elephant in the room that they were morbidly obese and had the most ridiculous diet you've ever heard of. I met with "no water" guy Sundays before the royal palms meeting for about 3 weeks. He was just there for the courts and wasn't really looking to change. He ended up getting kicked out on a relapse. I never mentioned anything about his health because it wasn't something I had been taught to do as a sponsor, but I knew this guy had no chance without getting his health in order as well. Afterwards I knew that not addressing his health was a mistake. If I really wanted to help people stay sober with a good quality of life, there were going to be times I needed to give people hard truths. I had to help the entire person. Taking someone through the steps a la carte was not always the most effective way to do things. So many men and women are out there relapsing from depression and don't know why. They end up turning to some form of street or prescription drug to feel better. They usually do this as a first move without even giving the mind and body a chance to catch up. The body needs time to recalibrate after using drugs for so long (took me almost a year) this can often feel like depression. During this period, you also need to give your body the proper nutrients and exercise to recover optimally. Quite a few people I came across claiming depression I would've bet that they were just unhealthy and malnourished. If they addressed their health, they probably would've felt significantly better, maybe even had a fighting chance at staying sober. Obviously, there are some with disorders that may need a medication to stabilize, though it is my opinion that these are far more infrequent than we are led to believe. Do not take this as medical advice, I'm not here to be your doctor, nutritionist or a personal trainer. This is aimed at the generally capable human without any major mental or physical disorders. There are no diet plans or workout routines in this book. You do not need to be a vegan, carnivore, cross fitter or intermediate faster but we will, and must, acknowledge our general health. Without it we have nothing.

-I'll have a free-range celery grasswich and some carrot fries. Oh and a diet water, thanks!-

In 2017 I spent a month in what would become one of my favorite countries to visit, India. Upon arriving there I quickly realized that there weren't really any meat options, everything was vegetarian. You had to search for a "Non-Veg" restaurant, this meant a gnarly rickshaw trip across town. At this time in life I was pretty much on a meat and potatoes diet. I didn't really eat that bad, but not that good either. My main concern was protein. Since I was a kid, I've always been into bodybuilding and weightlifting. Gym time was and still is priority number one in my day, so obviously protein was a big factor as well. *I'm gonna shrink!* was my first thought when I realized I was about to be forced into vegetarianism while in India. I wanted to keep an open mind, so I figured, hey, when in Rome... Let's eat some good Indian food then! Not only did I eat some good food, but it was some of the best food I have ever eaten in my life. The street food was so good I didn't even miss meat. I also experienced an unexpected side effect; I felt absolutely amazing after a week or so. My energy levels shot through the roof and surprisingly, so did my overall happiness. I felt really fucking good, inside and out. I didn't know if it was from eating so many vegetables, no meat, or the quality of the fresh produce. Who knows, but it definitely made a big difference. Back home I was eating about 220 grams protein a day and drinking half a dozen cups of coffee. I felt decent but always kind of bogged down. In India I was eating vegetarian and drinking a few small cups of chai, yet had more energy than ever. Plus my mood just felt sunnier. The better mood part really surprised me. Having more energy from seemingly eating lighter and all the veggies made sense, but the elevated spirit part is what impressed me most.

Back in the States, I immediately defaulted back to my burrito-centric diet, but now had a new appreciation for vegetarians and their food. Thanks India! That was a cool experience, but I'll take five carne asada tacos and a chicken quesadilla now please. I loved my meat. I thought vegetarians and vegans were frail hippie girly-man types. I wasn't interested. Nevertheless, within a day my energy level took a nose dive again along with my mood. Actually, right after my first meal back my stomach was messed up. Even when I tried to compromise and eat "clean" meal preps (chicken, broccoli and rice) I still couldn't get back to that high I had when I was eating Veg. The difference was like night and day. I couldn't deny or ignore it, I knew (my body) responded better with a plant-based diet.

Now I'm not here to convince you to become vegetarian or vegan. I'm only using this as an example of how what you eat directly affects your energy level. Which affects your mood, which will affect your relationships and productivity. Which can affect your job, and all of this affects your demeanour and how you look to the world and yourself. All of these things play a major role in whether you are going to be prone to depression and sickness or be happy and healthy. You don't have to look like Brad Pitt in fight club, but the healthier you are and better shape you're in, the better you will feel. The better you feel, the more confident you are. Confidence attracts (the right kind of people) which leads to better relationships. The better your relationships, the better your life in general. When you like your life, it's not hard to face it sober. Being in good shape says a lot about you, so does being in bad shape. See what I'm getting at? It's a compounding effect. Remember everything matters and sends ripples down the line. Good or bad. Let's face it, low confidence attracts lower people. It signals that you are afraid and are prey. Which leads to toxic relationships, crappier job positions, lower income, greater depression and back to the bottle. When your boss is considering the next person to promote and it's between the sloppy low energy unhealthy person or the high-energy positive confident one, who is he going to pick? Yes, you can still be a bigger person and have confidence and good general health, but you get my point. Forget about financial crap, it's just so much easier to stay sober when you feel good. It's not all about looks or size either. It's about getting the most out of your physical vessel and not letting it bring you down. There are people walking around in a delusion that they "love their life," but if they constantly have to be intoxicated to feel good and enjoy themselves, it's not their life they "love," but their life through the blurred lens of a substance.

-I'll have a double bacon chili cheeseburger, chili cheese fries, a large chocolate shake and a DIET coke please-

What is the optimal diet for you? Again, I'm not a nutritionist, and I'd be lying if I said I knew what exactly *You* should be eating. Everyone is different and even experts can't agree on what the hell everyone should or shouldn't be eating. Go on social media and start looking into any style diet and you'll be immersed into an echo chamber of posts related to and backing that particular diet. You'll have one doctor saying humans were meant to be carnivores, another saying we were meant to eat a plant-based diet. The truth is different people respond to different diets and everyone thinks theirs is the best. Personally, I don't like eating dead animals anymore because it aligns with my views and my body responds great to it.

People ask: What if you were on a desert island? If I was on a desert island, I'd first eat the coconuts and bananas. When that runs out then I'll eat the fish and animals and when that runs out then I'm eating YOU! If your grandma offers me a piece of cake that was made with eggs and milk, I'll eat it. There's no need for fanaticism. Simple as that. You don't have to be vegan to live a healthy happy life, of course, but I think in general, we can all agree that including plenty of fruits and vegetables in your diet is probably a safe bet. I won't get into what the perfect diet is because everyone is different, and I think your genes play a part as well. There are tests you can do to help find out your optimal diet, google "Dietary DNA test" and find a service near you, if you want. For now, what I will suggest is ditching sodas, sugary drinks and fast food completely. Drastically minimizing processed, instant, or "microwave dinners," sweets, and fried food. Maybe even learn to cook, using fresh ingredients and whole foods. If cooking isn't an option, pay the extra for quality food. Not bougie expensive food, quality food. Organic, free range, plant based, whatever it is that you're going to put in your body make sure it's quality. Even if you're fortunate enough to have a private chef, take the time to cook a meal with family and friends every once in a while. It does something good for the soul.

Here's another healthy bit that is good for the soul: Walking. Yep, good a good old-fashioned stroll. Since the beginning of man our primary source of activity and transportation has been walking. We were designed to walk not sit on our ass all day. Humans not walking is like a bird not flying or fish not swimming. Could you imagine? Picture a bird rolling out of its little nest and getting into a tiny plane to go get some worms. Then flying its little plane back to the tree, plopping back into her cozy nest to lay there and watch Nest Renovations on Bird TV while munching on processed worms. Ridiculous right? But isn't that similar to what a lot of us do with our cars? Currently I live in Barcelona, Spain. I left my cars back in LA. I walk and train everywhere, as most people do here. I love it, it makes me feel great. I average about 10-15K steps a day. I see old folks out for a stroll at 10 PM as well as kids. What I don't see much is obese people, at least nothing like in the US. I believe not having to walk any more has a big part to play in the decline of American health. As well as diet, and the healthcare system. Back in the United States walking is seen as a poor people thing, unless you're a teen or live in NYC. In cities like Los Angeles, if you tell people you don't have a car, and you walk everywhere, it's basically like telling them you're broke or crazy. I know plenty of people back home in the states that won't even walk a block, let alone a mile. They would rather drive around for 20 minutes to find a closer parking spot than to have to walk for 5 minutes.

COME FOR REHABILITATION LEAVE ON MEDICATION

The last subject I'd like to cautiously approach on just a tad is: Medication's. Especially regarding drug treatment. I won't go too deep on the topic, I am not a medical doctor. This is not medical advice. However, I was once on an insane number of medications prior to getting sober so I know the drill. I also was the owner of a drug treatment facility employing doctors prescribing meds to our clients. I was aware of every single client and their medications from start to finish. I saw some clients come in with no meds and leave on many. Others come in heavily prescribed and leave on none. I have also witnessed prescriptions being pelted out based off of 60 second zoom calls with clients that know the buzz terms to use for the meds they desire. I've seen countless addicts abuse the system and their meds. Treatment centers are also inclined to prefer meds as a means more for insurance authorization purposes, rather than an actual necessity of recovery in that human being. Try getting into, and through, a private-insurance-based drug treatment facility with no prescriptions. You'd have better luck pissing through a cheerio. It was common to see a client go into treatment with no medications and leave with a large ziplock bag full of prescription bottles. That is not an exaggeration. Disputes about client medications was a constant battle and one of the reasons I got out of the treatment industry. I was trying to get people sober, and it seemed like the drug treatment industry was just trying to get people medicated. Clinical departments are more worried about liability, insurance authorization and pacifying clients than people actually staying sober. After all, it is a business and they are employed to keep compliance and make the company money. Addicts are sold the illusion that taking these meds will pay their debt to the piper for the drugs they've been abusing for so long. Then everyone wonders why treatment is a revolving door. Why do people keep relapsing and going back? Partly because the addict is being robbed of the pain he needs to feel. The pain of withdrawal will instil the fear in his psyche that will keep him from ever wanting to do drugs again. We take the fear of fire away from an addict, then wonder why they walk straight back into the flames. I'll never ever forget the weeks of pain and sleepless nights during my withdrawal. I never ever want to go through that again. That fear overrides the good and helped keep me away. The treatment centers today: *Here's some Suboxone, Seroquel, Gabapentin and trazodone so you should sleep well and feel pretty good during your stay. Oh yeah, make sure to taper off once you leave.* What usually happens at the tail end of the taper? The withdrawals start coming and the addict relapses. Now he's trying to hide it for as long as he can till he gets fully strung out again, then it's back to the treatment center. I've been there, done that, too many times.

After numerous methadone detoxes, maintenances, and benzodiazepine prescriptions; I once asked my clinic doctor: "Doctor why can't I stay sober? What should I do? What are my options?" I'll never forget his stone-faced, ice-cold response: "You probably won't get sober. Your best option is to get on a (methadone) maintenance program." For the rest of my life? I exclaimed. "Yes" he casually said. "You don't think I can get sober another way?" I asked shocked and desperate for a more hopeful response. He answered me with a bone chilling "NO."

His demeanour reminded me of Agent Smith in *The Matrix* (hopefully he doesn't jump through this computer right now and grab me by the throat). I felt as if a judge had just handed me down a life sentence. A doctor pretty much just told me I was fucked. I didn't want to end up like all the old sickly methadone maintenance people showing up to the clinic looking like the walking dead. It hit me hard like a kick to the chest. I didn't want to live out the rest of my days addicted to a substance. But what could I do, he was a doctor right? Doctors can't be wrong, can they? I was taught growing up that you're supposed to listen to doctors "they know best." My parents thought doctors, police, and teachers were incapable of mistakes or lies. Lo and behold! The doctor was dead wrong. Not only did I get sober a few years after that pessimistic asshole's lame suggestion, but I would also do it without taking another psych med, benzo, opiate, or painkiller stronger than Advil ever again (knock on wood).

Was this doctor evil? No, he's just a human that makes mistakes and bad calls at work like we all do. Doctors aren't immune to having bad days either. Fatigue, frustration, and the blues affect them as well. They too have stress at home, or may find themselves not liking someone for whatever reason. Sometimes just like us they want to hurry up and go eat lunch too. We're all human, the only difference is that society has been conditioned to take a doctor's word as gospel. Unlike the mistakes of a barista, making your coffee hot instead of iced; the mistakes of a physician can alter the course of one's life.

Thankfully, in the case of my reptilian methadone clinic doctor, I don't obey very well and don't like others making decisions about my life. I don't just blindly believe anyone, let alone doctors, politicians, religious leaders, or teachers. Neither should you. Of course, if you get a tooth infection, take the antibiotics. I take the Ibuprofen over the Vicodin every time though. Try to avoid opiate medications at all cost. Even if you don't have any drug problems, that can easily change starting with just one opiate prescription. Use common sense though, obviously if you have a major back surgery, you may not be able to avoid it. Please use extreme caution. I have nothing against doctors or modern medicine. If you break your arm, go to the hospital. I'm mainly saying, before you take an anti-depressant ask yourself these questions; Could I be malnourished? Have I been sober long enough for my mind and body to recalibrate? Have I been exercising regularly? Have I been making the effort to spend time with family and friends? Have I been getting enough sleep? Have I been eating healthy, or has it been fast food daily? Have I been getting lots of fresh air and sunlight or am I cooped up in the house with blinds shut watching Netflix and scrolling social media all day? Have I done any type of service lately? Am I taking care of my hygiene or am I in dirty sweatpants and a stained shirt? Have I hit the barbershop or salon lately? When was the last time I had my teeth cleaned? Are my goals aimed at something truly fulfilling to me or are they all money-centered and materialistic? Did I just go through a major change in my life (divorce, job loss, death of a loved one) when it's natural to get a wave of depression? If you answered any of these in the negative sense, I would start running through the list and fixing those situations before I slapped on pharmaceutical handcuffs. Be honest, are taking pills in your case just the easier thing to do rather than putting forth the proper effort into solving the actual problem? Like the person that takes diet pills to lose weight before actually trying to exercise and lay off on the donuts.

Is it possible the depression you are in may just be your body's way of signalling you that something needs to be remedied? Like when you are tired and yawning, your body is telling you it needs to sleep. It's not telling you to take an Adderal. If your baby is crying in the other room, you don't turn up the volume on the TV; you go tend to the baby. If you are depressed it's doubtful that your body is telling you it needs a pill. What did everyone do before anti-depressants? Was everyone walking around depressed and suicidal 200 years ago? No. They had shit to do, they were active on their mission and purpose, that was the original anti-depressant. They weren't moping around the house all day by themselves napping, raiding the fridge and watching TV. This is the first time in history humans could behave that way. If you were unproductive and isolated, you were most likely going to die unless you were some type of royalty. People tended to be a part of the community and worked together with family and friends. They worked their trades to live and survive, not to make money for materialistic crap to impress people they'll never meet. There's a difference. Depression and anxiety have been on the upward trend in the United States recently. What do you think are some of the causes? Is it a culture of celebrity and consumerism? Could it be lack of productivity and the feeling of uselessness? Not having to work hard towards anything and easy access to everything? Lack of exercise and poor health? No sense of community or belonging? Materialism? Are we coddling our youth? Protecting them from getting their feelings hurt so much so that they have no resilience to adversity?

Take away: The quality of your diet, exercise and sleep can make or break you.

ON THE SPIRIT

-The Lion, the Snitch and the Wardrobe

The last couple of weeks I spent in the LA county jail crammed in a six-man cell that seemed to be meant for only four. I seemed to have landed in another housing unit that had its privileges taken away. You got one toilet paper roll a week, the paper was so thin it dissolved on contact with any moisture. It was gone by the third day, after that we used newspaper cut into little rectangular strips. We never left the cell at all, aside from the once-a-week shower which felt spectacular. All the other days we just took bird baths in the toilet. Most of the conversations I remember were while one of us was sitting on a toilet lathering up covered in suds. You had to bathe and wash frequently because deodorant wasn't a luxury we had in our cell. The feeling of clean fresh body after a workout was our only high. Working out and cleaning were also the only actions that gave you a little esteem. Normally you are supposed to be let out for yard once a day, but this particular module at this particular time didn't get that luxury either. I never saw the sun or sky once during that period. You don't realize how much little creature comforts mean to you till they're gone. But, aside from feeling like the Count of Monte Cristo locked away in a dungeon; we had a pretty good time. It was a mixed-race cell but everyone was from my area (the San Fernando Valley). All were waiting to get picked up by the prison bus, all but me. I was waiting for the rehab bus. "GALVAN ROLL IT UP!" *Finally! Give me a call when you get out!* I'll never forget the excitement of when the Royal Palms came and got me. I was so jazzed to get out, and sober at that. New beginnings were on the horizon. I was on a little high. At least until, on my way out they put me in a room and handed me my property back. I was handed a smelly bag of crumpled up hobo clothes. *Eww, damn...* I guess I had forgotten I was a street junky prior to my booking. I would've rather left in the jail clothes or even naked; how could I put this shit back on? Is this how I would have to show up to my new rehab? In some stinky tattered rags full of holes, they could smell me from a mile away.

You ever go to the beach and leave all your wet clothes in the trunk of your car to ripen with mildew for like a week?

Remember how they smelled? That's the smell I was putting back on. Well, that was the sum of everything I owned on earth. A dingy grey T-shirt that said *SI TV (from that comedy show I did)*, it was full of cigarette holes around the mid-section from when I would nod out with a cigarette in my hand. I kept that shirt and wore it proudly bragging to whoever would listen that I worked at a TV studio once. I thought about tossing it out and just wearing the wife beater I had on under. Unfortunately for some bizarre reason, it happened to be the undershirt I was stabbed in. It had two little slits covered in dry blood stains around the rib area. Why the hell was I wearing this? Covering my lower half was a baggy pair of jeans with even more cigarette burns. On my feet; a pair of socks and shoes that would make Oscar the grouch puke. The LA county jail leaves a distinctly putrid funk on your clothes, the kind of funk that doesn't wash off. It's like your clothes are haunted by a demon stench they either need to be thrown away or blessed by a priest and set on fire in a shallow grave. Sadly, there was no priest to cast my demon apparel back to the underworld. No change of clothes. No family or friends waiting for me at the gate with hugs and goodies when I got out. What I had was what I got; something that was actually worse than nothing. Humiliation.

    My socks, they were nuclear. Once at the rehab I would hand-wash them every day in the sink. Then hang them to dry overnight and wear them the next day, usually still damp. Even though I'd wring them out the best I could, they never really got a break long enough to dry. They always had a nasty mildewy smell. On a particularly hot day sitting in the royal palms basement where the groups were held, I noticed a foul smell. I heard a comment from another resident near me say something like "Damn! Who stinks?" I leaned forward discretely shook my leg a little bit and took a sniff. It was my smelly ass socks! I had good hygiene sober but I couldn't do anything about my clothes. I started to sweat as the anxiety and fear of embarrassment kicked in. I crept out of the group as if I was headed towards the bathroom. Instead, I ran upstairs to take off my socks and re-wash them along with my feet to try and somehow get through the rest of the day with dignity. Maybe I could go sock-less, or maybe try to steal a pair. While in the bathroom of our six-man room scrubbing and wringing out the socks in the sink, one of my room-mates walked in. He was a large native American guy. He had one of those pony tails with the sides of his head shaved, kind of goofy looking like a Simpsons character. He was known as a loudmouth and a snitch, not particularly liked by the other residents. He told on one of our room-mates for having a cell phone and got him kicked out, so he wasn't my favorite either. Anyways, he sat down on his bed, opened up a drawer and grabbed a gleaming white fresh pair of socks. He said "Hey buddy, do you need a pair of socks?" Then he tossed them at me. The ivory ball of crew socks came arching onto my lap before I could even answer. *Oh shit! Thank you!* I couldn't believe it, this guy just solved all my problems. You would have thought I just received Willy Wonka's golden ticket I was so happy. That made my day, it made my month. He just relieved me of so much anxiety and embarrassment. I was elated and so thankful for that man at that moment. A man I had despised 30 seconds earlier. It may seem like nothing to you, with your life time of having had clean clothes. However to me, at that time, it was like an act of grace. It touched me, almost made me cry. I had always been a dick to this dude and he just did the nicest, most helpful thing anyone had done for me in a long time. I said something like *I don't have any money to give you* or *I'll pay you back,* he just said "Don't trip, I got you." The dude didn't want anything from me, he was just being a nice guy (what a concept). I tried to hide my emotional confusion, but he seemed to understand where I was coming from. The man humbled me right on the spot. He taught me an important lesson.

On the streets and in gang life doing nice things for men you didn't know got you eaten alive. You only did things for other people if you got something in return. This was all new and just my first of many lessons in this new concept of being of service. The second would be about a month later on a night when I was restless and anxious from an overwhelming bout of cravings. I didn't know what I was craving more, the street life or the drugs. What do I do? I'm in the panic zone. I desperately did not want to relapse, but the streets were calling me. Crack and heroin were whispering in my ear "Fuck this lame rehab, let's get out of here. We can go score some rock and find some hood-rats. Let us sleep on the street tonight. It'll be spectacular" Then I remembered my sponsor saying: "When all else fails be of service." OK, but how? I can't get to a meeting. I have nothing to give, no money, no advice. It's not like I can volunteer my time at 10 PM in a rehab. I paced around my room stressed out, fighting the craving and wondering what to do next. Suddenly, the memory of that dude giving me the socks came to mind. At this point, I had hustled up a few outfits from the donation room and other residents. I grabbed a hoodie, some sneakers, maybe even a pair of pants I believe, and went back to that six-man room I used to be in. That's where all the new arrivals are, they probably could use some stuff.

What's up fellas does anyone want these? They don't fit

me anymore. I said, as I stood in the doorway with everyone staring at me.

An old black dude stood up: "Yeah, yeah I'll take em! These are nice!" I stuck around to chat and asked everybody how they ended up at the Royal Palms. I let them know I came in with nothing and straight off the street too, and that they were in a good place. They went on to tell me their stories, then we laughed and shared some street bloopers. I realized these were my people. It ended up being a really cool night. I walked in the room with anxiety and a frightening craving that I could not think my way out of. I had to act. I walked out on a pink cloud, grateful from head to toe. No more cravings, no more anxiety. There really was something to this concept of service helping you stay sober. You've got to give it away to keep it I guess. Later on that week, on my sponsor's suggestion, I took a service commitment at the Sunday night Royal palms AA meeting. It was something I really didn't want to do and couldn't see how making some coffee and announcements at a meeting could have anything to do with keeping a needle out of my arm. Little did I know what an impact it would make not only on my sobriety but my entire life. It actually ended up being kind of like my anchor to service and recovery. I kept that Sunday night commitment at the Royal Palms for over 18 years. Sponsoring people, bringing in speakers and getting to know all the people passing through that meeting has been one of the true joys of my life.

I was sad to give it up when I moved to Spain. That commitment is one of the only things I miss about LA (aside from the pacific and good Mexican food). That commitment also helped me implement a rule I had for myself I started that night with those guys in the 6-man room. Whenever I bought new clothes or shoes I would donate some old ones to the rehab. If I bought a new pair of shoes, I donated my least worn. If I bought two new shirts I donated two old ones. I tried to give as much as possible and hook people up the way I was hooked up when I got there. I could never repay Alcoholics Anonymous and the Royal palms for the gifts I received while there. The most important of those gifts being: the spirit of Gratitude. I believe it is the main ingredient in the recipe for a happy soul. How do we keep it? We stay in service.

I don't know what it is, but once you have recovered from addiction there is something fantastic that happens to your soul when you help another into recovery. It's like some sort of deep camaraderie that can turn two strangers into brothers after one conversation. My cousin Elvis who was deployed in Iraq says a similar thing occurs amongst war veterans. Maybe the act of service to another addict feels so good because it was what we were missing all along. Connection, community and service.

SERVICE IS FOOD FOR THE SOUL

What can you do in your community to be of service? Here's just a few ideas (for addicts):

- As soon as you finish this process, pass it on to another that may need it. Share your experience and answer any questions. Never be pushy, just be available to help.

-Find a local state-run rehab or shelter and donate some clothes, food or other items they might need.

-Take time to chat and get to know a few of the individuals, maybe even take one under your wing.

-If you're in a 12-step program go to some meetings and find the newcomers. Make them feel welcome and at home.

Give them your number. Offer to help in any way (within reason) i.e. rides to meetings, sponsorship, give em this book, show them how to fill out a resume, how to open a checking account etc. You'd be surprised what basics people don't know when they're fresh off the streets. I needed help with all of these things when I first got sober.

- If you're not a 12-step person maybe just practice being friendly. Smile, say hi to people, complement them, spark up a conversation centered on them. Stop acting scared like people are going to bite you, pretend everyone is an old friend.

- Call friends and ask how *they* are doing, listen to *their* problems, not yours.

- Do something cool for a stranger. When you're in line for coffee or something maybe pay for the guy behind you. Be a cool example of a human, even if just for a moment. Add up enough moments and we just might get there.

- If you're really brave try my favorite: If you see a seemingly mentally stable panhandler outside of a store, buy him a pack of cigarettes and a beer. That's what he really wants. Maybe even throw in a candy bar or some food. If possible, stop and talk to the fellow human (not at them) but like a friend would. About sports or a cool truck in the parking lot, whatever. Making someone who is in a bad spot feel normal for even a brief time goes a long way. Use common sense though.

- Shoot a text to an old friend and tell them how they positively impacted your life. Don't worry we all know how tough you are already... Show people you got a cool side too.

- Do as many kind acts as you can anonymously and without expectations of anything in return.

Even though you are able to work this program without the attendance of 12-step meetings, they are a good a place to find those in need of help. There should be no conflict for anyone to attend "open" meetings and meet people. At least it shouldn't be a problem for anyone whose true aim is only to be of service to the addict or alcoholic still suffering. I am hoping in time we can integrate within a 12-step community or form one of our own across the globe for anyone that needs help available in person, over the phone or on line all hours.

Don't get being of service confused with people pleasing. You aren't expected to be a pushover or "the nice guy" that everyone dumps their garbage on. You are giving out of strength and integrity, not weakness. You pick and choose what calls to you. Even though your action will benefit others, don't be mistaken; this is for you. You are helping yourself, by helping others. You may feel like an imposter at first don't worry that will pass. You will soon find joy in the actions of service, then, you won't be faking it. Finding ways to be of service is absolutely VITAL in one's recovery. It should be vital in the life of every human being. Oh well, we're not here to change the world, just you. But for every person changed the place gets better and better. I cannot stress enough how important the service part of this program is. It is what the firehose is to the fireman. If you leave out the service part of this program or fail to find ways of being of service, your likelihood of succeeding plummets. Even if you do stay sober or kick your vice, you may still find yourself miserable. Service to other humans, especially those you are uniquely suited to help, is our purpose. It's the patty in your burger, the meat in your taco, the main character in your film. Without service the spirit is missing in your life. Helping others is the key to unlock a meaningful existence.

HIGHER POWER

Tolerance and an open mind. Let's see where you're at. We've come a long way since the Spanish Inquisition, but I think we still have a little ways to go. Quite a few people still don't like to think that maybe, just maybe, it's ok for other people to believe in something different than they do. Don't worry I am not here to change your beliefs in a higher power or religion. I only want to encourage the co-mingling and appreciation, of people with different interpretations of the human experience. So before you call the thought police or throw this book across the room at your cat, hear me out.

When it comes to your higher power, this is an entirely personal matter. Whether you believe in a deity or not makes no difference in this work. It's a B.Y.O.B program (Bring Your Own Belief). This is a program of action; do this, and you get that. Simple. It won't meddle with your faith. If anything, it will improve it. The actions in this program could be considered a service to yourself and the greater good of the people around you. What god wouldn't like that? One of the aims of this program is to truly be non-biased and encouraging of other's personal beliefs. Hopefully its participants can follow suit. You don't have to agree with other's beliefs, but we should be able to; agree to disagree and remain cool. Even friends. Think of others like your friends that are fans of a different ball team than yours. *How could you like that team? They suck! Our team is the best! Wait let's grab a hot dog first. Want anything?* Frankly, AA, NA and CA are supposed to be non-biased non-religious programs as well (at least according to their literature). The higher power part of the program is supposed to be subjective. However, its members are the choke point of these principles, and it doesn't always seem to be a program of free belief in many meetings. Religious members can have a way of dominating the culture of a local meeting hall in such a manner that the 12-step group appears to be an arm of the church. Not that there is anything wrong with religion, but because sometimes the feel of a church or religion can repel those that would otherwise want the help. If you walk into a meeting with a bunch of people pushing your religion you'd feel right at home. What if you walk into a meeting with a bunch of people pushing a different religion that you're not comfortable with?

No one wants to be told what to believe. It's our right. There should be a place where everyone can leave their religion and politics at the door and get down to the level of human helping human. While I do understand that the deep nature of addiction, and recovery from it, can be seen as a spiritual dilemma. I also think it can be done in such a fundamental and pragmatic way as not to conflict with anyone's beliefs, or lack of. Just like physical exercise, this program can be done without any friction to faith. It's all action. Imagine going to a local gym to lift weights and being politely obligated to pray with a religion you didn't belong to. Then being chided if you chose not to pray. Would you go back to that gym again?

There are not as many free, non-religious programs to get sober as you would think. Oftentimes going to a 12-step meeting is the default for someone trying to make a change. When that seems like a turn off then it's back to the streets. I was this way. I would wander into a meeting hoping to be struck sober, but would leave after being weirded out by people cornering me trying to hold my hand and pray. *Chill bro give me some space.* The meeting was indistinguishable from a prayer group. I'm not discouraging prayer. I am discouraging pressing adults to do something they didn't go somewhere to do. Sure, you can opt out of prayers in a meeting, I never have, doesn't bother me. But I can see why others would be uncomfortable. I've also seen people opt out and it's definitely awkward. Why put someone in that position? You might be thinking: "Maybe a little prayer or church would do them good." Maybe. Maybe it wouldn't. Let's just help people get sober first then they can decide for themselves. You never know what that person's past might have been like. Maybe they had a horrible experience at a religious school. Some had a holy book forced upon them via a leather belt by a drunk parent. People need to find their own paths. Sometimes it will lead back to their family religion. Others will convert to another faith. Some will be forever atheist. All are ok. Who cares what other adults are doing anyways? Are you going to convert the world? You can't even convince someone your football team is better. Let's focus on the most important person in our life, ourselves. We can't help anyone if we're fucked. The better off we are the more good we can do on earth. Everyone's conception of god likes people doing good. Even those that don't believe in god can still believe in good. Consider this book a vehicle, it will help get you wherever it is you choose to go on your journey.

G.O.D = GET- OUT- DO SOMETHING ABOUT IT

"Insanity: Doing the same thing over and over expecting different result"- Albert Einstein

I've been working a 12-step program for almost 20 years now and a while back I had this notion. That all these different people in the program with various higher powers and different religions seem to all be having, or not having, these "spiritual awakenings" not based on how strong their beliefs were, but based on the actions they took. In other words; people that did the work, got the results. People that did no work and just relied on their beliefs got their crack pipe back. Even atheists with no belief still got the results when they did the work. Those that came in ready to work and had some sort of belief system seem to have the easiest path. Of course, all with a faith will attribute their success and experience to the deity they have in their minds eye. However, I think the actual work *they* did doesn't get enough credit. Maybe god provided the trees, but it was still the man that had to cut the wood and build the house. Regardless of your beliefs, it seems YOU still have to do the work. Many devout are offended at that notion that their belief alone is not enough and effort on their part is required. They also seem to think that their higher power will be offended as well if they believe that they too have a part to play in their own success. I like to think that if there's a god he's probably a little more tolerant and chilled than a teenage ball hog that wants to take all the credit. Truth be told it didn't seem to matter how deeply one believed in their god. How often they went to church or how "holy" they acted. How much religious music they listened to or how much they donated. The fact that they didn't cuss, eat pork or how often they went to meetings didn't matter either. The simple fact is: I've seen them all reunite with the dope man again if they didn't put in the work.

The only thing that seemed to matter in this particular situation (of staying sober or not), was whether or not they did the step work whole-heartedly. People definitely get sober outside of 12-step programs, I'm sure of that. However, I'm not too familiar with those situations. I'm just reporting what I've seen in my experience. Non-believers don't seem to have much problem doing the work once they get past the religious undertones. It's the believers that have a hard time accepting they have to do some work. As if god is supposed to just take care of it if they pray and believe hard enough. I've witnessed people follow this belief to their own death. That's why this issue is such a hot topic in my mind, people die over this stuff. They usually feel like they already have a strong enough connection with their higher power simply based on faith. Even when I point out that it must not be sufficient enough since they were just drinking themselves into oblivion and snorting meth a few days prior. They stonewall me and repeat the same cycles of relapse over and over. Most chronic relapsers are that way due to a fixed state of mind. The fixation is usually an interpretation of their faith; as if to try something different would be the equivalent of a betrayal to their god. They had their beliefs prior to attempting to get sober, but still couldn't stay clean and had no real notable progress to be able to rationalize their "God's in the driver seat" way of going about life. Some "normal" people can live like that. Their lives just naturally line up in a harmonious fashion. Not the addict. As much as he would love to be in this category, it doesn't seem to ever play out very well. The addict gets his county check or beats a court case and claims

"Divine intervention!" "God is on my side!" Then goes on a bender with his money and freedom only to lose it all once again. If God was in the driver's seat, they definitely choose the wrong times to take back the wheel.

    Their problem was not an insufficient belief in God. It was their lack of belief in themselves. They too wield power; to either fix or destroy their own life. In 12-step programs they preach "Powerlessness" not realizing some are going to take that all too literally. Yes, in our active addiction we are powerless. Sober, we are still powerless over the effects drugs and alcohol have on us once we ingest them. However, when we remain separated from drugs long enough we regain our power of action and decision. As a result, we also get the consequences that tag along. Out of the thousands of people I've personally worked with, and the even larger number I've been acquainted with; the only ones that actually stayed sober (with a quality of life) were the ones that did the 12-step work thoroughly. Whether they believed in a higher power or not. The ones that had strong beliefs but did no work still got loaded every time, it was as plain as day. Are the 12-steps magical? No, it's just a process that when done thoroughly can relieve a spiritual malady. The process in this book contains the same recipe for relief, without as many barriers. Can this relief be achieved without this book or a 12-step program? Sure, although I wouldn't even know where to tell someone to start. I have never seen a real hardcore drug addict get, and stay, sober any other way. Doesn't mean it hasn't happened, I don't know everyone on earth. I've had friends that did lots of drugs and crime but stopped via church, birth of a child, falling in love, etc. But they were a slightly different breed. I don't think they had ever stepped into the depths of true hardcore addiction. The *Real ones* are a different story. We require a psychological exorcism of sorts to get our demons out. This process is like an exorcism for the *Real addict*. It works so well when it's done whole heartedly, there's really no reason to reinvent the wheel.

Do you have an inner voice that guides you? How many are there? There's usually the one telling us to wake up in the morning; then the other voice is telling us "Just 5 more minutes sleep." Wait, would that make us the third party listening to the other two? Then there's our body who is kind of like a silent partner but can override decisions we want to make. We seem to get tired, sick, hungry, achy or injured at all the wrong times. Thoughts, feelings, voices, oh so many choices. Is one voice ever always wrong and the other always right? Not usually. So how do we know which one to listen to at any particular time? Can one be good and one bad? Can one voice get stronger and the other weaker? If it could get weaker could you kill it? "If it bleeds we can kill it!" Points if you know what movie that's from. That's not all. Every once in a while, there's another messenger that comes out and gives us a clear strong direction. It could be with deep emotion, stillness or involuntarily. This voice or feeling doesn't seem to be coming from the usual suspects. Some associate this player in our internal cast of characters with their gut instinct, or the deity of their faith. Some will even say it comes in the voice of a dead loved one. Personally I just refer to it as my instinct. Pretty generic I know. I don't mean the type of "instinct" as in to procreate, or care for your child. I'm talking about that gut instinct from the 4th dimension; your *spidey sense* if you will. This seems to be the most reliable and the one I always try to listen to. Though sometimes it doesn't tell me anything, more like; it takes over. This phenomenon has saved me from potential death, great injury and heavy prison time. I do believe this instinct can grow stronger, but I don't think it can be called upon at will. Could this "instinct" be a transmission from God? A message from the ether? Some of the core writings in this book were scribbled in frenzies of instinctual non-thought. In case you haven't noticed; I'm not a writer. I'm just relaying the message. Half of the work has been separating the wheat from the chaff and filling in the blanks. I can tell you without a doubt what is definitely not the word of God. The crap that comes from my mind. The mind should never be confused with "the instinct." The mind will tell you all kinds of weird stuff and get you in a wreck. My mind is telling me right now: *Why are you writing this? No one is going to read it.* Yesterday it was telling me: *this is the best book ever!* How can you tell what was written by my mind and what by the "instinct"? If it sounds dumb, that was probably me.

What does this have to do with a higher power? I don't know, I guess that's up to you. I'm not here to debate whether God talks to you or not. How would I know? Regardless of what I think, makes no difference. Makes no difference what anyone thinks, because we all agree on one thing: We need to overcome our addiction. That's the main goal. After that we can all branch out any which way. What I am trying to drive home is; WE make all the little choices that make up our life. WE are responsible for our lives here on earth. At the very least, our responses to our current situation. If you're fat, no amount of praying is going to get you in shape. No amount of money is going to get you fit. God can't do push-ups for you. God's also not going to smack a churro out of your mouth either. YOU need to build the discipline and do the necessary work required to change your life. As an adult your life is in your hands. If you need a job, you can sit at home and pray all day and night; maybe even sacrifice a goat, you still won't find a job (unless you sell the goat meat). Only by networking, job searching and putting forth the effort will you find work. The same goes with getting sober or rid of whatever vice you have. Action, action and more action will always be the precursor to the best results. My favorite time to start acting on something: Now. Then once you get sober or whatever it is; you can show your gratitude to whoever you want. The fact is: Faith, without works is dead. It even says so in the Bible, and book of Alcoholics Anonymous. On the flip side works without faith is not dead. If you make yourself run 2 miles, do 200 push ups and 200 squats a day every day for a year you will get stronger. Regardless whether you believe you will or not. If you plant some orange seeds then do all the necessary work you will get an orange tree. It doesn't matter if you pray for mangoes or apples, or even if you believe nothing will grow at all, you will still get oranges.

WHO DO YOU BELIEVE IN?

I'm certain of nothing. I'm not even sure I'm certain of that- Anthony Bourdain

People all over the globe that have a different faith than yours seem to be getting along just fine. Countries like Japan, Netherlands, France, Sweden, Korea and many others that are largely secular aren't burning up into flames and the people seem to be generally happy. While in India, a man overheard me ordering some food from a street vendor and asked: "Are you an American?" I confirmed and we both started chatting. Turns out he worked at a call center for a major bank in the states and dealt mostly with Americans so he spoke good English. He invited me and my family to have dinner at his house with his family, I'm not one for turning down dinners so we went. It was a great night, we ate and talked for hours. We must've touched on every topic under the hot Indian sun. One topic that came up was religions. I was shocked when he didn't know who the hell Jesus was. I mean he kind of seemed to recognize the name but definitely wasn't familiar. It was like asking my kids if they knew who Marlon Brando was. They seemed to have heard the name, maybe, but still give you a blank stare. I hadn't travelled much yet and still had that naïve belief that the things I learned in the USA everyone else on Earth must be familiar with as well. This guy didn't have any more details about Jesus than I had about Ganesh. But wait! This guy and his family were great people, and seemed to be genuinely happy and contented, without Jesus. Hmmm... does that mean he's going to Hell? Of course not. I'm just giving you an example of how small my world and perspective was at one point. Still is. The more I learn the less I seem to know. I'll probably read this in a few years and think: *What an idiot!* At least that's the goal, keep learning. I strive to learn more every day, even if it shatters an old lifelong belief or misconception. I love to be proven wrong! I'm lying. But I do feel growth and progress when I can disregard wrong information for the truth. It burns going down but feels good after.

A few years back at my Sunday night Royal Palms meeting, a man went up to the podium and started preaching as if he was in church. He was trying to do a full-blown sermon. Keep in mind that this was a newcomer meeting. The guy preaching wasn't a preacher, and probably had only been sober a week or two. Yet he thought he had all the answers (no, the man wasn't me). He was going on and on about how the book of Alcoholics Anonymous was based on the Bible and how everyone needed to just go straight to the Bible instead. The Royal Palms has hundreds if not thousands going through that meeting every year, so you get all types. I'm used to it so I let the guy say his piece but after going over his share time by almost five minutes I had to stop him. I was the secretary of the meeting (for those unfamiliar it's basically service position where you organize and facilitate the meeting) so it was my responsibility to politely shut down people rambling on, so other people can get a chance to share. Another responsibility of anyone facilitating an AA meeting is to make sure the integrity of the traditions and ethics are upheld. While people are free to practice any religion they choose AA does not want anyone pushing their religion on the group. As you know by now that's not something I'm in favor of. Individuals' beliefs are an entirely private matter. Forgive me if I seem to be singling out Jesus, I mean no harm or insult. I think we could all benefit from some of his teachings. Especially his followers. It's just so happens Christianity is the major religion in the area I grew up, so it's obviously the majority reference.

I didn't want to embarrass the guy or cause a scene, so I pulled him to the side after the meeting. In a respectful manner I shared with him that "the god of his understanding" is a personal matter and AA doesn't endorse or promote any religions. I asked if he could dial down the preaching a little and try to keep it as general as possible when speaking at the podium as the format of the meeting suggests. The thing about some meetings is anyone can get up and share. You can have a guy with 2 days sober get up and share something completely false. But other new people in the meeting aren't aware the information is false, or that the guy sharing is newer than they are. Or you can have someone show up at newcomer meeting to give AA a try, then have some dude out of his mind get up to the podium and ramble on forever. It's up to the secretary to gently make sure the blind don't start trying to lead the blind.

The newly sober man grew visibly upset and irate as if I had insulted his mother. In a strong tone and volume he barked "I BELIEVE IN THE LORD AND SAVIOR JESUS CHRIST AND I'M NOT ASHAMED OF THAT" as I started to respond (while making hand gestures to chill and lower his voice) before I could get a sentence out he went on " I DON'T CARE WHO HEARS IT! I'LL LET THE WHOLE WORLD KNOW!" Finally I was able to speak and I tried to explain to him that it was great he found solace in Christianity and Jesus. The meeting is full of Christians. Nevertheless there are Catholics, Muslims, Jews, Atheists, Hindus and the secular as well. AA doesn't want to offend or get involved in those matters. Plus, we don't know what peoples past experience with any particular religion is. We don't want to scare off any newcomers thinking we are a church or religious organization. "Well, that's on them, the book of AA was based on the Bible and Bill W. was a Christian," he fired off.

My reply was that while Bill W. may have been Christian and a white man in the early 1900's America of course the Bible was influential in his life and writings. The Bible itself was influenced by other books, that's not saying much. The authors of the AA book make it absolutely clear that "AA is not allied with any sect, denomination, political organizations or institutions." The book and steps were written to be interchangeable with any higher power. That in itself would be going against the Christian beliefs. It's not a religious book at all. AA goes to great lengths to make sure it's an all-inclusive program. I even pointed to the poster of the 12 traditions on the wall trying to explain why we relied on them to keep the program running without conflict. The man was not hearing me and looked at me as if I was Lucifer himself trying to suppress the name of Jesus. Dr. Bob and Bill Wilson themselves could have risen from the dead and given the explanation and the man would probably just call them demons.

After all, the reason AA and the 12-steps were created was because Bill left the Christian based Oxford group and it's 6-step program because it was too evangelical and religious. As his wife Louis puts it: "They kicked us out for focusing too much on alcoholism and not enough on Christ." Bill knew how off-putting religion could be to some people and wanted to help as many as possible by making AA all inclusive. He used the word "god" in sort of a generic manner along with the term higher power. In the end we had to agree to disagree, as I have had to do with many similar discussions like this one. I've had this same debate many times with my buddies in 12-step meetings over the years. The authors of the AA book tried hard to steer away from conflicting with anyone's conceptions of a higher power. It is the religious members who take it upon themselves to persist on imposing "God" onto others. Bill Wilson was onto something with his original ideas. The book of Alcoholics Anonymous and its spin off 12-step programs have helped millions of people. It's safe to say AA changed the world. But even still, there are plenty of addicts that slip through the cracks. This book hopes to be the net that catches them.

Do you believe in a higher power or higher self? If you believe in a higher power describe your concept in full detail. If you believe in aiming towards a higher version of yourself describe what that self would be like in detail. If neither and you have a different concept describe it. Save these writings.

OVERVIEW
(Resentment, sex, and fear inventories)

If you're serious about changing your life, you'll find a way. If not you'll find an excuse- Jen Sincero

Now comes the "action" we've been talking about all through this book. This next process is the heart of this program, the difference between relapsers and those that stay sober. You've got to the gym, are you going to work out or just watch? Not sure where you stand yet? That's OK, try this, read through it and commit to just doing the first part (The list) if it starts calling you, keep going. Just do the next thing indicated, then the next and so on. When you start it will be interesting and can even be fun, but when you get in deep it will definitely start to drudge up emotions. It will take a toll on you. When it starts stinging you know it's working. Even working on my inventory for sometimes only 10 minutes a day wore me out mentally. I stayed committed to do a little every day and got through it. Next thing I knew,

I had finished this monumental inventory of my life. I felt like I reached the peak of a mountain and had this amazing view of my life. It was one of the most life changing things I've ever done. My actions and behaviors started to make sense now. In the Breakdown of our life, we get a peek at our moving parts, we see the how-and-why things are working the way they are.

My entire life, as far back as I can remember was ran on fear. I didn't realize fear was in the driver seat till I did my inventory. I always knew something was off but couldn't quite put my finger on what it was. In the inventory we get to take a look behind the curtain. Why did I have so much fear? My life wasn't anywhere near as bad as some of my friends. Maybe that's why they were my friends? I don't see my childhood as traumatic at all, yet I can see how it shaped my thinking. Not to speak badly of my mother, but my first memories were of her snorting powder through a rolled-up dollar, her being in major distress, which she would later confirm was someone beating her and getting taken to the hospital. Lots of sex around and in front of me. Someone getting stabbed and bleeding out on our front porch. Me and her coming home to our apartment robbed and ransacked by her ex-boyfriend and my dad spending the night to protect us. There are some others, but these are the earliest and sufficient enough to get my point across. Now these aren't things I saw or see as traumatic, nor as bad parenting from my mother. In fact, those early childhood years in which these memories occurred were the only years I was actually close with my mom. That was like our era. I can't ever be mad at those early days, she had me as a teen and was doing what she could. Even though there are no hard feelings, these memories still played a part in my make up. They instilled a fear in me. Not against anyone in particular, just like a heightened general fear of people. As if my little fear gauge was turned up a few notches higher than the average kid. Even a few years later when my mother married my stepfather and settled into a more stable life, I was still way out of whack. There was no turning it off. I was either severely shy or hyper as hell and wouldn't listen to anyone. I didn't fit into normal life. Not fitting in caused me to build up resentments towards my peers, parents and life itself. I hated life and the fact I was even born. It wasn't until that first drink of alcohol that the fear and stress seemed to melt away. I could finally breathe.

Whenever white coats, pant suits, girls, or curious cats asked me about traumas in my life, I never really saw myself as having any. The things that stuck out as traumatizing to me, were actually harms I had inflicted on others. People these days seem to throw everything in the category of trauma. I once had a woman trying to check into one of my sober livings with Xanax and other prohibited meds. She said these meds were needed because she had severe anxiety from trauma. When the house manager and I asked what the trauma was, she said it was from being born via caesarean section. Listen, I'm not here to judge, but if the most traumatic thing to happen in your life was your birth... and you need to be on high powered meds because of it; I can't help you. But, I do recognize now that certain incidents and the accumulation of others have helped assemble the roster of fears in me. As well as strengths, behaviors, habits and dislikes. For instance, the countless fights, broken noses, teeth, concussions, stabbings shootings and other mayhem, has left a bad taste in my mouth for "going out." In fact, it's safe to say I hate going to bars and clubs. I used to force myself to go out on the weekends just so I could be "a part of."things. After a while though I gave into my homebody tendencies and started to embrace it. This habit of staying in during the nights helped me propel my life forward as an adult when all my other peers partied away their 20's and early 30's. I saved money, stayed healthier, kept out of trouble, and was able to focus on building up my life. Some will see certain characteristics as defects, others will see them as strengths. The important thing is you need to see what it is you're working with.

Once you do this Overview inventory process, it's like you dump out the box of puzzle pieces of your life and starting fitting them together. Once you are done you can see the whole picture and identify the problems. Then you can actually make sense of things and start the healing process. Otherwise, you are just taking shots in the dark at generic issues hoping to fix your problems. The issues may be more complicated and way deeper. The world has enough people walking around dysfunctional and fucked up with absolutely no idea why. It seems like people know they have some issues to deal with and just hire a therapist as if that's the cure-all. "Now I just pay my money and show up once a week to my appointment and life will be great!" I don't want to downplay therapy, it can be a helpful tool in our box as well. But ask yourself: would my therapist take me on and meet with me for free till we got to the bottom of things? Probably not, right? That's because he/she is not as invested in your well-being as you are (or at least should be). Care paid by the hour only goes so far. An hour. Sometimes we have to take responsibility for our own well-being. That's when we can make a real difference. Besides, it's your life, you should learn about it sometime. You might actually like it after all.

I saw that the engine of my life was fuelled by a mixture of fear and resentment. A person run on resentment and fear can hardly produce anything other than calamity. When our actions are rooted in fear and resentment on a day-to-day basis; we end up planting little seeds of destruction everywhere we go. What do seeds of destruction sprout? Maybe it was interactions with our spouse that are run through with tones of jealousy (fear), insecurity (fear), or resentment of something they did in the past. Visits to a parent's house or with family that start out polite and end in outbursts of argument and tears, fuelled by a lifetime of resentment. Meetings with our boss where we stumble our words and say stupid things because our mind is bogged down by inferiority (fear), worries about losing our job (fear), or disapproval (fear). Or, maybe we meet up with a friend for a fun night out but we decided to work into the conversations things they did or didn't do in the past that we were still upset about (resentment). An argument starts and our night is ruined. Now we have a falling out with our friend and we vent (resentment) to others about the incident spewing out more negativity. After all, we must let everyone know we were (resentful) "wronged." Have you ever laid in bed at night going over what you should have said or done in an argument *ad nauseam*(resentment)? Sometimes even an argument from months ago. Then you ended up not getting enough sleep and ruining the next day? The next morning you show up to work tired and late, to top it off you didn't have time to grab something to eat so you'll be hungry and agitated soon as well. You have a bad day at work, so you come home and take it out on your spouse or roommates. Do you see how these problems can keep compounding on each other?

FEAR

There is nothing either good or bad, but thinking makes it so... -William Shakespeare

We are all too familiar with the word fear. There's fear of heights, fear of people, fear of water, fear of clowns, and fear of everything else under the sun, including Heliophobia (fear of the sun).

People seem pretty comfortable letting you know their fear of spiders or their fear of heights. Maybe they mention to you in conversation their fear of public speaking, or how frightened they were watching *The Conjuring* movie. Some even seem to wear their fear like a badge or token of their quirky personality. Those are the easy fears. When was the last time you heard someone boast in conversation that they were afraid you weren't going to like them? Have you ever heard someone say; "Guys I'm afraid of being left out, can you include me more in the conversations?" Not often right? But it's a feeling we've all had. Or when the co-worker everyone likes suggests a restaurant that you hate, you don't say "I actually hate that place but I have a fear of missing out so I'm going to go anyway." Pretend you're at the bar chatting with someone, when out of nowhere they say: "Wow cool story. I actually don't care, but I have this fear of being rude, so I'll keep listening." Imagine how much time and effort would be saved if people just told you whether or not they were attracted to you. Say you meet a guy or girl and you are instantly infatuated by them, they're beautiful and charming. But you say nothing of course, even go out of your way to make sure you don't show any signs of attraction. You might even make an effort to ignore them. Why do we do that? Wouldn't it make sense that we just tell the people we like, that we like them? The fear of rejection is a strong one. I guess the more obvious fear is the awkwardness after, if things don't go right. Oh well... like I tell my kids: a closed mouth doesn't get fed. Learn to speak up or be prepared to lose everything you want to those that do.

JULIA GULIA??

As a teenager I had a huge crush on a friend. This girl and I partied together all the time, but I never told her, or even hinted that I liked her. Even weirder, I knew she kind of liked me too but she wasn't saying anything either. We were just both in fear of speaking up I guess. Weird right? Our fears are what cause all the time-consuming formalities we put people through to vet out bad partners. Unfortunately, we probably miss out on some good ones in there too. We try so hard to protect ourselves from heartbreak, women especially do this, only to still end up getting played or heartbroken anyways. As if we can control who is going to betray us or not. Or like getting to know someone really well first, lessens the chance of them "doing you wrong." It's usually the people we know best that do the most harm. In my opinion things are either going to work out or not, might as well give it a shot. Having dated plenty of women in my life, I feel like many are in such fear of one-night-stands, being mistreated, getting their hearts broken or ending up with a "loser" that they try to super filter and sterilize their interactions with men. They wear their failed relationships on their sleeves. He must be: tall, rich, handsome, alpha male that is dominant but also kind and empathetic. He's got to love his momma but not too much! Oh and love animals but also be ready to kill one! He has to be super masculine but also very sensitive to my feelings. Every man has felt the torture chamber of contradictions trying to appease a woman. In many cases for a man to "just be himself" would surely mean roasting in the fire. One of the biggest fears on earth is the fear men have of women not liking them. Men are driven by their sexual urges. Take away a man's sex drive, you take away all his life force.

Most men can look wealthy at face value and say the right combination of words to get past the woman's vulnerability gatekeeper. They can spot the women that are looking for love and others who are looking for lifestyle. Then once they get what they wanted, they move on to the next woman leaving the previous one upset and dumbfounded. *How could I get played?* She asks herself crying to her friends. *He was so nice and I was so careful. I thought he was Mr. Right. Why does this keep happening to me? Maybe all guys are just dogs.* The problem is the fear-based model many women use to pick men is easily hacked by guys that know what they're doing. I wish I could give you a woman's perspective but I can't give what I don't have. I tell my daughters that when they like a guy, they should not be afraid to approach him and let him know. If you're already acquainted let him know fast, or go up and meet him. I tell them to do this because there are probably lots of good guys that like them but are just afraid to let them know or just don't know how to say it. If the girls only rely on guys approaching them, then they're mostly only get the guys with the skill of approach. Who has the skill of approach? You guessed it. So, I teach them to speak up and take matters into their own hands. Over caution, hesitation and fear often leads you down just as bad as path as the one you were trying to avoid in the first place. I'm not saying you should start going up to every person you think is cute or voicing your fears to everyone, I'm just illustrating how some form of fear is woven into our everyday lives. I want to drive home your awareness of unnecessary fears so they can be identified as they pop up. Optimistically you'll be able to catch yourself about to do, or not do, something out of an irrational fear, and act on the contrary.

When I was newly single I met a girl in a coffee shop. She was cute and seemed to be cool, so I introduced myself and got her number. We went out the next day and had a "great time." That night I had mentioned we could probably grab coffee and hang out the following day. The next day arrives and she asks me what time I'd like to meet her for that coffee. *Damn... I forgot I had the kids during the day.* So I texted her and suggested we hook up in the evening or maybe the next day. I then watched my phone screen as the typing bubble appeared and disappeared several times over. Finally, I receive a text long as The Declaration of Independence. The woman went on about how if I didn't like her, I should just say so, and how I should keep my word as a man and so on...WOW, that was unexpected... but I gave her the benefit of the doubt and replied with: *Chill. It's all good. I'll hit you up later today and we'll meet up.* I know what you're thinking, I should have recognized that huge red flag right away. Well I did. Being newly single and eager just to get out of the house made me a little more pliable at the time though.

Anyways, a couple hours go by and then DING! DING! DING! My phone starts blowing up. All at once I get a bunch of screenshots of old Facebook pictures of me with my ex-wife and kids. Since my older kids followed me on social media I thought it would be in bad taste to start deleting family pics just because my ex was in them. Plus I didn't really give a shit. This woman then followed up the pics with a college thesis length text on what a liar I was and how she was going to tell my wife that I was cheating on her. Not to mention some other kind words she had for me. I explained the reason those pics were still on my page, and that my ex-wife was fully aware her ex-husband is probably dating people. I politely said I couldn't continue this conversation and proceeded to block her number. *Phew, I dodged a bullet on that one* I thought.

Later that evening, I received yet another series of screenshots. This time from my ex-wife. The woman from the coffee shop went online to various local Facebook groups and blasted pictures of me with the caption "Are we dating the same guy? Richard Galvan" with a bunch of red flag emojis surrounding the text. A woman in one of the groups recognized me and sent screenshots of the post to my ex-wife. As well as the brutal roasting of me in the comment section. My ex was obviously humiliated, as was I, since the woman that recognized me was a family member (in law).

What a mess! Why did this happen? I knew this woman less than 48 hours. This wasn't a story of love, passion, heartbreak, and an affair. This is a story of a needy, insecure woman, pent up with resentment and fears shooting herself in the foot. Like I said, I thought she was cute and cool. I had no issues. She sabotaged herself by letting her fears and insecurities run the show. I'm sure we all have a similar story to this one. I think it's safe to say we have all screwed something up needlessly because of some irrational fear we had. *Irrational* being the key word. We want to keep fear out of the places it's not needed. We want to walk the Earth giving off vibes of confidence, and love. In that we will attract good fortune and the right people. While at the same time repelling the insecure and needy.

FEAR OF PEOPLE UNLIKE OURSELVES

As ashamed as I am to say this, as a kid growing up in the 80's & 90's I had certain amount of default American adolescent homophobia. The kind that was issued to young boys by their peer groups and lack of understanding. At least that's how it was for me as a kid, the worst and most common insults were either geared towards your mother or labelling you as gay or a "fag." I was a heterosexual boy and had never been harmed by any homosexuals, nor did I even actually care who or what other people liked as long as they weren't stealing my girl. So why did I demonize this group as a kid? Social acceptance. I didn't want to be outcasted by my peers (another major fear). I just wanted to fit in like everyone else. I was too weak to say: *Who cares if he might like other dudes, leave him alone!* So, I joined in the teasing. Having said that, to anyone I hurt as a kid I apologize. I was just an ignorant follower, feel free to reach out, there are some I owe an amends to but can't find.

I have had many experiences on the street but one of the most interesting hats I've worn was that of what some would call a pimp. And no, we were not sex trafficking. We were there to protect them and collect street taxes. What might come as a surprise to some, is that these prostitutes took great pride in being "Hoe's" and even glamorized it. Much in the same way underground culture glamorizes drug dealers and mobsters. They loved it and were proud to be there, at least the ones I dealt with. My friend who happened to be a gay cholo had just been put in charge of the trans and gay prostitutes that worked on Santa Monica Blvd. in West Hollywood. He asked me to help him run it because we were already hustling together in the drug game and had been through some dangerous situations so he knew he could trust me to have his back. During that time, I got to know a lot of gay and trans people. This experience changed me in a few ways. No, it didn't turn me gay or curious. It did make me see how badly prejudiced people were. Even just having a gay friend my mom even accused me of being gay. I also realized that just because someone was gay or trans didn't mean they were bad or weird in any way just because they liked the same sex. Also, that there were more "straight men" that were secretly homosexual than I ever could have imagined. There's a hell of a lot of people living in heavy fear and shame out there. I also did of course come across many weirdos and a few predators on the streets. The weirdos were weirdos because they were weirdos, not because they liked the same sex. There were plenty of straight weirdos too. Same went for the predators, in fact all the predators I came across were straight men not any of the gay or trans people I encountered. In fact, we were there to protect them because they were the prey and constantly being attacked and robbed. Which brings me to the next observation; these people have it rough. I never realized how cruel people were to them. I felt bad and it pissed me off after a while once some became like friends. Do I want drags in scandalous nun costumes doing story time to my children? Hell No! I don't want straight women in scandalous nun costumes doing story time to my kids either. Again there are weirdos in every category that can give the rest a bad name. Try not to judge an entire section of mankind by a few radicals in the public eye. Be fearless and make being kind cool again. Protect the vulnerable. Keep an open mind, and don't ever let the crowd turn you into a shitty person.

ORIGIN STORY

The mind is its own place, and in itself can make a heaven of hell, and a hell of heaven... -John Milton

When I was a kid I used to love comic books. Some of my favorite characters were Wolverine and Gambit from The X-Men. The Punisher, Daredevil, Batman, and Spawn too. One thing they all had in common was a cool origin story, and none of them were stories of a nice peaceful life. They were all forged in tragedy and turmoil. I heard somewhere; a life without tragedy is a tragic life. Let's stick with; a smooth sea never made a good sailor. So what is your origin story? Ask yourself the following questions and write down the answers. Have fun with it, write it in the style of a comic or hero story if you want. Are the memories of your childhood happy or sad? What, if any, tragedies or hardships did you have to overcome? Did the people that were supposed to love and care for you treat you well? If you were treated bad, did you have a part to play in that? Did you feel like you belonged at school, at home and in life in general? Remember it doesn't matter whether your parents or siblings think you had it good or bad, the way you experienced and perceive things is *your* reality. At least for now, that may or may not change. Whether you think your childhood was good or bad or in-between we need to lay things out to get a clear picture. Relying on our brain firing off random memories at various times is like trying to watch a movie in random 30 second clips. We need to take a look at your childhood experiences and acknowledge the way they have affected your adulthood. It is also very helpful to go a little deeper into the background of your parents or primary caretakers as kids. What were your mother and father like? What was their childhood like? Did they pass on what was taught to them? If you were raised by family members or guardians, describe them as well.

 I have friends who seemingly had a much harder childhood than I did, but they didn't appear to be as negatively affected. They must've been just wired differently than I was. Sometimes that's just what it boils down to in my opinion. My five daughters all have very different personalities and temperaments. I didn't assign personalities, they were born that way. My oldest daughter Isabel has been calm and mellow since birth. While my second youngest Venice was born with her energy turned up full blast. They are all very different by nature. I am well aware that I was a sensitive kid. The world seemed to have a harder effect on me than it did on others. There's always a flip side to the matters we think are curses. Kind of like the superheroes I mentioned, they wouldn't have become superheroes without the tragedies that preceded. The Punisher would just be The Regular guy, if he didn't suffer the loss of his family at the hands of criminals, prompting him to join the battle against wrong doer's. Would Batman have become Batman if he didn't lose his parents? Would Daredevil be Daredevil if he wasn't blind and could see like everyone else? No, he'd just be another lawyer but because he was blind his other senses were heightened to compensate. Those comparisons might not be the best or make you feel any better, but they hold a point. The point is; it's our choice what we do with our hardships, either we can become zeros, or heroes. Our days of bitterness and feeling sorry for ourselves must end now.

THE GROUCH AND THE BRAINSTORM

"Resentment is the number one offender. It destroys more alcoholics than anything else." Page 64, Alcoholics Anonymous. To normal men and women, a resentment might be great fuel for competition, it may even drive one to success. However, for the addict, the path of indulging resentments leads us straight back to the pipe. The addict doesn't build an empire on a resentment like the instance between Lamborghini and Ferrari. The addict catches resentment and destroys friendships, careers and even families. He needlessly holds onto pain -years- even decades old, pride won't allow him to forgive, so his or her loved ones end up paying the price for wrongs they didn't do. What does someone have to gain by holding on so fiercely to these resentments? It truly is: drinking the poison hoping the other person dies.

With resentment comes the urge for revenge- in hopes of leading to some type of *justice*; and it's the justice (I feel) is the carrot dangling at the end of the stick. The powerless crave justice for the wrongs done to them. It gives us a sense of power. People don't seem to be very critical of those they feel are much less fortunate and in no position to take anything from them. It's those that they see as competition or above them that they get *so mad* at. So then, doesn't that bring their opinion of themselves into the hot seat? Doesn't it become more of an *insecurity* or *self-esteem* problem- more than the actual offense?

If a 90-year-old senior citizen gives a darling compliment to your spouse, you think nothing of it. When a younger than you, beautiful specimen of a human gives the same compliment- it's a different story. The compliment didn't change, the threat to our security did.

I could be wrong, but to me- it's all an inside job.

Many addicts seem to be over-thinkers, and/or emotionally sensitive; give someone like that a small resentment and they'll work wonders with it. They ruminate on the smallest offense, incubating them in their head till they've grown it into a sinister plot or conspiracy theory. Like nurturing gardeners tending to a seedling. These offenses could have been unintentional, but in the addict's mind-they were premeditated with malicious intent. They go over in their head what they're going to say to the offender again and again *Just wait until I see them again!* Using untold amounts of mental energy, planning and rehearsing the scene in their mind. Once primed and in position-they unleash their wrath on the offender. Often the offender wasn't even aware they had done anything wrong, or had completely forgotten about the incident. The addict never really gets the satisfying results they are looking for, and definitely never looks as cool as imagined; they usually just end up embarrassing themselves or making their own situation worse. I'm sure there's an addict right now that just got fired, dumped or in a jail cell-wishing they would've just *let it slide*. It's usually not until *after* we blow up, that we in a way, *sober up* and see things clearly. So, in that sense stewing on a resentment is like a cheap high of sorts. Think about it. Consider how much time we spend stewing on resentments that have absolutely no effect on our lives. A meaningless waste of energy.

In order for civilization to thrive, people need to get angry about certain things; your sister's back handed compliment is not one of them. Wouldn't we all be a little better off if we let more inconsequential things slide? Every single *perceived* offense does not need to be avenged. I once knew a woman that seemed to keep massive records stored in her head of every single person that ever offended her and was just waiting for an "I'll show you" moment. But why? What do we have to gain in these tiny useless acts of vengeance? What happens when it's ourselves we are mad at? What type of behavior does that lead to?

Sometimes I think when people don't have "actual" problems to solve in life- they create them. They start finding problems, and it's usually the people closest to them that become the focus of their attention. I wonder if that's just a first world issue.

"If we were to live, we had to be free from anger. The grouch and the brainstorm were not for us. They may be the dubious luxury of normal men, but for alcoholics these things are poison." Page 66, Alcoholics Anonymous.

When a person gets caught up in addiction, it's common for them to fall behind in life. It's like they entered a party in the twilight zone and finally decided to step out *years* later, realizing the rest of the world had moved on. They get sober and see their peers with stable jobs, families, homes and seemingly great lives. Meanwhile, the addict is starting over, filling out resumes for fast food jobs and telemarketing agencies- hoping to land anything just to put a few bucks in their pocket. The pressure is intensified if they have a child or are middle-aged. Years behind, they get frustrated and feel they need to hurry and catch up in life. This leads them to either give up- or cut corners and participate in shady hustles for money. When they do get their hands on some money, instead of using it to pay down debts, buy a car, rent an apartment or invest- they instead buy things to *look* wealthier. Take a peek into the closets of any sober living, you won't find the clothes of the down and out. On the contrary, you'll most likely find designer clothes and name brands. There seems to be no in-between, the addict is either flaunting money or dead broke. With money- they feel on top of the world -*I've made it! Bow before me you peasants!*- They spend as if there's no tomorrow, at the same time they start to slack off on their obligations. They feel they no longer need to be bothered with such wastes of time like- going to work or school. They also no longer feel the need for the people that helped them get back on their feet; their memory seems to have been wiped clear of their low times. Gratitude gives way for hubris and greed. Broke- they're mad at the whole world -*WHY ME? What did I do to deserve this?*- Entitlement and resentment kick in. They start acting out as if they were still using; maybe selling drugs, stealing or hanging out with the *old crowd*. Both ends of the spectrum typically relapse and have to start back at square one, this time a little older and with an even bigger bag of resentments. The cycle then starts over.

We either humble ourselves or life does it for us.

INVENTORIES

Let's get humble. We're going to make an inventory of all our resentments.

First, we get some paper and just make our list of people, places, things, we're resentful towards. Then we'll get another sheet paper (probably quite a few) and write the name of the person we resent. The next line we will answer "Question 1," next line "Question 2" and so on.

RESENTMENT INVENTORY
Directions:

Get a couple notebooks and pens first, and for the next few days start making a list of every single person, place, thing, institution or ideal that you resent. When I say "resent" you don't necessarily have to be mad, it can be things that just slightly sting you. Put it all down. Everything! Mom, Dad, siblings, mailman, the boy that embarrassed you in kindergarten, the cool kid in high school, the girl that didn't notice you, the sheriff, political party, your family dynamic, your big ears, being born poor, being born rich; whatever comes to mind put it on the list. When in doubt, put it on the list. If it popped in your head it's taking up space. Better safe than sorry, you can cross it off later if needed. The more thorough you are the better pay off in the end. As you go about your day more names will pop up, write them in your notes or voice notes and put them on your paper list when you get home. The length of the lists vary, mine was over 500 and each name might have more than one resentment. Just make it thorough and remember, don't cheat yourself. Most find that the harder the resentment, the more joy you will find after its removal. Treat the situation like you would an infection or infestation. All roaches must be eradicated. If even one lives it will have babies and you'll have a house full of cockroaches again in no time. It is also important to be aware that although we may *feel* that we have been wronged, we must be prepared to face the fact that some of the *wrongs* were just perceived. Even though they felt very real to us, the actual wrong may have never occurred. We don't want to downplay *or* exaggerate, we want to find out what was our fault, as well as what wasn't. Once we drop the weight of our past, we will be significantly stronger in the present.

Now that you have your list, answer these 4 questions for each name. You'll need to start this on a new sheet of paper.

Question 1: What is the resentment?
Write briefly what the resentment is.

Question 2 : How did it affect us?
We write in the second section below the resentment, which one of these were affected. Did it affect our:

Confidence: did it damage your confidence, pride, self-esteem, or dignity? Embarrassment falls into this category. For example: if your boss berated you in front of all of your co-workers, or your spouse started an argument in front of others and humiliated you.

Goals: did it get in the way of you trying to achieve something? Maybe a job promotion, life-goal, completion of a task, acquiring of something, or even ruining a special night.

Safety: were you or your loved ones put in danger? Was someone harmed or almost hurt?

Money: were you affected financially? Did you lose money?

Family & friends: did it somehow affect your relationship with family or friends? This includes co-workers and acquaintances.

Relationships: did the resentment affect your relationship with a partner, fling, love interest, or spouse.

Question 3: What was our part?

It's time to find out what part *we* played in the resentment. Never mind what the other person did, what did *we* do? Even if it was 90% them and 10% us. We almost always played some part. Obviously there are situations like a child being harmed, where the child has no fault. But, an adult getting black out drunk and being assaulted does have a part to play. Examine each situation logically and with an open mind. Just because you played a part does not always mean you were at fault.

We ask ourselves:

What was my part: what part did I play in this? What wrong did I do in this situation? What am I not admitting? What did I do to set this in motion? Did this really happen or was it an assumption or opinion?

Where was I being Selfish: Were others affected as well? Was I only concerned with my agenda?

Have I done the same: have I ever done the same thing? Am I expecting someone else to not do something that I've done before?

What am I afraid of: did this trigger a fear in me? Fear of harm, fear of death, fear of criticism, financial fear, fear of losing a loved one.

Many of my resentments were of things I only perceived, and never actually happened in reality. There were quite a few people I was resentful towards just because I *thought*, that they thought, they were better than me. None of these people ever actually said these things to me, these were just conclusions I jumped to in my head from my own insecurities. For all I know they could have thought highly of me and were just nervous. But in my mind, they thought they were better than me, and I treated them with contempt for a perceived insult. Women I had never even asked out, in my mind didn't like me, and had already rejected me in my imagination. Even though, they had done nothing wrong and had no idea. Some I had never even spoken to.

Here are a few incidents I didn't think I had a part to play in but got a better understanding after I did the inventory.

One night in high school I was at a house party when a rival gang member snuck up behind me and hit me in the back of the head with a full bottle of vodka knocking me out cold. While I was on the ground I was stomped out. I was hospitalized and out cold for a couple days. I had a concussion, broken nose, fractured cheek bone, knocked back teeth and a few other injuries. My head was like a basketball and I even had a clear distinct shoe imprint on my head. Does any kid deserve that severe of a beating? Maybe not, but did I have a part to play in it? You bet. First and foremost; anyone who joins a gang knows you are going to take beatings and maybe even be killed. If you weren't prepared to deal with that you should have joined the church instead. What else was my part? I tried to start an altercation with that gang member earlier on but he backed down. His girlfriend then got involved and I insulted her as well. Next, I didn't even belong at the party in the first place, I crashed it with a friend. The kids that threw the party even offered me some alcohol to take if I left because they knew I was going to start shit and ruin the party. Back then everywhere I went I started or instigated fights and it was known. I was also heavily intoxicated from heroin and alcohol. If I was sober none of this probably would've happened. I may or may not have deserved what I got, but I definitely played a major role. I laid out all the ingredients that would cook up that incident. We usually do.

Here's another example: I was robbed Narcos-style for my Rolex in Colombia. Sitting in a taxi headed to my Airbnb in Medellin, all of a sudden, I hear loud roars of motorcycles surrounding the taxi. *What the fuck is going on?* As I'm sitting in the passenger seat with the window rolled down the driver gives me a frightened look as he comes to a stop. Next, I feel a jab into my stomach and hear a man start yelling in Spanish. I look down and there's a pistol rammed into my stomach so far it feels like it's under my ribs. I look around for a second still unsure my next move. The driver was yelling: "He wants the watch! Give it to him!" I was stuck in the passenger seat with a gun shoved in my torso surrounded by armed men on motorcycles. There was nothing I really could do but give up the watch, or get shot and have him take it anyway. I unclasped the watch and handed it over to the gunman. As I was pulling the tight fitting watch off of my wrist, I could see panic in the gunman's eyes. He was starting to shake and looked like he was about to shoot me and flee. I gave him the watch seemingly in the nick of time, the gang then sped off in a loud roar of engines. Can you guess my part in all this? I'm sure you can. Why the fuck was I wearing a Rolex in that part of Colombia? No one ever asks for it when a crime happens, but sometimes if they don't use common sense like I didn't that day, they are "asking for it."

One big resentment that I considered myself to have no fault in, was towards a man named "Dee." My girlfriend at the time and I met Dee while buying some crack cocaine on Skid Row. He was a dealer that I had become acquainted with. One day he invited us up to his motel room to crash because we didn't have a place to stay for the night. All evening, we smoked crack, weed, and drank. At the end of the night my girlfriend and I slept on the bed, Dee slept on a chair. Around 4 or 5am my girlfriend called me into the bathroom. She was crying, and told me that Dee had been forcefully touching her in the night and stole some money. "He kept shoving his hand into my pants" she whispered, with her eyes red and in tears. "He took the $20's out of my cash too!" Furious, I woke Dee up ready to kill him and asked if he touched her? I forgot to mention Dee was about 40 years old, over 6ft 250 to 275 pound big ass black dude. My girlfriend and I were 17 or 18, and I was probably 150 pounds soaking wet and strung out. I always carried either a gun, straight razor or ice pick. That day I think I had some type of knife. I honestly don't remember what I had that day. I just remember pumping myself up for whatever was about to happen.

When Dee came to and realized what was going on, he frantically tried to calm me down. He was denying everything. Seeing I didn't believe him, and that I was only getting more upset, he slowly pulled out his bag of crack and said something like: "Chill, chill, chill, let's have a smoke, let's talk about this." As he was saying that, he looked me right in the eyes and dumped out the cigarette cellophane full of crack on the table. Then he slowly stuffed as much crack as he could into a pipe and handed it to me. "Here man chill, let's talk." He knew how to solve the riddle and get past the troll, he got me. We ended up sitting there smoking crack for the next hour or so while my girlfriend sat off to the side humiliated and scared. I can only imagine how she must've felt. How can I be smoking crack and sitting with this guy listening to his bullshit? For those unfamiliar with the effects rock cocaine can hold on someone, it is overwhelmingly powerful. You get "stuck." The all-mighty grip of the crack takes over your brain. You can hardly talk, all you can think of is smoking more crack. You will do anything to get more, so the only person with rock wields a special power over you. I was "stuck," and Dee was feeding me rock after rock trying to smooth his way out of the situation. I was powerless. I was in too much of a daze to even make out a sentence, let alone fight or do anything to bring some type of justice to the situation. There were many different paths I could have taken to bring resolution or make my girlfriend feel better. Smoking crack with her abuser, and allowing him to bullshit his way out was definitely not it. I just added insult to the injury. She was so angry and disappointed in me. I let her down. We were never the same again.

So, did I have a part in that situation? Yes. Sure, he was a sexual predator, thief and drug dealer, and no I didn't steal any money or molest anyone. But what I did do was put us all in that situation. If I wasn't buying drugs, we wouldn't have ever met him. We wouldn't have needed a place to stay if I didn't spend all of our money on drugs. If I didn't start smoking crack with the guy, I could have at least got her out of there. I set this traumatic night up for all the players. She was the victim, and I was an offender as well. I played a part and owed her an amends. For years I had selective memory and only blamed Dee. I never thought I had any faults in that. I also omitted the part where I was smoking crack with him, whenever the thought came to mind. I had to examine the incident with an open mind to see the truth and admit my faults. In the third column we forget about what other people did, and only concentrate on the parts we played. This may be much more difficult to do in severe situations such as a rape or someone harming your children. Without a doubt there are situations where no one but the aggressor is at fault. Nevertheless, though there may be no fault, the situation should still be faced and analyzed to help us be freed from it and to see exactly how, who, and what, was affected. We may owe an amends.

There is nothing anyone does to deserve to be victims of such crimes. Nor is there any justification on behalf of the assaulters, but the sad truth is, there are serial killers, rapists, molesters, abusers and thieves out there preying on people. We need to behave in accordance with such realities.

Here's an incident that put a couple people in my inventory. Not because they did any harm to me personally but because they put me in a bad situation, both victim and offender. In the early 2000's I lived in a town called Pacoima. In Pacoima there were housing projects where everyone would buy crack or PCP. Even my mother used to score from those projects back in her day. Anyways, one night a girl wanted to hang out with me. I told her I was in the projects, and I would meet up with her later on. She asked what I was doing there, and I told her I was just hanging out getting high with so and so (I said the names of the guys I was with, guys she knew were bad news). She then said; "I'll be over there in 30 minutes!" *No! Don't come, just wait, I'll call you after.* Of course she didn't wait and showed up. There was about eight of us, all gang members standing out front of a house across the street from the projects. Three of the guys were friends of mine, the others were just acquaintances that I definitely did not trust. All were serious dudes known for being crazy and violent. She pulled up like an idiot, blasting music and yelling. "Wasss upppp!" I thought to myself: *Oh my*

God...she's gonna get herself killed. As soon as she stopped the car one of the dudes pulls out a gun. He ran up to the car pointing it at her and telling her to get out. I tried to calm everyone down and let them know she was cool, and I knew her. They chilled out slightly, but not homeboy with the gun. The guy was smoking PCP, weed, doing coke and drinking all night long. He was high as hell, there was nothing any of us could really do to stop him without possibly getting shot ourselves. So, with the gun still pointed at her face, he instructed her to get back in the drivers seat as he jumped in the passenger side. As she shut the car door, she looked at me with eyes I'll never forget. The expression on her face was full of fear and confusion, and with the gun still pointed at her head they drove off. I could still see the black tears from her mascara running down the caked makeup on her face. Scared, teary eyes locked in with mine as the car pulled away. I had noticed her hair was done and she was dressed for what she thought would be a fun night of partying. Instead, it ended up being a traumatic night. She ended up being assaulted. Next time I saw her she didn't want to talk about it. She stopped me right away when I even tried to ask what happened. Now as much love and sympathy as I still have for her, I would like to use this instance as an example that will hopefully help someone else get through a hard instance in their inventory. I would, and have, used many rough incidents in my life as well to better get my point across so I hope no one takes this in bad taste.

No, she did not deserve what happened to her. Did I have a part to play? Yes. Could I have done more to help? Possibly. But did she have a part to play in it too? Should she have been driving to the projects in the middle of the night to get high with a bunch of gang members? Even after she was warned not to come? Even though there were people that she knew were dangerous? Now here's the even harder question I struggle with: If this happened to my daughter, (after consoling) do I point out the part she played or let her live thinking she was 100% victim? I'm sure if you ask 100 people their opinion on the matter you will get many different viewpoints and lots of fierce disagreement. This is the type of painful examination we must allow ourselves if we want to be freed from the painful experiences. The more painful the experience, the more strength and honesty you will need to get through it.

Question 4: What harm did we do?

For example;
List:
Joe
Lacy
Mom
2nd grade teacher
Lady at grocery store
High school bully
Etc...

Inventory:
Name- Joe
Question 1- He was telling lies about me

Question 2-Confidence, Goals, Family & Friends

Question 3- What he said about me wasn't fully a lie. I was very late and rude to him. I would be upset and say the same things if I were in his shoes. I was afraid of him making me look bad in front of everyone.

Question 4- I talked crap about him and made him look bad

You don't have to write all the labels, it doesn't have to be pretty. This won't be turned into any teacher. This is for you.

For example,

Lacy- She cheated on me

Confidence, goals, Family & Friends, Relationships.

I wasn't spending much time with her, I was treating her bad, I didn't show up to her birthday party, I had cheated in the beginning.

I cheated on her, I embarrassed her, I caused emotional harm, I broke her phone.

List any and all harms you may have caused.

In the fourth question, we list all the harms we did to the "offender." That includes physical, mental, emotional and financial. Some resentments can have no harm. Like if you are resentful towards the police, you don't have to list things like; I like to play N.W.A.'s *Fuck the police* rap song. But you should list things like; I called a cop a scumbag devil man for writing me a fix-it ticket. Harms like punching a person, or maybe if you stole something of theirs are pretty easy to identify. But there are some harms that take a little more thought to uncover. For instance, say your resentment is towards an ex. Maybe they cheated on you or it was just a bad relationship. Once again you may or may not have any fault, most likely you will if you were in a relationship with them. We try to ask ourselves some questions like this: Did you ever cheat on them? Did you have any questionable friendships? Were you doing all you could to stay intimately connected? Did you do all you could to grow the relationship, or did you allow things to get stale? Were you argumentative or holding onto bitterness? Were you supportive to the things important to them? Did you treat them well and as if they were special? Was there anything really harmful that you have said that may have stuck with them? Had the relationship actually ended long ago but you guys were just holding on out of some sort of co-dependency? Remember we are not looking for things that would "justify" their behavior, we are just aiming to hold ourselves accountable for *our* harms and deficiencies. Not everything you come up with is an actual "harm." Some things they won't think are harms, but in your heart you don't feel right about them, therefore they should be addressed. Some things you won't think are harms, but to them they are. It's better safe than sorry, we want to make sure our side of the street is completely clean. It's better to list it and it be nothing than to leave it out and have a tiny stain. Those stains add up. Even if it's just the smallest pin sized infraction in your mind, why not get it out? Make sure you dig deep and be completely open-minded and honest with yourself. List 'em all. The reward is your freedom but it can also be the price you pay.

Certain religions have instilled guilt and shame in people from a young age, for character traits they were born with. As good as it may be for everybody to have a decent amount of humbleness, or at least self-awareness in their actions; I also think this can go overboard in a lot of people giving them low self-esteem, right off the bat.

There is no reason (in my opinion) for anybody to be brought up with the burden of guilt on their conscience before they have even done anything wrong. I think this introduction of default guilt can lead to a sort of a spiritual sickness, breeding resentment, and shame.

Get rid of guilt and sin. The "seven deadly sins" are thread throughout our character and personality to some degree, whether we like it or not. In fact, these are just features of every human being. *Discipline* in these features should be pushed, not guilt about them. Our lives are driven by *desires*- our level of discipline in them, is the valve which controls the number of consequences. Many of the things that make us unique as individuals are comprised of these so called "sins." To think of these as some sort of spiritual failure does us no good and only harms our spirits more. Acceptance and discipline I believe is the solution.

SEX INVENTORY

This part is called the sex inventory, not just *sex* sex, but relationships as well. A huge portion of our lives, our happiness and our sadness, is in direct correlation to the quality of our intimate relationships. There is no such thing as a flawless relationship, that would make for a pretty boring life in my opinion. We thrive best with certain amounts of chaos, turmoil, and problem-solving. I don't mean toxic, dysfunctional type chaos. I mean the type of dynamic that breeds fun and growth; think Lucy & Ricky from *I Love Lucy*. Just picture how crazy you would go if you had a partner that agreed with you 100% of the time, did everything you did and obeyed everything you said. Ideally, both partners should grow in their own fashion while still remaining compatible with each other in a complementary way. That's just my opinion, I'm no expert on relationships. This isn't a marriage counselling book. There are no hard and fast rules here on relationships, nor will we go any further into the topic. This inventory is meant to analyze *your* past behavior in relationships. It's all about you. The goal is to improve upon yourself, therefore bettering your future relationships. In doing that, you can have a better life; thus making it easier for you to stay sober and free of harmful vices.

You wouldn't buy a house without first doing a home inspection right? You'd want to see if there are any leaks, holes in the walls, electrical problems, plumbing or structural damage. You've got to know what you're working with and you can't fix a problem that hasn't been identified. So, we will run a similar diagnostic of our intimate relationships. You may *think* you have a good idea of what went wrong in a past relationship, but most are in for a much-needed wake up call. Personally, I was brought to tears when seeing my behaviors in black-and-white.

We will lay things out like the previous inventory. First make a list of all sexual partners and relationships then answer the questions below.

Question 1: What was that relationship like?

Question 2: Why didn't it work out?

Question 3: What harm did I do to this person? Was I ever selfish, dishonest, jealous, bitter or cruel? Did we cause any physical or emotional harm? Did I have a negative effect on this person's life?

Question 4: What was my motive? What was your motive at Heart? Did you want this person for their good looks, success, a specific body part, social ties?

Question 5: What could I have done better?

After the analysis of each person we ask ourselves : Do I owe this person an amends? If so, we will add them to our repair list later on in the book.

Once we are all done and have reviewed our conduct, we spend a few minutes meditating on what our ideal relationship would look like; how will we contribute to their lives and conduct ourselves. We write down on paper the type of person we want to be like in a relationship. We ingrain this ideal into our brain, we make it a part of our psyche. We acknowledge how we have harmed those in the past and become willing to make amends when the time is right. Some things cannot be fixed, but we can make sure we never repeat the same mistakes again. It's best to add these ideals to your daily prayer or goals for a while. Especially when we start a new relationship.

FEAR INVENTORY

WRITE YOUR LIST OF FEARS. STOP ACTING ON THESE.

NEXT TO YOUR FEARS, LIST THEIR OPPOSITES. START ACTING ON THESE.

NOTE: DON'T BURN OR DISPOSE OF YOUR INVENTORY UNTIL AFTER YOU MAKE YOUR AMENDS LIST (THAT'S COMING NEXT)

Once finished with the resentment and sex inventory (and read through till the *end of this section*) we do a critical overview of both. The goal is to identify our most common forms of fears. This works well when done with a trusted friend but can be done alone as well. We note the fears that seem to be shaping our lives. Fear of harm, fear of death, fear of criticism, financial fear, fear of losing a loved one, and any other more specific fears that spawn from those. "As far back as I can remember I always wanted to be a gangster." We all remember that line in the movie *Good Fellas*. Well, when I was a kid I felt the same way. Not because I was some tough little boy, but because I felt vulnerable. The gang members in my neighborhood seemed to have things figured out. They were feared, nobody fucked with them. Everybody fucked with me. Everyday me and my friends would go play at Pony park which was at the end of my block. It's now a much nicer area, but in the 80's and 90's it was a shit hole. Not the worst in LA, but still had a bunch of rowdy kids running around trying to kick my 10-year-old ass. I remember one kid no one would fuck with, because his older brother was in the local gang. It was like he had a VIP pass and had instant respect amongst all the neighborhood kids. He never got pulled off the swing by the legs or trash and rocks thrown at him like I got.

One time I got in a fight with one of the little goons and I accidentally beat him up. I used a move I always did back then, I bent his finger back till he submitted, then I started punching him in the face. Strictly out of fear. The kid started crying and said he was going to a bring his other friends and jump me. Immediately I stopped and started panicking. *NO I'M SORRY! I'M SORRY!* I was scared for weeks and avoided the park and my own street. Luckily when I did see him and his friends again nothing happened. I hated the feeling of being powerless, even though I didn't know that's what it was. I thought I was just weak. I was tired of being afraid. I wanted people to be afraid of me. I wanted to be around people that were stronger and meaner than I was. I was tired of being a bullied, dork nobody.

Not that I ever became some big gangster... but having protection and the ability to protect my peers quenched something in me. Also, that human urge to be a part of something, and I wasn't good at sports so being a gangster satisfied both my fear and brotherhood deficits. My main fears were of harm and of criticism. More specifically, the fear of being taken advantage of, fear of looking weak, fear of humiliation, and fear of not belonging.

I remember fearing and hating my mother's boyfriends and the way they treated me. I wished that my father would beat them up or do something. I used to always think, whenever I was older and bigger I would find and beat the shit out of them. I saw that everybody including my mother's boyfriends were afraid of the local cholos. I had fantasies of becoming a cholo myself and sicking the others on the people I hated in life. I felt powerless. As they say the over trait often conceals its opposite. My biggest fear back then was you thinking I'm a punk or a bitch. Maybe this fear came from feeling powerless at school, the streets and at home. Maybe I was just sensitive or out of my element.

I also believe that the natural self-awareness everyone is equipped with was dialled up way too high. Perhaps I could've fitted in great at a small midwestern prairie school in the 1800's. However, in a hugely diverse, complicated city like Los Angeles (even in its smaller sections) I felt out of place. Maybe that's what caused me to be introverted and awkward. Or possibly it was the other way around? Maybe I felt out of place because, I was always so "in my head" which caused me to be awkward. Feeling weak killed my confidence at school and stronger more confident kids could smell it, making me prey to bullies. Eventually I was able to adapt and toughen up. To do that I had to go against my default personality. My natural temperament was to be nice, easy going and funny. Isn't it strange how being a nice kid can get you hurt sometimes? I had to become violent and cold. I developed a persona that was almost the complete opposite of my true character. When you live like that it only further fucks you up on the inside. My life was forever altered by my fear of being "a bitch." In other words, fear of what other people think. I never had much of a fear of physical harm, I feared humiliation.

That same fear of what other people think, would rear its ugly head into my sober life as well. This time it was the fear of being poor. Even worse: looking poor. The inventory helped me see how the deep shame I felt in my homeless years rolled over into an insecurity in my sobriety. The degrading feeling of old friends and family seeing me panhandling. Store clerks giving me the side-eye waiting for me to steal or shoo'ing me out of their store. Walking around dirty and stinky, wanting to clean up but not being able to. It's a completely different existence. I've had some crummy experiences in life but the shame I went through during the worst of my homeless periods was the most devastating to my psyche. This insecurity of mine has gotten much better in the past few years, but it ain't gone yet my friends. I still have this little voice in my head that whispers to me every once in a while: She thinks you're broke. I understand why some rappers go overboard on gold and flash. They probably have a similar insecurity.

THE MATRIX

Have you ever been to the mall and seen a group of teens that all look the same? Same haircuts, clothes and shoes, aside from assorted colors they all look like clones of each other. Adults do it too sometimes. It almost reminds me of something in an episode of the twilight zone. Nothing new can be introduced into the community accept in small drips. Changes usually stem from pop culture then trickle down to the people. Or the alpha of a group sets the trends then the others will follow like sheep. Have you ever felt like switching your style up, or trying something new, but you tested it out and got clowned by your peers? Or even worse you knew they'd ridicule you, so you didn't even try? That's fear. It's like you get a notification from your subconscious to upgrade, but your fear kicks in and deletes it. Fear doesn't like change. Every time you give in to fear it incubates and grows stronger. Our given friends, and family can be like the proverbial crabs in a bucket when it comes to our growth. I use the word "given" because we were born into our family not by choice and most of our friends were provided to us by the schools or neighborhood our family provided. I am by no means saying this is a bad thing. I am just pointing out that sometimes the people around us aren't people that we would've picked ourselves if we had the choice. It's wise to go out and pick friends that push you in a positive way, encourage your growth and make you stronger. Are "given friends and family" stunting your growth? Did you ever have the urge to date that kinda weird strangely attractive person but you knew your people wouldn't approve, so you killed the notion? What if you would've been happy with that person? Or maybe you bought a new jacket you loved but one of your peers made a stupid comment, so it now sits in your closet collecting dust. Do you have a longing to move to the beach, mountains or another country but "you can't" because you're too tied to family or work? All these things separately don't seem like much of a sacrifice to be around loved ones. Cumulatively though, not doing a bunch of things that are calling you can kill the spirit. One can become like the caged lion sleeping all day covered in flies. He's safe, fed and cared for but somethings missing. He's a lion in flesh but not in spirit. Now he's just a cog in the wheel of a business.

Don't ignore your instincts they are trying to guide you. Those were all ideas and desires you didn't choose to have. They were sent down to you from the ether or whatever you want to call it. Either way they were messages left in your inbox from an unknown sender. We don't get to choose what comes down the pike. All we can do is choose whether to indulge, ignore or act. Self-defeating thoughts we ignore and replace with redirection and positive action. What would happen if we went down that rabbit hole and followed more of those thoughts we call "dreams"? Ok, maybe if you're a 40-year-old convict fresh out, working construction; your dream of becoming president of the United States probably won't happen. But you can be president of your own construction company and live a hell of a good life. One of the common things I notice when working with newly sober addicts or convicts; their confidence in themselves to do anything positive is shot. I was the same way. Most don't have any deficiencies in intelligence or potential, they just lack belief in themselves to do anything good. It's a fear. Was that fear instilled in them before or after drugs and crime? If a kid grows up to be a criminal or addict most will assume they were abused, impoverished or a mental defect. What if they were just geared to believe they weren't anything? That may be one of the most disgusting abuses of all. I'll take some type of physical abuse and confidence, over non-abuse and a dead spirit any day. Let's root out these self-defeating fears and smash'em. Remember: *If it bleeds we can kill it!* If you're an addict starting over you have an advantage. Don't believe anything different. There are so many directions you can go, you just have to kill the self-defeating fear that is telling you I'm full of shit right now. The person in the unfulfilling job living to work, chained by their car, house and lifestyle is trapped. That person still has to make an escape, you're already out. That's a freedom of its own, a fresh start. I've seen the "miracles" happen, it only takes 3 ingredients: Belief in yourself, action and a little luck. If you believe in yourself, you'll keep the action going long enough for the luck to eventually happen.

Fuck that cookie cutter life. If you're a *real addict* it wasn't meant for you anyways, or else we wouldn't be here going through this book together. I'm talking to you! There's no middle road for us. It's either a beautiful life or the gutter. Living to work and letting social media or TV do the living for you is the gutter too. Who needs to travel? I'll just watch the travel channel. My life sucks so let me watch the Kardashians and get lost in their lives for an hour. Don't be that guy/girl. If you can hustle your way through the streets and institutions, regular life people are easy. You just have to have confidence. Your confidence will get stronger, fake it till you make it for now.

Shake things up. Get out of the old environment for a while. Sure, you'll miss some people and upset others, but you can't make everyone happy. Plus, if they really had our best interests in mind, they would want us to be fulfilled and live out our best lives, right? When we bought a new house and had to move my girls to a new school, in a new district, they all cried because they thought they were going to lose their friends and would miss them. They were in major fear. What ended up happening was they kept those friends and added new ones, new friends that would add to their lives. Same thing happened when we moved to Spain. With social media it's easier than ever to stay connected. I always tell them; you never lose real friends, only fake ones. Their fears didn't come true, yours probably won't either.

    Are you in a group of family or friends clinging to each other for security, or out of insecurity? If not great. This is for the: "My parents had a hard life and I owe them mine, so now I've got to sit it out in this crappy town till they die." I tell my kids the only thing they owe me is to live out their best life and full potential. That's it. They owe me nothing else move anywhere you want, I'll follow or visit. I'm their biggest fan and roadie, not the other way around. I will happily die alone in bed if they are out doing all they can to max out life. Are you nobly sacrificing a chance at the life you're supposed to be living out of obligation to someone else? If so, is it time to start lovingly telling people to fuck off. Start following the trail of crumbs that mystery of a subconscious is dropping for you. "There's beauty in the unknown and beauty in what may be, beauty in the promises of tomorrow, and beauty in all we cannot yet see"- Erin Forbes

IF YOUR LIFE WAS A MOVIE, WOULD PEOPLE FALL ASLEEP IN THE THEATRE?

Home is not where you are born; Home is where all your attempts to escape cease- Naguib Mahfouz

Are you living the same few days of life over and over? Ever watched that movie Groundhog Day? Are you afraid to live the life you want because you don't want to let down family or friends? Isn't not living up to your maximum potential letting them down anyway? Take a look at your wardrobe and style, is it the same style you had from high school? Or a decade ago? Do you have what I like to call Uncle Rico syndrome? When clients would come in and all their energy, references, excuses and even their style were centered in the past; I would jokingly say they had Uncle Rico syndrome. In the 2004 comedy movie *Napoleon Dynamite,* the main character Napoleon has an uncle named Rico. Uncle Rico appears to be in his late 30s and is constantly talking about his high school football days. "If the coach would have put me in the game we would've won state... I could've went pro.. If only things went different..." Uncle Rico's peak in life was high school, so he's stuck living in the past. Like a time loop. Instead of creating new pinnacle moments, he's obsessing on how things could have been. He goes even as far as to try to use a time machine to go back to the year of "the big game." We all know an Uncle Rico, or an Al Bundy from *Married with Children* and if you don't, it may be you. Are you stuck in the past? If so, maybe it's time for some drastic changes. High school is over, life is in session now.

I like to think to myself: These are the good years. But my best times haven't even happened yet. Maybe your frame of thought is: I'm comfortable with my life now. I'll just leave it. The problem is comfort now, only leads to discomfort later. Life is always changing, don't just assume things are always going to be how they are today. Be proactive. If you're not swimming, you're sinking. Though the descent may be so gradual that you won't notice till you're looking up from the bottom. Besides, is the story of your life capped out where you're at right now? This is your peak? So the rest of the episodes of your life are going to be re-runs? Being content with one's life is great, but contentment can morph into stagnation and discontentment in the blink of an eye. Remember happiness isn't something you can hang onto for very long. If you remain motionless in your life it leaps out of your hands like a rabbit and runs for the fence. It's a constantly moving target and needs to be continually pursued. Often indirectly, or by proxy. Don't rest on your laurels, stimulate your mind and soul with new experiences and ways to be of service to others. This book isn't meant to be a set of directions to a destination. It' a re-evaluation. This is a guide to a mindset of infinite possibilities. You can go through this book every year and have a new experience. A new attitude, and a different world opens up.

    To me, stagnation is radiation. That goes for mind, body and spirit. As well as the human experience in general. For me, rolling into change and swapping out life elements comes easily. I guess that's the positive side effect from a life of chaos. I've never really lived anywhere for more than three, maybe four years straight in my entire life from baby till now. I've moved from town to town, parent to parent, family members, friends, jails, homes, hotels, institutions, the streets, even to different countries. What this did was force me to get out of my comfort zone as a kid and to get used to making new friends and adapting to new situations. As an adult I feel comfortable and confident anywhere on earth. You can drop me off like The Terminator in a bolt of lightning butt-naked anywhere on the planet and I'll be OK. Your grandmother might be yelling in the background "But children need stability!" (If you have kids). I have five daughters, they've lived in the projects in LA to one of the richest neighborhoods in the country. They've been all over the world and make friends everywhere they go. No matter where you go the fundamentals are still there and relatively similar i.e., school, exercise, play. But at the same time a whole new experience. The girls can go get groceries and cook for themselves (although we usually cook together). They can book and take flights, trains, buses, Ubers and rickshaws by themselves and navigate around anywhere on the planet. They are more interested in collecting passport stamps rather than purses. My function as a parent is to release them into the adult world as good humans. To love and teach them to think for themselves and live out their unique path. They get their "stability" from me being solid, I am their constant. It's not some wood and drywall structure in Reseda they need to call home. I am their home. A structure can easily be swapped out, I can't. Everyone these days wants to eat and do what "Humans were evolved to do." Do you think humans were evolved to live in a square house in one place their entire lives? I could be wrong but I'm sure that's a relatively new thing in the history of our existence. Look, I'm not giving up WiFi either... I'm just trying to get you to rethink what you've been told you're supposed to be doing. No one *knows* anything, especially me. We're all winging it. But that's where the good stuff lies. Let's go do something new. Someone's already doing that other stuff. I'm fortunate enough to be able to spend more time with my kids now than most parents are, I'm a single stay at home father. Do I regret not keeping them in the same home with the same group of friends from preschool to high school like the norm? No way, and neither do they. Besides with social media they are all still friends with the real ones and have a bigger network worldwide with no problem keeping in touch.

16 CLUMSY AND SHY

I was dating this woman recently, beautiful. I saw her and I was, like: *Yes please.* Then I started to get to know her. She was so ingrained with all these firm beliefs it was hard to even casually talk to her. She grew up a Muslim but wasn't really practicing, yet still held firm with certain dogmas. Even though she lived completely contradictorily. She would get upset and argue certain things like: "You should never move a kid out of their school!" But when I would ask why or who told her that? She didn't really know. She just "knew." She had a two-year-old kid. I have five kids the oldest being eighteen right now and the youngest is two. I know it's a dick move, but I explained to her that she's still a new parent; I've been a parent for eighteen years and have moved kids out of schools so I know it can work out well. I am well aware my thinking is not right for everyone, but it is a good option for some. Just as keeping kids in one place can work out well too. My only argument was to keep an open mind. But she was completely adamant that her belief was the correct one. Without even knowing *why*! That's my point.

So many people are walking around the world pushing their beliefs on their kids, family and friend but don't even know why. Maybe they heard it from their parents, or their holy book, or even just a social media post. But they don't know *why*. They don't realize their beliefs aren't actually "theirs" they are just hand-me-downs. They're just regurgitating something they heard but have no experience in. So why would you listen to them? My step-mom tried to tell me all these reasons why I shouldn't start a business when I wanted to open our dance studio. She had never started a business before, why was she telling me these things? FEAR. That's why. People are either afraid you're going to fail or afraid that you're going to succeed. Either way both are scary to them because: they aren't doing anything they weren't programmed to do. No, you don't have to move around as much as me, (I am definitely not the model parent) but try to switch it up here and there. Shake hands with change. You can start out with small things like changing gyms or running new paths, take a different route to work, maybe even try biking there. Go work for another company (some studies say employees that stay in companies over 2 years get paid 50% less than those that jump ships) or start your own company. I don't know, again these are just random suggestions, this is not meant to be financial advice. I'm just trying to get you to re-think. This isn't a "Get rich" book, this is an En-rich book. Sure this book can help you get wealthy, indirectly. It can also help you get poorer too (if that's a weird aim of yours) but either way your life will be *richer* if you follow it. If you live in the city maybe move to the country, mountains or beach. Hang out with a completely different group of friends, make new ones. Donate your old wardrobe and buy a new one. Start meeting new people for God's sake.

Speaking of that I have a challenge for you. Get comfortable with rejection. I don't care if you're married, divorced, single or in a relationship. Start talking to strangers (of both sexes, it doesn't have to be flirty). The more people you know the bigger your life will grow. If you're like me, I had very bad social anxiety my whole life. It still tries to creep in, but now I can win the battle. The only time I was comfortable talking to women, strangers or even being around more than two friends at a time was when I was high or drunk. So, when I got sober I didn't have that crutch anymore and hadn't developed the skill to cope with it. I was a grown man having to learn basic social skills I should've picked up in kindergarten. I felt like I did when I finally had my first driving school lesson. I walked into the driving school a grown man in a wife beater, dickies shorts, tattooed up and buffed out from county jail burpees, only to find myself in a room full of tiny 16-year-old Asian kids with their parents. Time had passed me by. Once again I was behind. Many addicts have to play catch up in life and are slow learners. Yet once they grasp hold something they will excel.

I read and listened to audio books like *How To Win Friends And Influence People* by Dale Carnegie and *How To Talk To Anyone* by Leil Lowndes. I challenged myself to meet five new people a day. I challenge you to do the same! Whether it be on the street, store, gym, work, or wherever, meet someone. You don't have to get their life story or make friends. Even if it's just saying *hi* and giving a compliment or asking a question. As for single people, I used to tell myself: *I'm going to try to get five rejections today and that's OK*. Even if I just went up and said: *My name is Richard I just wanted to say hi and meet you.* I'm no

Casanova but it worked sometimes and I bombed others. At least I took some action and met a lot of cool people I'm still in touch with. I know a guy that every girl I've spoken to about him thinks he's handsome, but he's too nervous around girls and avoids them. Then he complains he can't find a good woman. I know women in the same situation. It's fear. Plain and simple.

I used the same type of method when I was pitching my business. I said I'm not going home till I get at least five rejections, sometimes I'd get ten. When I made getting 5-10 rejections a day my goal I didn't feel like a bum at the end of the day if everyone turned me down. I felt like I accomplished a bit of progress because I knew I only needed one *yes*, and it was bound to happen sooner or later. Each rejection was one step closer. In the end I made plenty of business connections, or got plenty of girls' numbers, but those are the booby prizes of the challenge.

The real goal of the exercise isn't money or mates, it's to walk the earth freely with golden confidence and no fear of your fellow man. To be able to be a part of a community anywhere life may take you.

I've since (mostly) lost my fear of rejection or at least now it's easier to stomp it out. It still takes effort- the older I get the farther I drift from connection with the populus.

I've had my kids do the 5-rejection challenge, if they can do it so can you. Many people dream of lives they'd rather be living with people they'd much more prefer to be living it with. Instead accept their unsatisfactory reality rather than face rejection, change or some other form of fear. Are you one of these people? So many lives being directed into the dirt by fear. Remember how I told you my life had been ran on fear? Fear is a foe with many faces.

My biggest loss in life? All the people I was too shy to meet. Go write out ALL of your fears. Don't be afraid.

THE END OF THIS SECTION.

REPAIR
(Making amends)

The only man who doesn't make mistakes is the man who never does anything- Theodore Roosevelt

Now that you've rid yourself of resentments and got a good look at some of the harms you've done, it's time we right our wrongs. If you've done your inventory whole heartedly you should be pretty eager to make amends. If not you probably half-assed it or you're only two years old and haven't harmed anyone yet. You wouldn't be my two-year-old though, cause she's definitely bitten a few kids at preschool. Either way, hand this book back to mommy, or come back when you get honest enough to truly look at your part in the inventory. If you're feeling crappy about all the ways you've hurt people, then you're in the right place and ready for some amends. Doing this amends process will change your life.

First, we make a list of all those we've harmed.
1 Making the list

2 After making the list, transfer to index cards. Write each name on an index card. Below it write the harm you did.

Start by getting the names of those with harms in the Overview list and sex inventory. Then start writing people's names, just the names (for now), of those you harmed. Don't hesitate and start wondering if you did or didn't do some harm, or whether or not it was justified. Just write the name anyway and keep it going. Set aside some time for the next few days (even if it's only ten minutes at a time) to write names and meditate on those you've harmed. You don't need to go deep and re-live the incident, just write the name then move onto the next. You can start out by asking yourself: Who did I harm in elementary school? Yup as far back as elementary, farther if you can remember (I doubt you were harming people before elementary but you're a savage if you were). Did you make fun of a kid and hurt their feelings? Were you horrible to your aunt or a teacher? Did you steal from a store? Did you push your little brother down a flight of stairs and claim "he just fell"? Yeah this is when you become free from those things. Once done with one section of life, go onto the next section; Who did you harm in middle school? Then high school, then college, then your 20s, 30s, and so on till you get to present day. Include family, work, and friends. Also institutions, stores you stole from, houses vandalized, even random bar-fights. All harms. Don't worry about whether you can make the amends or not, just write it. If it pops in your head for a second write it. Be diligent and thorough. Take as much time as needed don't rush. Squeeze out all the names possible. But DO NOT LOSE MOMENTUM. It should only take a couple days at most. Once done with the list, grab some index cards, or cut sheets of paper into 6 equal sized rectangles then cut them out. If you're lazy as hell do it on your computer or notes app. Remember though, there's magic in actual writing.

Each card gets one name on the front, and on the back, all the harms you did to the poor guy. Take a moment and think about what harms you did to this person and write it out. You don't need the whole back story, just a general description. Enough that you could recall the incident when reading later.

Once you have the cards done divide these names into three categories.

Categories:

A) Easy– amends you are willing to make immediately. These are the easy ones you'll knock out first.

B) difficult– this is the list of people you are not quite ready to make amends with or are still very raw about. This list will also include large financial amends. Basically, the ones you don't want to do yet.

C) Impossible– these are the ones you can't do, either because the person is dead or making amends would harm yourself or others.

3. Making the amends:

Now that you have your cards organized and finished, start with the easy list. Pause for a minute, make sure your head is clear and free of resentments or irritations. It's better to wait than to go into an amends disgruntled. Do a different person first. If possible, contact the person and make an appointment to meet up. The amends should be done face-to-face. Unless you live in Minnesota and your person lives in Australia, then a call is OK. Never text unless absolutely necessary. Don't bitch out. Face the people you harmed, look them in the eye. Don't rob them, or yourself of a proper amends. You will get more out of it as well. Before you meet, again take a moment for a few deep breaths. Leave all hard feelings and resentment at the door. When face-to-face let them know that this is something of a personal nature and ask if it's a good time. We don't want to make an emotional amends to someone right before they walk into an important meeting or anything like that. Once we have the green-light, sit down with the person and start off with something similar to this: "Hey Joe, there's something that's not sitting right with me. I'm the one that broke your TV last year and I want to apologize and make things right. What can I do?" Keep it simple. After you've said your part, shut up and LET THEM TALK. Don't say anything until they're done, let them get out everything they need to. Again, let them say everything they need to say.

Once you've done all your easy amends, it's time to move on to the difficult ones. This is where you'll have to take a leap of faith, and trust that the most dreaded amends are the most rewarding. These are the ones with the most weight, and the heaviest rocks on your back. The ones that made me cringe to even think about making, are the ones that set me free. Oddly enough, even our financial amends, even though we may not feel bad or have any emotional connection with a credit card company or old drug dealer, we can find huge relief in these as well. You'd be surprised the weight these hold and relief they can bring, even the stupidest ones. Hitting us in our wallet hurts the most. We all feel like we can't afford any more financial burdens, but somehow paying our debts and righting ourselves with the universe seems to end up paying off for us financially in the end. Call it good fortune or good karma, however you want to see it. A new life waits on the other side, but you're going to have to conquer your fears to get to it. No guts, no glory. Swallow your pride, and go for it!

If the person wants you to pay them back, and you are able to, then pay them promptly. Get it out of the way. Look at it as you're buying back your freedom. Because you are. It's their money after all. If payment, arrangements are needed then make them. People's reactions will vary. Some will break into tears and forgive you on the spot. Some will be angry and make unreasonable demands. Use your best discretion. Obviously, it's not OK if someone demands to sleep with your wife in reparation for a girlfriend you stole in third grade. Most importantly make sure to never blame the other person in any way. Regardless of what really happened, shut up, vent it to your dog when you get home. This is our amends and it's meant to clean our side of the street only. No matter what the other person did to set things in motion, that is of no concern to us right now. Avoid mentioning their part at all cost. To do so will result in a ruined amends and disaster.

The other person may even surprise you with admitting and apologizing for their part as well. Hold your tongue. Gracefully accept their apology and reiterate that it was not your intention to provoke any guilt in them.

We should be prepared and willing to do all we can, even when it stings, to make things right. Many amends will make you extremely uncomfortable and require a good amount of discipline and bravery as well as sacrifice. However, on the other end of those amends is the relief we never knew we needed. The other end of that discomfort is a new life. The release of burden will give you a high and supply the fuel needed for the next one. Some will deplete the tank and leave you drained. Keep going. Make sure to allot a decent amount of time for each amends. You don't want to be rushing through one to go make another. These can be very intimate occasions and each one should be treated with the utmost respect.

One of my most dreaded amends was to a long-time enemy from back in the day. I got into some heavy altercations with this man and his friends. I ended up doing something pretty bad to him in retaliation for him and his friends jumping me in an ambush. They had a girl I liked call me and ask to meet up. When I got to the meeting spot a car pulled up. Instead of the pretty girl it was a bunch of dudes that jumped out of the car. Instead of doing the smart thing like heading in the opposite direction, I ran towards the altercation. I was also drunk and high. In those days I would have rather died than run from anyone. This unfortunate twist of events sent me to the hospital with a broken nose, knocked back teeth and concussion. Yes those three injuries happened often. I remember looking at my face in the mirror that night; it felt as if I was staring at some sort of disfigured monster in a movie. I looked like the elephant man. My face was all swollen and bloody, nose broken and smashed. I remember lifting up my fat swollen lip to unveil my teeth that were knocked in all different directions. I couldn't stop from rubbing them with my lacerated fat tongue. When I fell I must've chomped down on my tongue. I came in and out of consciousness that night. Somehow I got from the street, to my friend's house, to the hospital. Like I was teleported from situation to situation in the blink of an eye. It's funny how the most horrible of experiences end up being the most valuable. Sometimes I feel like I seek out shitty experiences. Maybe because without them life would be like a boring movie.

It was a risky amends to try and make. It almost fell into the *Do not do if you will injure yourself or others* category. As much as I didn't want to do it, I knew it had to be done. I told myself that I would put out the effort to find him and see how it goes from there. I would try my best to make the amends but if it seemed risky, I would find some other way to rid myself of the burden. I ended up getting ahold of him through a mutual acquaintance. I gave him a call and felt out the situation first to make sure he'd be cool. I kind of had to make a mini partial amends over the phone to let him know this was a well-intentioned meeting and not a set up. When we met, I mustered up the balls and made the amends. I just spit it out and waited for a reaction. He looked at me, shook my hand, then gave me a big strong hug. He followed with a genuine apology for what he did as well. I felt a huge rush of emotions and relief. What for years was a heated resentful feud turned into a feeling of love and respect for the man. I think he felt the same way I did, he seemed to have a look of relief on his face as well. I left that encounter with a new freedom of spirit, I was walking on clouds. I knew without a doubt that this process was for real. After that the other "hard" amends were much easier to make. Not all went as well as that did, but I now understood the significance and power of what I was doing.

Making amends to an enemy or nasty relative might seem easy compared to some of the financial amends. Don't worry these won't be as bad as you think, but it can be just as rewarding. As I mentioned before you may even see your financial situation get *better* as you start paying other people what you owe them. Funny how that works. If you don't, and never will have the money to fully pay back a huge amends, be creative. Ask if there's any other way you can make it up, maybe intern or volunteer. You never know where that door may lead. Maybe allot yourself a set dollar amount every month for restitutions split up between a few people i.e. $100 to Jimmy, $200 to Willy, $200 to your uncle. Do what is within your budget but be honest with yourself. Sacrifice some luxuries on your end to make it work, but don't take food out of your kid's mouth. You should be the one shouldering your sacrifice, not your family. Sell some things if you have to. Maybe even offer them something of value instead, again, be creative. Be honest with yourself and do your best. I promise it will be worth it.

THE IMPOSSIBLE LIST

As I mentioned previously my Nana and Papa were the sacred jewels of my life. I loved and respected them more than anybody on earth. Their passing away was my biggest fear, growing up. Nevertheless, in my peak addiction even though I always liked to think I never disrespected them, that was a delusion, because I stole money from them and caused enormous amounts of grief.

Heroin is a nasty drug and compels you to do things you would never normally do, the whole time hating yourself as you're doing them. I still remember the first time I stole from them. I had known for years where my Nana stashed her money but never touched it. I found it once when I was younger, just snooping around like a dummy. It was in a green box in her closet, the box had a silicone breast padding she used because she had a breast removed from cancer. The first time I looked in the box I felt something shifting around under the plastic mould. I lifted the mould and found about $10k in $100 dollar bills. I put it back right away and didn't touch it again. That is till one really, really shitty day. Only a true dope fiend will appreciate this one. I sprung up around 4 am to shoot up my morning fix, which unfortunately was only 1 heroin balloon, (2 was preferred). One balloon was enough to get me well so I could go hustle up some money downtown and buy more. As I was sitting on the toilet setting up my spoon, needle and everything else I needed in my ritual for shooting up, I carelessly tried to rip open the balloon with stuff in my hands. Normally the heroin is in solid form, this time however it was powder. The balloon ripped open and the powder cascaded between my bare legs and into the pee filled toilet. I fumbled to grab at it but watched hopelessly as it dissipated into the disgusting yellow water. My heart sunk and I was thrown into an instant panic! I almost started crying as I cursed God. I was already in withdrawal and needed that shot to get well, now it was gone. I had no dope, no money, and the busses weren't even running yet to get down town. It would be hours before I could get down there and hustle up money to get more. Like I've said when you're sick, seconds feel like hours. My mind and body was in an involuntary panic, I didn't know what to do. The thought came into my head that I could take $100 from my Nana's stash and then replace it later today and no one would even know. My brain locked into that idea and closed out all other thoughts, it was the fastest solution to put out this fire. A few seconds later I was army-crawling into my Nana's room, slowly, quietly like a ninja, past her bed and on down towards her closet door. I silently slid open the mirrored door, grabbed the box, rolled on to my back, put the box on my chest, lifted the lid, felt around under the mould and slipped out one

$100 dollar bill. Got it! Then I slowly put the box back and slithered my way out of the room like the snake that I was. I threw on my shoes and hoody and ran out of the house, it was still dark out, just me and the yellow glow of the street lights. I ended up replacing the money that night like I said I would, and the next time, but then eventually I didn't. One $100 bill at a time became 2, then 3 then more. The more drugs I bought the higher my tolerance got, I couldn't go back to a $100 dollar a day habit. Every so often I would hit a lick and replenish what I could but eventually I drained almost all of their money. The dreaded day came when they discovered what I had done. I happened to be in jail at the time. What a scum bag I was. I know I ruined their golden years and their final days. My Papa died while I was in jail and my Nana passed while I was in rehab. Neither got to see me get my life together, and that was all they ever wanted from me. They didn't care if I was rich or poor, they just wanted me to be a good respectable man. An amends to them was something most needed in my soul. But how? They are both no longer with us.

 What I did was take my Nana and Papa's amends card to the cemetery where they were buried. I brought some flowers and sat down next to their headstones which are side-by-side. I greeted them and began my amends. I read off the list of things I did, and wanted to apologize for. I made an emotional plea for forgiveness and swore to live my life in a way that would make them proud. I promised to show my children and grandchildren the type of unconditional love that they showed me. I assured them that their efforts on me were not in vain, and that I now understood my mistakes and was grateful for all they had done for me. I cried at their gravestones that day and although they weren't there to forgive me, I knew I had turned my life around and was no longer that dumb kid. They wouldn't want me walking around carrying guilt, I wouldn't want my kids to either. I knew they would just smile and say not to worry about anything in the past; what mattered was I was doing good now and with that, I forgave myself. I still to this day try to live my life in honor of them. I know they'd be mighty proud of me for writing this book. Once it's done, I'll go back and drop them off a copy, maybe even read them a few pages, the lighter stuff of course. They probably wouldn't get what it's about, I'd have to just say: *Nana it's a book to try and help people get off drugs like I did.* She'd probably just put an arm around me and say: *Well, that's good then honey, I'm sure it will.*

We have to be creative with our *impossible* list. If you robbed a liquor store 20 years ago and you now support a family (obviously if you confessed it would not do any good and only bring harm to your family), maybe you might make the amends to a random liquor store in another town. You wouldn't want to get into any details, but maybe just tell the owner when you were a kid you made a bad mistake by taking money from a different liquor store and want to make things right. I'm sure they've been robbed before and took a loss, an amends and some cash would probably be respected and appreciated. The same can go for different crimes, just make the amends to a different victim somehow if circumstances won't permit you to do it with the actual person. Possibly read the amends to a priest, maybe make an anonymous donation. I'm not going to tell you whether or not you should confess or turn yourself in for an old crime or wrong you did, I don't know the situation and it's none of my business. All I can say is, if you are no longer that person anymore and nothing good would even come of it, then don't, I wouldn't. But you still have to make things right somehow. The world would probably be better off if you found a way to make some reparations and do some good out there. If it's weighing on you heavily and there are people that need closure and justice, then maybe it's a good idea. Again, I don't know, that's between you and your maker. If you have done everything thoroughly up until those very last hard amends, the answers will come to you. Will you be brave enough to take action?

For personal suggestions, anonymous amends or just to say hi, send me an email at galvan@theaddictscores.com or visit theaddictscores.com I look forward to hearing your stories and helping in whatever way I can.

Find me on instagram @casablancaxsl

EVOLVE
(The daily overview)

Once you've done as many amends as you could, or maybe halfway through, start doing your daily overview at the end of the night. This will ensure we don't pile on more dirt as we go. We want to try and keep our resentment, fear, and guilt in check, no matter how good or "bad" life gets. It's best to do a daily cleaning so things don't pile up. Who cares if you have millions in the bank if you are miserable. Who cares if you look good on the outside if you feel like shit on the inside. Who cares if you're an expert on the subject being discussed but are afraid to speak up. You'll be surprised how much of a self-esteem and confidence boost you'll get from repairing your past. We want our mind, body, and spirit to all be in a state of progress. If it ain't all right, it's all wrong. You work out to keep your body healthy and strong right? But are you going to leave your mind stagnant and weak? Some people stop working their mind once they get out of school and just leave it to stale out, they assume the problems they have got to fix at work or home is sufficient. That's like assuming the activity you get from walking around work is sufficient exercise. I'm sure in some lines of work it is, but usually we need to supplement extra exercise and extra learning.

What about our spirit? Should that be neglected as well? Would we not benefit greatly from continually working towards strengthening and growing that precious glow inside of us? Yes, this too (whatever it actually is) can grow stronger or become weak. The same way running a mile will exert your body, reading books, good conversations and solving problems will work your mind; actions of service and repairing your wrongs will strengthen your spirit. Each one is vital to our well-being and each one needs to be pushed to progress. Like they say: if you don't use it you lose it, and you don't want to lose or let any of these things degrade. When I can squeeze in some amount of exercise, learning and service in my day it lines me up and something magic happens. It is in these peak states of alignment that I gain the most progress in life. When I'm aligned, I'm on fire, my mind is primed and ready to receive its direction from the ether. To get in that state of alignment I usually just have to have those three things be in a state of active progress. Even if it's just hitting the gym that morning, maybe get some reading done in a book that opens your mind a little. Then do something really loving for your partner, kids or, better yet, something kind for someone you don't know. You don't have to move mountains to get the juices flowing, just work on each one every day. Yes, every day should be the aim, grow or go. Make them a Must in your day. Of course, none of us are perfect (definitely don't expect me to be). Keep in mind; you can't stay clean from yesterday's shower. You can't stay primed of yesterday's actions. Sure, your state of mind may linger a day or so, but it's easy to go sideways. Irritability, restlessness and discontentedness can kick back in fast, that is why we have our final action of the day: The Overview.

This is a very simple effective exercise to do at the end of your day that will change your life and it'll only take you 5 minutes. Once you're settled in at the end of your day grab a piece of paper (I do it in the Notes app) and just write down any resentments you picked up during the day and run through the same questions as your resentment inventory. Doesn't have to be neat or exact, just a brief little inventory going over your day. The goal is to see our errors and make tiny improvements day by day.

DAILY OVERVIEW

MORNING- Your goals and or prayers.

NIGHT-
Did you pick up any resentments? Do a quick inventory.
Did you do any harms? Were you a dick to somebody today? If you have a small amends you need to make, shoot out a text or make a quick call.
Did you accomplish your goals for today? If not, why?
Do you have your day planned out for tomorrow?

Did you do your best today? Is there something you can improve and do better tomorrow?

Tie up your loose ends, maybe read for a few, say your prayers or goals then hit the hay. Remember, goals and prayers are only gratified when combined and harmonized with thoughts and actions.

THE FIVE VIRTUES

To be in harmony with these five fundamental virtues is to be in harmony with your source. Whether that be god, self, nature- these virtues are your target direction. Everyday, every hour, every minute we have a choice. We are either heading in the direction of one of these five virtues or their opposite. One who builds out their life using these virtues as its foundation will surely be successful on their paths. If you notice these virtues are the harder options to take compared to their opposites, then consider that the easier in the long run is always the harder option in the beginning. All roads lead through pain; either pay it up front or double it up on the back end. It is best to always pay our prices upfront.

Ignoring one is ignoring all, they overlap and intertwine with each other. You don't need to do anything perfectly, just do your best to improve each day. The best is whatever you can do that day. A little bit of effort consistently, plus plenty of time is all it takes. Too hard, too fast, it slips right through your hands. Take it easy; don't be too hard on yourself; remember- the steady pace wins the race. I'll be right behind you, don't wait up; you can be a front runner- I'm just here to make sure the slowest man finishes.

1.) Love: (as a verb). Service to your fellow man. Forgiveness. Correcting your mistakes. Kindness. Protecting. Effort. Be polite but hold boundaries. Giving without expectation. Making frequent quality time with your loved ones a priority.

2.) Courage: Action. Learn to say No. Change. Embrace discomfort. Open-mindedness. Doing the right thing no matter what. Be decisive but know when to pivot.

3.) Honesty: Being true to oneself (not being afraid to end bad relationships/jobs not only for you but them). Trustworthy. Admitting when wrong. Being honest about your opinions so as to not mislead people.

4.) Discipline: Sticking to plans, moving towards goals. Constant learning. Doing beneficial things you don't want to do. Not procrastinating. Proper hygiene. Keeping your word. Living by your codes.

5.) Health: Daily exercise. Eating for nutrition rather than taste (gold if you can squeeze in both). Hobbies. Nature. Conscious deep breathing. Meditation or quiet time. Reading.

Part Four:

BECOME WHO YOU ARE

WHAT IF I'M WRONG?

Do you ever ask yourself: What if I'm wrong? I feel like this is an essential question that should be constantly running in the back of one's mind. I'm not talking about being indecisive, or not executing your decisions with confidence. No. I'm talking about a regular re-evaluation of our opinions, beliefs, relationships and current life situation in general. All aspects should be contemplated at some point, every so often. Like a diagnostic run to confirm everything is still in good working order. Sometimes we've grown into a new person, but are still in our old life. How can we tell? Well, we've got to ask ourselves the tough questions every once in a while, questions that should make you cringe. What if I'm wrong about my career choice? Do I still love this industry? Would I do it for free? Can I do this for another thirty years? What if I'm wrong about my religious beliefs? Am I even open to consider this or has my religion put so much fear in me that I can't even question it? Did I find this religion on my own or was it passed on to me from my parents and or community? If I was born and raised in another country, such as India or Iran, would I belong to a different religion?

What if I'm wrong about the way I eat? Am I out of shape? Am I just eating the same comforting foods I grew up on? Am I eating the foods I eat out of taste and convenience rather than what is best for my body and mind? What foods would be better for me? Why aren't I eating that way? Am I being stubborn, cheap or just undisciplined? What if I am wrong about my partner? Am I treating them the best way I possibly could? Am I still in love or just attached? Do I really want to spend the rest of my life with this person? If I could be with anyone else given the opportunity, would I leave? If so, am I doing my partner a disservice by leading them on? Am I with this person because I'm afraid of change or just because I don't want to hurt them? Am I just afraid I can't do better?

What if I'm wrong about the city or country I live in? Am I just here because it's where my parents raised me? If so did they just move to the country because *they* liked it or was it the only place they could afford? Am I just staying here because of my family and friends? If it wasn't for my family and friends would I move somewhere else? Am I just afraid of change? Or afraid to upset people? Out of the thousands of cities and hundreds of countries on earth does the town I live in now, bring out my full potential? Could I possibly be happier and more successful somewhere else?

Here's another tough one that needs to be asked every once in a while: Are my closest friends really my friends? Or are they more like a friendly enemy I can talk to? Do they honestly have my best intentions at heart or do they seem to be harboring resentment? Have you outgrown them? Is there a mutual reciprocation or is it all take, take, take? Am I a taker? Is there something, or someone, that is tying you together? If so, if you took that away would you still be good friends?

These are all tough questions to ask yourself and may bring about some answers that you don't want to face, but yet, there they are. Will you face them and make the necessary changes to better your life, even though the road to the other side might be a tough one? Or will you take the easy route sweeping it under the rug and put the blindfold back on, hoping things work themselves out? Ladies and gentlemen these are the choices that shape our lives.

NOW WHAT?

Ok so you made it this far, now what? If you have worked The SCORE program thoroughly, you will undoubtedly have had what can only be referred to as an awakening of the spirit. If you haven't, why not, what have you got to lose? Being freed from a lifetime of resentment and guilt along with admitting and amending our faults, has cleared away the blockage that was obstructing our view. The view of our true essence. Guilt, resentment and fear, hijacked our spirits, it turned us into something else. That "something else" saw the world differently. Jaded, grim, sullen. Like we had on a pair of sunglasses that were way too dark. Now we took them off and it was nice and bright outside. The color of the world was restored. Mental clarity. Not only do we see our lives front to back more clearly, but now we have a better picture of our *self* and realize we weren't that bad after all. We become intimate friends with *ourselves* once again, a relationship some of us lost long before we could even remember. Our lives, past and present make a little more sense now. *Ok now I get it.* Our future is seen like a movie that is starting to get good, we eagerly wonder what's next? On this journey of our life, we've taken the pebbles out of our shoe and dropped the heavy load we were carrying. Now we meet the road refreshed and ready to go. We stepped outside, the sun hits our face as we looked up into the sky, we squint our eyes and we take in a deep breath. Now what? Well my friends that's entirely up to you. I've given you the best of me, in order to do that I had to give you my worst. I welcomed you into my dirty home to share with you the messages of my misfortunes. My contribution to this life contains no glamour, no Lamborghinis or stacks of cash, the bloodletting of all the demons in my closet was done on one knee, in service and gratitude.

 The constant feeling of death lurking over my shoulder that I've had since a teen now has some leverage over me. Not of my death, but that my end will come before my children know the man that was their father. I have many lessons I've yet to teach them; mostly in the form of- what *not* to do. The paths to stay away from, harsh lessons their dad learned the hard way so they don't have to. Stories they're too young to understand right now, but my wishes are that the words on these pages meet their eyes at the right times. I hope when they read these words they hear my voice, as if I'm talking to them while on a walk or car ride together. I hope the strangers that read this book finish as friends, if you can feel the words in this book then we are in a way connected, because then it was written for you too. Back to our question: Now what? As an old crack-head we called Mr. Cash used to say: "I bought you the books, took you to school, betta not come back a daaamn fool." Of course no one is expected to follow this program perfectly.

I myself can only hope to come close on my best days. Working the program outlined in this book will make you happier, that I can promise. If that's what you're after. Personally, I find too much happiness to be neutering. I like to build the house but I can't live in it too long, I'd rather burn it down and build something new. I prefer the warm lick of the flames. I think it's in the chaos where I'm most comfortable. When things get too calm I start getting antsy. I find sleep easier with the back pack on the bus, over the blonde in the bed. Maybe one day that'll change. The good thing about this program is, it's like having a key to your friend's house you can always go back to when you're hungry and tired. It's pulled me out of some ruts and got me back on track before I did too much damage.

To this concept of a program, and the men whose shoulders it stands on- I am eternally grateful. I take no credit. I didn't create the jalapeño, the tomato, the onion, the cilantro, I just blended them together and served you salsa. As the old saying goes: in order to keep it you must give it away. What is it that we're trying to keep? This *thing*, whatever it is, I believe it's love in disguise, or in one of its many forms. The love of oneself, it's a feeling that we want to keep. Sure, you feel love for your grandma or your children, and would die for them, but do you treat yourself with as much tenderness as you treat them? Do you have as much love and affection for yourself as you do for other people? Our prior actions and the way we treated ourselves suggests not. Once you've felt that feeling of loving *yourself* as much as you love your child, the world changes. It's a feeling most people only *think* they've felt. Posting a quote on self-love to your social media page is not it, a self-care day is not it, a girls/guys night out to "do you" is not it. Those may be great but don't mistake them for the profound feeling that is a deep love for oneself. It's a feeling that when you have it, it reverberates to everyone around you. The same way someone walking around full of anger gives off tense repelling vibes that you can feel, a person filled with love has the opposite effect. Like when we see someone who almost appears to be glowing.

It's not a feeling you can put a leash on though, it slips away and must be found over and over again. Once you've felt it, you know love is more than just a chemical reaction to motivate procreation and care for your offspring. Love and its byproduct- service, is the fuel for our soul. I'm not talking about walking around like some idiot thinking he's enlightened telling everyone you love them. Love isn't a poet, it's a warrior. Deception is conveyed through words, love is conveyed through action. Love is a strength, it's not proven during the good times, it only reveals its strength during the worst. It's only at the bottom where you can look up to find out who truly loves you. They'll be the only ones still there. All you really need is one to hang on with you. Most will never go far enough down to really find out. It's probably better that way. I've been left alone down there a few times, you never quite come back up the same. It's like the difference of Christmas as a kid believing in Santa Claus and presents; to the Christmas of a 40-year-old man that knows it's just an account draining bunch of work to make the ones that still believe the lie happy. But there is a silver lining, a very special one. No one loves stronger than the one that knows the loneliness of not having anyone. Only those that have ever looked up to find themselves all alone know love's true significance; just as only those that have been poor know the value of a dollar.

Love to me is protection. Not just shielding one from harm but being strong enough to allow your loved ones sufficient amounts of harm to grow strong themselves, so that you are no longer needed to protect them. Love sets the bird free, it doesn't keep it in chains. Love is bringing out the best in those around you, not putting them down. Love is telling someone what they need to hear not what they want to hear. Love is the ability to endure discomfort for the greater good. Love is dangerous, it's exposing your vulnerabilities. It's like going into battle with no armour and no sword, trusting you won't be hurt. It takes true strength and courage to love. I'm not talking about attachment, or dependency, which is what most people mistake for love. Holding someone hostage because you don't want them to leave isn't love, it's the hand of fear with a velvet glove on. Fear is the twin brother of love, they come as a package deal. When you get love you also get the fear of losing that person. It can be hard to balance the two. Fear is giving the man a fish, so he always needs you. Love is teaching the man to fish so he can eat forever without you if he wants.

Love is the true spirit of service. Service, making the new person feel welcome; not just in recovery, but with work, school, family and friends too. Fear is ignoring or acting "too cool" when the new man walks in; that attitude hurts the whole world. Service is giving freely of what has been given to you. Fear is withholding information so others won't take your job. Service is giving without expecting anything in return. Service is a genuine compliment to a stranger. Service is making someone having a bad day laugh. Service is taking a friend out to lunch just because. Service is leaving somewhere better than how it was when you arrived. Service is putting your phone on silent and giving someone your full attention. Service is treating the bus boy with the same respect as the owner. Service is not talking bad about people behind their back, and shutting people down when they try to do so. Service is praising someone behind their back and giving them a good name to live up to.

Love and service commands respect. Genuine respect. When you live your life in such a way you open the doors for the right people and opportunities. At the same time you repel those that are toxic. The venomous can't stand to be around such a presence, it makes them feel uncomfortable. We avoid petty arguments, we admit when we are wrong. If a lie unconsciously escapes our mouth, we excuse the mistake right away. All your life's problems will not go away, but now you are on solid footing, ready to tackle whatever comes at you. When you live your life with such integrity people can talk bad about you, but no one will believe them anymore. You become a solid person. Your confidence is magnetic. Your eyes are of a brighter wattage. You become the only thing you could ever truly be: YOU.

GRATITUDE

Today at 3:41am, I was jolted awake by a horrible stench... Oh my God what is that? I grabbed my phone off the nightstand and opened the home screen for some light. I shined the light of the phone over my two sleeping toddlers and noticed my three-year-old's shorts were wet. There was what looked like chocolate pudding smeared all over her thigh, the bed, blankets, and her sister; who she was cuddling. Only it wasn't chocolate pudding, it was baby poop! Holy shit... Literally... Ok, here we go... So, I turned on the bathroom lights letting enough glow in to clean everything up without waking the babies. Just as I got us all cleaned up and was dead tired about to go back to sleep- I see a set of open eyes staring at me. "Daddy! Daddy!" One wakes up the other and within three seconds they go from eyes opening, to scooting themselves off the side of the bed. Great, now we're wide awake and ready to play at 4am. That's how my morning started.

Ok, let's brush our teeth and go make some breakfast... I said to the kids in a zombie like state. Chasing kids around by myself and cleaning up oatmeal flung all over the place before the sun is up, was less disgusting, but an equally challenging feat. Recently divorced, I was back to being a single dad again. I had been a single dad before with my oldest daughter Isabel. She was a mellow kid, very easy to care for and went everywhere with me. My two youngest are a different story. 1 kid is easy, 2 kids is a circus, but 5 kids... it's a mad house. The two little ones are sweet on their own, but together they combine to form a tag team of destruction. As you're changing one's diaper, the other is running into the kitchen opening drawers. One is playing with blocks peacefully, the other comes in like Godzilla and destroys everything, enraging the other; now there's a fight. They go head-to-head in a battle of bites, scratches, and hair pulling. Soon both are crying. My toddlers have the energy and temperament of Tasmanian devils, so next we were off to the park to let them play and run wild. It was only 9 am and I already felt like this day had gotten the best of me. I even half-jokingly sent a text to their mother saying: *I don't know if I'm cut out for this fatherhood thing anymore.* She was on her way to LA for the next four days, so it was all me with the kids. My other three teen daughters live with me and help, but they each come with their own individual issues; it's still a lot of work.

Standing at the park in a daze pushing my daughter on the swing, I contemplated how I was going to get through the next four days- and the rest of my life. It had already been a rough week. The divorce, caring for five kids, the sale of my company, moving to a new country and starting a completely new life; my brain felt like it was humming and buzzing. I had hardly slept the past few days and was especially grouchy that morning. *Ok Richard, stop acting like a bitch snap out of it!* A few kind words to myself, then I stopped and took a moment to take some deep breaths, look around and try to re-ground myself. I looked over and saw what appeared to be a caregiver, he was walking up to the playground pushing an old lady in a wheelchair. The old lady had some type of breathing apparatus and bruises on her shrivelled skin. She was in bad shape. My kid jumped off the swing and ran to the slide, as I followed her, I crossed paths with the old lady. I posted up next to the caregiver and lady to watch my daughters play on the slide apparatus. I said: *Buenos Dias* and tried to spark up a conversation hoping they spoke some English. Unfortunately, the lady only spoke Spanish but the caregiver's English was decent. I asked how their day was going and the caregiver said "She likes to come to the park and watch the children play." I looked at the lady as she smiled at me. The three of us gazed upon the playing children for a few moments. Then I had to run over to spot my daughter climbing a rope ladder.

Playing with the girls, I was contemplating what the caregiver said, and looked over to see the cheer in the old lady's face; not only in her face but in her eyes. Her face was a dishevelled wrinkly mess but the sparkle in her eyes and smile was powerful. "She likes to come to the park and watch the children play." I kept hearing in my head. The lady was drawing joy out of the sight, the same sight I was looking at with disgruntled eyes. Kids playing at the park, not just any kids, my kids. They were healthy, happy children playing on a nice sunny morning. What could be more beautiful? There was nothing wrong in our setting; we weren't in a concentration camp, we weren't dying in a hospital bed, we were playing at a beautiful park in Barcelona. The only wrong thing was taking place in my head. Remember Shakespeare's "There is nothing either good or bad but thinking makes it so." A sentence spoken by a stranger, a look in an old lady's face, and a thought in my head, transformed the way I saw the playground and my day. My mentality flipped from bitter to grateful. My physical exhaustion melted away too, I was now in a sunny energetic mood. I thought: *Wow how ungrateful was I just a few minutes ago bickering about my day. I bet that lady would give anything to be back in my shoes, playing with her children and able to do anything we wanted for the rest of the day.* My eyes started watering at the thought that one day I might be a frail old man confined to a wheelchair, yearning for the days of my youth; grasping to recall the memories of my daughters' childhood. Wishing I could do it all over again, but this time around I would savor every glorious moment- good and bad, for there is beauty in both. Both are what make up our lives, and if you took away either it wouldn't be the same. I'd probably think back to what a fool I was to ever waste a moment. I'd probably wish I gave more hugs, more kisses and more talks. I would've eaten meals a little slower, been in less of a rush to leave, gone on more walks- *It's a nice day kids, let's get out of the house.* Less criticism and more praise, less time worrying and more days just enjoying time together. Sometimes I think back to the days when my oldest was small and used to lay down and fall asleep in my arms while watching a movie. I'd shut off the TV, give her a kiss, then hug her tight and fall asleep too. Those were golden times, precious moments; life in its most beautiful form. She has just turned 18, that'll never happen again- ever. Just memories now. Hopefully I can hang on to them; something to keep my spirit alive when *I'm* that old frail man in the wheelchair. I have to constantly remind myself to cherish each day, because you may never know when you're experiencing something for the last time. Something you to take for granted now. Always remember Richard, happiness and sadness lies in our perception.

-It's never a bad day if the sun is setting down Sherman way...

THE END

www.ingramcontent.com/pod-product-compliance
Lightning Source LLC
Chambersburg PA
CBHW070537010526
44118CB00012B/1154